# 1st Workshop on Statistical Parsing of Morphologically Rich Languages 2010

# (SPMRL 2010)

AA005259

**Held at NAACL HLT 2010**

## Los Angeles, California, USA
## 5 June 2010

**ISBN: 978-1-61738-683-1**

**Printed from e-media with permission by:**

Curran Associates, Inc.
57 Morehouse Lane
Red Hook, NY 12571

**Some format issues inherent in the e-media version may also appear in this print version.**

Copyright© (2010) by the Association for Computational Linguistics
All rights reserved.

Printed by Curran Associates, Inc. (2010)

For permission requests, please contact the Association for Computational Linguistics at the address below.

Association for Computational Linguistics
209 N. Eighth Street
Stroudsburg, Pennsylvania 18360

Phone: 1-570-476-8006
Fax: 1-570-476-0860

acl@aclweb.org

**Additional copies of this publication are available from:**

Curran Associates, Inc.
57 Morehouse Lane
Red Hook, NY 12571 USA
Phone: 845-758-0400
Fax: 845-758-2634
Email: curran@proceedings.com
Web: www.proceedings.com

# Foreword

The idea of organizing this workshop was sparked following very interesting discussions that occurred during EACL09 among various researchers working on statistical parsing of different types of languages. Indeed, an opportunity to discuss the issues that we were all experiencing was much needed, and it seemed such a good idea that we decided to take advantage of IWPT'09, which was held that year in Paris, to organize a panel on this topic. We planned to have presentations on the various issues faced by this small emerging community, which would allow us to share our sometimes similar solutions for parsing different languages.

Inspired by the idea of organizing such a meeting, but without knowing quite yet if there was any sense in comparing, for example, Modern Hebrew and French parsing issues, Deirdre Hogan (Dublin City University) suggested that - should the panel be successful - we ought to organize a real workshop. She was right. We had an extremely successful and animated panel discussion. We were surprised to see the extent to which the IWPT'09 audience chose to contribute to the discussion instead of taking a break from the long presentation sessions. This encouraged us to pursue these attempts at providing a forum for discussing such matters even further, and to create a new community of shared interests. This workshop is the result of our common will to do so.

We believe that the issues faced by researchers involved in statistical parsing of morphologically rich languages are not always well known outside of this small community, and that the kind of challenges that we all face require a more thorough introduction than we could possibly provide in this foreword. Therefore, we decided to include here an elaborated preface which presents the current state-of-affairs with respect to parsing MRLs and frames the various contributions to our workshop in relation to it. The overview should act as a primer for those who are not experienced in the subject and yet wish to participate in the discussion. All in all, we are proud to have 11 very nice papers presented in our proceedings that will help advance the state of the art in parsing MRLs. In order to obtain sufficient presentation slots, we asked our authors to choose between different modes of presentation, we are glad the authors involved in 3 papers accepted to present them as posters.

Finally, we would like to express our gratitude to the many people who encouraged us on this journey: Harry Bunt, Alon Lavie and Kenji Sagae from SIGPARSE which fully endorses this project; Joakim Nivre who heartily encouraged us to launch our workshop, Eric de la Clergerie who agreed to give us a slot at IWPT'09 and Josef van Genabith who very kindly chaired our first panel, all of whom constantly advised us during this year - this was precious to us. More than 20 very busy researchers agreed to review for our workshop - without their commitment this would have been plainly impossible. We further wish to thank Kevin Knight who kindly agreed to give a talk on a pressing topic, morphology in SMT, in this workshop, and Dan Bikel, Julia Hockenmaier, Slav Petrov and Owen Rambow, who willingly agreed to engage in our panel discussion. Last but not least, we want to thank Laurence Danlos - whose team, the Alpage project, is funding our workshop - for believing in our project from the start.

Best regards,

The SPRML2010 extended Program Committee

- Endorsed by SIGPARSE, the ACL Special Interest Group on Natural Language Parsing.
- Sponsored by the INRIA's ALPAGE PROJECT.

**Organizers:**

Djamé Seddah, INRIA/University of Paris-Sorbonne (France)
Sandra Kübler, Indiana University (USA)
Reut Tsarfaty, Uppsala University (Sweden)

**Program Committee:**

Marie Candito, INRIA/University Paris 7 (France)
Jennifer Foster, NCLT, Dublin City University (Ireland)
Yoav Goldberg, Ben Gurion University of the Negev (Israel)
Ines Rehbein, Universität Saarbrücken (Germany)
Lamia Tounsi, NCLT, Dublin City University (Ireland)
Yannick Versley, Universität Tübingen (Germany)

**Review Committee:**

Mohamed Attia (Dublin City University, Ireland)
Adriane Boyd (Ohio State University, USA)
Aoife Cahill (University of Stuttgart, Germany)
Grzegorz Chrupała (Saarland University, Germany)
Benoit Crabbé (University of Paris 7, France)
Michael Elhadad (Ben Gurion University, Israel)
Emar Mohamed (Indiana University, USA)
Josef van Genabith (Dublin City University, Ireland)
Julia Hockenmaier (University of Illinois, USA)
Deirdre Hogan (Dublin City University, Ireland)
Alberto Lavelli (FBK-irst, Italy)
Joseph Le Roux (Dublin City University, Ireland)
Wolfgang Maier (University of Tüebingen, Germany)
Takuya Matsuzaki (University of Toyko, Japan)
Yusuke Miyao (University of Toyko, Japan)
Joakim Nivre (Uppsala University, Sweden)
Ines Rehbein (Saarland University, Germany)
Kenji Sagae (University of Southern California, USA)
Benoit Sagot (Inria Rocquencourt, France)
Khalil Sima'an (University of Amsterdam, The Netherlands)
Nicolas Stroppa (Google Research Zurich, Switzerland)

**Invited Speaker:**

Kevin Knight, University of Southern California/Information Sciences Institute

**Panelists:**

Dan Bikel, Google Research NY (USA)
Julia Hockenmaier, University of Illinois at Urbana-Champaign (USA)
Slav Petrov, Google Research NY (USA)
Owen Rambow, Columbia University (USA)

# Table of Contents

# Workshop Program

**Saturday, June 5, 2010**

09:00-09:15 **Opening Remarks**

Statistical Parsing of MRLs: Workshop Preface and Overview

*Statistical Parsing of Morphologically Rich Languages (SPMRL) What, How and Whither*
Reut Tsarfaty, Djamé Seddah, Yoav Goldberg, Sandra Kuebler, Yannick Versley, Marie Candito, Jennifer Foster, Ines Rehbein and Lamia Tounsi

09:15-10:30 **Dependency-based parsing of MRLs** (Chair: Reut Tsarfaty)

*Improving Arabic Dependency Parsing with Lexical and Inflectional Morphological Features*
Yuval Marton, Nizar Habash and Owen Rambow

*Two Methods to Incorporate 'Local Morphosyntactic' Features in Hindi Dependency Parsing*
Bharat Ram Ambati, Samar Husain, Sambhav Jain, Dipti Misra Sharma and Rajeev Sangal

*Application of Different Techniques to Dependency Parsing of Basque*
Kepa Bengoetxea and Koldo Gojenola

10:30-11:00 **Break**

11:00-12:15 **Constituency-based parsing of MRLs** (Chair: Djamé Seddah)

*Modeling Morphosyntactic Agreement in Constituency-Based Parsing of Modern Hebrew*
Reut Tsarfaty and Khalil Sima'an

*Factors Affecting the Accuracy of Korean Parsing*
Tagyoung Chung, Matt Post and Daniel Gildea

*Direct Parsing of Discontinuous Constituents in German*
Wolfgang Maier

12:15-1:40 **Lunch Break**

**Saturday, June 5, 2010 (continued)**

1:40-2:30 **Invited Talk** (Chair: Reut Tsarfaty)

*Morphology in Statistical Machine Translation: Integrate-in or Tack-on?*
Kevin Knight

2:30-3:00 **Improved Estimation for parsing MRLs** (Chair: Yoav Goldberg)

*Handling Unknown Words in Statistical Latent-Variable Parsing Models for Arabic, English and French*
Mohammed Attia, Jennifer Foster, Deirdre Hogan, Joseph Le Roux, Lamia Tounsi and Josef van Genabith

*Parsing Word Clusters*
Marie Candito and Djamé Seddah

3:00-3:30 **Break**

3:30-4:45 **Rich Morphology and Lemmatisation: Short Papers and Posters** (Chair: Jennifer Foster)

*Lemmatization and Lexicalized Statistical Parsing of Morphologically-Rich Languages: the Case of French*
Djamé Seddah, Grzegorz Chrupała, Ozlem Cetinoglu, Josef van Genabith and Marie Candito

*On the Role of Morphosyntactic Features in Hindi Dependency Parsing*
Bharat Ram Ambati, Samar Husain, Joakim Nivre and Rajeev Sangal

*Easy-First Dependency Parsing of Modern Hebrew*
Yoav Goldberg and Michael Elhadad

4:45-5:45 **Discussion Panel: Dan Bikel, Julia Hockenmaier, Slav Petrov and Owen Rambow** (Chair: Sandra Kübler)

5:45-6:00 **Concluding remarks**

# Statistical Parsing of Morphologically Rich Languages (SPMRL) What, How and Whither


**Reut Tsarfaty**
Uppsala Universitet

**Djamé Seddah**
Alpage (Inria/Univ. Paris-Sorbonne)

**Yoav Goldberg**
Ben Gurion University

**Sandra Kübler**
Indiana University

**Marie Candito**
Alpage (Inria/Univ. Paris 7)

**Jennifer Foster**
NCLT, Dublin City University

**Yannick Versley**
Universität Tübingen

**Ines Rehbein**
Universität Saarbrücken

**Lamia Tounsi**
NCLT, Dublin City University



## Abstract

The term Morphologically Rich Languages (MRLs) refers to languages in which significant information concerning syntactic units and relations is expressed at word-level. There is ample evidence that the application of readily available statistical parsing models to such languages is susceptible to serious performance degradation. The first workshop on statistical parsing of MRLs hosts a variety of contributions which show that despite language-specific idiosyncrasies, the problems associated with parsing MRLs cut across languages and parsing frameworks. In this paper we review the current state-of-affairs with respect to parsing MRLs and point out central challenges. We synthesize the contributions of researchers working on parsing Arabic, Basque, French, German, Hebrew, Hindi and Korean to point out shared solutions across languages. The overarching analysis suggests itself as a source of directions for future investigations.


## 1 Introduction

The availability of large syntactically annotated corpora led to an explosion of interest in automatically inducing models for syntactic analysis and disambiguation called *statistical parsers*. The development of successful statistical parsing models for English focused on the Wall Street Journal Penn Treebank (PTB, (Marcus et al., 1993)) as the primary, and sometimes only, resource. Since the initial release of the Penn Treebank (PTB Marcus et al. (1993)), many different constituent-based parsing models have been developed in the context of parsing English (*e.g.* (Magerman, 1995; Collins, 1997; Charniak, 2000; Chiang, 2000; Bod, 2003; Charniak and Johnson, 2005; Petrov et al., 2006; Huang, 2008; Finkel et al., 2008; Carreras et al., 2008)). At their time, each of these models improved the state-of-the-art, bringing parsing performance on the standard test set of the Wall-Street-Journal to a performance ceiling of 92% $F_1$-score using the PARSEVAL evaluation metrics (Black et al., 1991). Some of these parsers have been adapted to other language/treebank pairs, but many of these adaptations have been shown to be considerably less successful.

Among the arguments that have been proposed to explain this performance gap are the impact of small data sets, differences in treebanks' annotation schemes, and inadequacy of the widely used PARSEVAL evaluation metrics. None of these aspects in isolation can account for the systematic performance deterioration, but observed from a wider, cross-linguistic perspective, a picture begins to emerge – that the morphologically rich nature of some of the languages makes them inherently more susceptible to such performance degradation. Linguistic factors associated with MRLs, such as a large inventory of word-forms, higher degrees of word order freedom, and the use of morphological information in indicating syntactic relations, makes them substantially harder to parse with models and techniques that have been developed with English data in mind.



*Proceedings of the NAACL HLT 2010 First Workshop on Statistical Parsing of Morphologically-Rich Languages*, pages 1–12,
Los Angeles, California, June 2010. ©2010 Association for Computational Linguistics

In addition to these technical and linguistic factors, the prominence of English parsing in the literature reduces the visibility of research aiming to solve problems particular to MRLs. The lack of streamlined communication among researchers working on different MRLs often leads to a *reinventing the wheel* syndrome. To circumvent this, the first workshop on Statistical Parsing of Morphologically Rich Languages (SPMRL 2010) offers a platform for this growing community to share their views of the different problems and oftentimes similar solutions.

We identify three main types of challenges, each of which raises many questions. Many of the questions are yet to be conclusively answered. The first type of challenges has to do with the architectural setup of parsing MRLs: *What is the nature of the input? Can words be represented abstractly to reflect shared morphological aspects? How can we cope with morphological segmentation errors propagated through the pipeline?* The second type concerns the representation of morphological information inside the articulated syntactic model: *Should morphological information be encoded at the level of PoS tags? On dependency relations? On top of non-terminals symbols? How should the integrated representations be learned and used?* A final genuine challenge has to do with sound estimation for lexical probabilities: *Given the finite, and often rather small, set of data, and the large number of morphological analyses licensed by rich inflectional systems, how can we analyze words unseen in the training data?*

Many of the challenges reported here are mostly irrelevant when parsing Section 23 of the PTB but they are of primordial importance in other tasks, including out-of-domain parsing, statistical machine translation, and parsing resource-poor languages. By synthesizing the contributions to the workshop and bringing it to the forefront, we hope to advance the state of the art of statistical parsing in general.

In this paper we therefore take the opportunity to analyze the knowledge that has been acquired in the different investigations for the purpose of identifying main bottlenecks and pointing out promising research directions. In section 2, we define MRLs and identify syntactic characteristics associated with them. We then discuss work on parsing MRLs in both the dependency-based and constituency-based setup. In section 3, we review the types of challenges associated with parsing MRLs across frameworks. In section 4, we focus on the contributions to the SPMRL workshop and identify recurring trends in the empirical results and conceptual solutions. In section 5, we analyze the emerging picture from a bird's eye view, and conclude that many challenges could be more faithfully addressed in the context of parsing morphologically ambiguous input.

## 2 Background

### 2.1 What are MRLs?

The term Morphologically Rich Languages (MRLs) is used in the CL/NLP literature to refer to languages in which substantial grammatical information, i.e., information concerning the arrangement of words into syntactic units or cues to syntactic relations, is expressed at word level.

The common linguistic and typological wisdom is that "morphology competes with syntax" (Bresnan, 2001). In effect, this means that *rich morphology* goes hand in hand with a host of *nonconfigurational* syntactic phenomena of the kind discussed by Hale (1983). Because information about the relations between syntactic elements is indicated in the form of words, these words can freely change their positions in the sentence. This is referred to as *free word order* (Mithun, 1992). Information about the grouping of elements together can further be expressed by reference to their morphological form. Such logical groupings of disparate elements are often called *discontinuous constituents*. In dependency structures, such discontinuities impose *nonprojectivity*. Finally, rich morphological information is found in abundance in conjunction with so-called *pro-drop* or *zero anaphora*. In such cases, rich morphological information in the head (or co-head) of the clause often makes it possible to omit an overt subject which would be semantically impoverished.

English, the most heavily studied language within the CL/NLP community, is not an MRL. Even though a handful of syntactic features (such as person and number) are reflected in the form of words, morphological information is often secondary to other syntactic factors, such as the position of words and their arrangement into phrases. German, an Indo-European language closely related to English, already exhibits some of the properties that make parsing MRLs problematic. The Semitic languages Arabic and Hebrew show an even more extreme case in terms of the richness of their morphological forms and the flexibility in their syntactic ordering.

### 2.2 Parsing MRLs

**Pushing the envelope of constituency parsing:** The Head-Driven models of the type proposed by Collins (1997) have been ported to parsing many MRLs, often via the implementation of Bikel (2002). For Czech, the adaptation by Collins et al. (1999) culminated in an 80 $F_1$-score.

German has become almost an archetype of the problems caused by MRLs; even though German has a moderately rich morphology and a moderately free word order, parsing results are far from those for English (see (Kübler, 2008) and references therein). Dubey (2005) showed that, for German parsing, adding case and morphology information together with smoothed markovization and an adequate unknown-word model is more important than lexicalization (Dubey and Keller, 2003).

For Modern Hebrew, Tsarfaty and Sima'an (2007) show that a simple treebank PCFG augmented with parent annotation and morphological information as state-splits significantly outperforms Head-Driven markovized models of the kind made popular by Klein and Manning (2003). Results for parsing Modern Standard Arabic using Bikel's implementation on gold-standard tagging and segmentation have not improved substantially since the initial release of the treebank (Maamouri et al., 2004; Kulick et al., 2006; Maamouri et al., 2008).

For Italian, Corazza et al. (2004) used the Stanford parser and Bikel's parser emulation of Collins' model 2 (Collins, 1997) on the ISST treebank, and obtained significantly lower results compared to English. It is notable that these models were applied without adding morphological signatures, using gold lemmas instead. Corazza et al. (2004) further tried different refinements including parent annotation and horizontal markovization, but none of them obtained the desired improvement.

For French, Crabbé and Candito (2008) and Seddah et al. (2010) show that, given a corpus comparable in size and properties (*i.e.* the number of tokens and grammar size), the performance level, both for Charniak's parser (Charniak, 2000) and the Berkeley parser (Petrov et al., 2006) was higher for parsing the PTB than it was for French. The split-merge-smooth implementation of (Petrov et al., 2006) consistently outperform various lexicalized and unlexicalized models for French (Seddah et al., 2009) and for many other languages (Petrov and Klein, 2007). In this respect, (Petrov et al., 2006) is considered MRL-friendly, due to its language agnostic design.

**The rise of dependency parsing:** It is commonly assumed that dependency structures are better suited for representing the syntactic structures of free word order, morphologically rich, languages, because this representation format does not rely crucially on the position of words and the internal grouping of surface chunks (Mel'čuk, 1988). It is an entirely different question, however, whether dependency parsers are in fact better suited for parsing such languages.

The CoNLL shared tasks on multilingual dependency parsing in 2006 and 2007 (Buchholz and Marsi, 2006; Nivre et al., 2007a) demonstrated that dependency parsing for MRLs is quite challenging. While dependency parsers are adaptable to many languages, as reflected in the multiplicity of the languages covered,[1] the analysis by Nivre et al. (2007b) shows that the best result was obtained for English, followed by Catalan, and that the most difficult languages to parse were Arabic, Basque, and Greek. Nivre et al. (2007a) drew a somewhat typological conclusion, that languages with rich morphology and free word order are the hardest to parse. This was shown to be the case for both MaltParser (Nivre et al., 2007c) and MST (McDonald et al., 2005), two of the best performing parsers on the whole.

**Annotation and evaluation matter:** An emerging question is therefore whether models that have been so successful in parsing English are necessarily appropriate for parsing MRLs – but associated with this question are important questions concerning the annotation scheme of the related treebanks. Obviously, when annotating structures for languages with characteristics different than English one has to face different annotation decisions, and it comes as no surprise that the annotated structures for MRLs often differ from those employed in the PTB.

[1] The shared tasks involved 18 languages, including many MRLs such as Arabic, Basque, Czech, Hungarian, and Turkish.

For Spanish and French, it was shown by Cowan and Collins (2005) and in (Arun and Keller, 2005; Schluter and van Genabith, 2007), that restructuring the treebanks' native annotation scheme to match the PTB annotation style led to a significant gain in parsing performance of Head-Driven models of the kind proposed in (Collins, 1997). For German, a language with four different treebanks and two substantially different annotation schemes, it has been shown that a PCFG parser is sensitive to the kind of representation employed in the treebank.

Dubey and Keller (2003), for example, showed that a simple PCFG parser outperformed an emulation of Collins' model 1 on NEGRA. They showed that using sister-head dependencies instead of head-head dependencies improved parsing performance, and hypothesized that it is due to the flatness of phrasal annotation. Kübler et al. (2006) showed considerably lower PARSEVAL scores on NEGRA (Skut et al., 1998) relative to the more hierarchically structured TüBa-D/Z (Hinrichs et al., 2005), again, hypothesizing that this is due to annotation differences.

Related to such comparisons is the question of the relevance of the PARSEVAL metrics for evaluating parsing results across languages and treebanks. Rehbein and van Genabith (2007) showed that PARSEVAL measures are sensitive to annotation scheme particularities (*e.g.* the internal node ratio). It was further shown that different metrics (*i.e.* the Leaf-ancestor path (Sampson and Babarczy, 2003) and dependency based ones in (Lin, 1995)) can lead to different performance ranking. This was confirmed also for French by Seddah et al. (2009).

The questions of how to annotate treebanks for MRLs and how to evaluate the performance of the different parsers on these different treebanks is crucial. For the MRL parsing community to be able to assess the difficulty of improving parsing results for French, German, Arabic, Korean, Basque, Hindi or Hebrew, we ought to first address fundamental questions including: Is the treebank sufficiently large to allow for proper grammar induction? Does the annotation scheme fit the language characteristics? Does the use of PTB annotation variants for other languages influence parsing results? Does the space-delimited tokenization allow for phrase boundary detection? Do the results for a specific approach generalize to more than one language?

## 3 Primary Research Questions

It is firmly established in theoretical linguistics that morphology and syntax closely interact through patterns of case marking, agreement, clitics and various types of compounds. Because of such close interactions, we expect morphological cues to help parsing performance. But in practice, when trying to incorporate morphological information into parsing models, three types of challenges present themselves:

**Architecture and Setup:** When attempting to parse complex word-forms that encapsulate both lexical and functional information, important architectural questions emerge, namely, what is the nature of the input that is given to the parsing system? Does the system attempt to parse sequences of words or does it aim to assign structures to sequences of morphological segments? If the former is the case, how can we represent words abstractly so as to reflect shared morphological aspects between them? If the latter is the case, how can we arrive at a good enough morphological segmentation for the purpose of statistical parsing, given raw input texts?

When working with morphologically rich languages such as Hebrew or Arabic, affixes may have syntactically independent functions. Many parsing models assume segmentation of the syntactically independent parts, such as prepositions or pronominal clitics, prior to parsing. But morphological segmentation requires disambiguation which is non-trivial, due to case syncretism and high morphological ambiguity exhibited by rich inflectional systems. The question is then when should we disambiguate the morphological analyses of input forms? Should we do that prior to parsing or perhaps jointly with it?[2]

**Representation and Modeling:** Assuming that the input to our system reflects morphological information, one way or another, which *types* of morpho-

[2]Most studies on parsing MRLs nowadays assume the gold standard segmentation and disambiguated morphological information as input. This is the case, for instance, for the Arabic parsing at CoNLL 2007 (Nivre et al., 2007a). This practice deludes the community as to the validity of the parsing results reported for MRLs in shared tasks. Goldberg et al. (2009), for instance, show a gap of up to 6pt $F_1$-score between performance on gold standard segmentation vs. raw text. One way to overcome this is to devise joint morphological and syntactic disambiguation frameworks (cf. (Goldberg and Tsarfaty, 2008)).

logical information should we include in the parsing model? Inflectional and/or derivational? Case information and/or agreement features? How can valency requirements reflected in derivational morphology affect the overall syntactic structure? In tandem with the decision concerning the morphological information to include, we face genuine challenges concerning how to represent such information in the syntactic model, be it constituency-based or dependency-based. Should we encode morphological information at the level of PoS tags and/or on top of syntactic elements? Should we decorate non-terminals nodes and/or dependency arcs or both?

Incorporating morphology in the statistical model is often even more challenging than the sum of these bare decisions, because of the nonconfigurational structures (free word order, discontinuous constituents) for rich markings are crucial (Hale, 1983). The parsing models designed for English often focus on learning rigid word order, and they do not take morphological information into account (cf. developing parsers for German (Dubey and Keller, 2003; Kübler et al., 2006)). The more complex question is therefore: what type of parsing model should we use for parsing MRLs? shall we use a general purpose implementation and attempt to amend it? how? or perhaps we should devise a new model from first principles, to address nonconfigurational phenomena effectively? using what form of representation? is it possible to find a single model that can effectively cope with different kinds of languages?

**Estimation and Smoothing:** Compared to English, MRLs tend to have a greater number of word forms and higher out-of-vocabulary (OOV) rates, due to the many feature combinations licensed by the inflectional system. A typical problem associated with parsing MRLs is substantial lexical data sparseness due to high morphological variation in surface forms. The question is therefore, given our finite, and often fairly small, annotated sets of data, how can we guess the morphological analyses, including the PoS tag assignment and various features, of an OOV word? How can we learn the probabilities of such assignments? In a more general setup, this problem is akin to handling out-of-vocabulary or rare words for robust statistical parsing, and techniques for domain adaptation via lexicon enhancement (also explored for English and other morphologically impoverished languages).

| | Constituency-Based | Dependency-Based |
|---|---|---|
| Arabic | (Attia et al., 2010) | (Marton et al., 2010)† |
| Basque | - | (Bengoetxea and Gojenola, 2010) |
| English | (Attia et al., 2010) | - |
| French | (Attia et al., 2010)<br>(Seddah et al., 2010)<br>(Candito and Seddah, 2010)† | -|
| German | (Maier, 2010) | - |
| Hebrew | (Tsarfaty and Sima'an, 2010) | (Goldberg and Elhadad, 2010)† |
| Hindi | - | (Ambati et al., 2010a)†<br>(Ambati et al., 2010b) |
| Korean | (Chung et al., 2010) | - |

Table 1: An overview of SPMRL contributions. († report results also for non-gold standard input)

So, in fact, incorporating morphological information inside the syntactic model for the purpose of statistical parsing is anything but trivial. In the next section we review the various approaches taken in the individual contributions of the SPMRL workshop for addressing such challenges.

## 4 Parsing MRLs: Recurring Trends

The first workshop on parsing MRLs features 11 contributions for a variety of languages with a range of different parsing frameworks. Table 1 lists the individual contributions within a cross-language cross-framework grid. In this section, we focus on trends that occur among the different contributions. This may be a biased view since some of the problems that exist for parsing MRLs may have not been at all present, but it is a synopsis of where we stand with respect to problems that are being addressed.

### 4.1 Architecture and Setup: Gold vs. Predicted Morphological Information

While morphological information can be very informative for syntactic analysis, morphological analysis of surface forms is ambiguous in many ways. In German, for instance, case syncretism (*i.e.* a single surface form corresponding to different cases) is pervasive, and in Hebrew and Arabic, the lack of vocalization patterns in written texts leads to multiple morphological analyses for each space-delimited token. In real world situations, gold morphological information is not available prior to parsing. Can parsing systems make effective use of morphology even when gold morphological information is absent?

Several papers address this challenge by presenting results for both the gold and the automatically predicted PoS and morphological information (Ambati et al., 2010a; Marton et al., 2010; Goldberg and Elhadad, 2010; Seddah et al., 2010). Not very surprisingly, all evaluated systems show a drop in parsing accuracy in the non-gold settings.

An interesting trend is that in many cases, using noisy morphological information is worse than not using any at all. For Arabic Dependency parsing, using predicted CASE causes a substantial drop in accuracy while it greatly improves performance in the gold setting (Marton et al., 2010). For Hindi Dependency Parsing, using chunk-internal cues (*i.e.* marking non-recursive phrases) is beneficial when gold chunk-boundaries are available, but suboptimal when they are automatically predicted (Ambati et al., 2010a). For Hebrew Dependency Parsing with the MST parser, using gold morphological features shows no benefit over not using them, while using automatically predicted morphological features causes a big drop in accuracy compared to not using them (Goldberg and Elhadad, 2010). For French Constituency Parsing, Seddah et al. (2010) and Candito and Seddah (2010) show that while gold information for the part-of-speech and lemma of each word form results in a significant improvement, the gain is low when switching to predicted information. Reassuringly, Ambati et al. (2010a), Marton et al. (2010), and Goldberg and Elhadad (2010) demonstrate that some morphological information can indeed be beneficial for parsing even in the automatic setting. Ensuring that this is indeed so, appears to be in turn linked to the question of how morphology is represented and incorporated in the parsing model.

The same effect in a different guise appears in the contribution of Chung et al. (2010) concerning parsing Korean. Chung et al. (2010) show a significant improvement in parsing accuracy when including traces of null anaphors (a.k.a. *pro-drop*) in the input to the parser. Just like overt morphology, traces and null elements encapsulate functional information about relational entities in the sentence (the subject, the object, etc.), and including them at the input level provides helpful disambiguating cues for the overall structure that represents such relations. However, assuming that such traces are given prior to parsing is, for all practical purposes, infeasible. This leads to an interesting question: will identifying such functional elements (marked as traces, overt morphology, etc) *during* parsing, while complicating that task itself, be on the whole justified?

Closely linked to the inclusion of morphological information in the input is the choice of PoS tag set to use. The generally accepted view is that fine-grained PoS tags are morphologically more informative but may be harder to statistically learn and parse with, in particular in the non-gold scenario. Marton et al. (2010) demonstrate that a fine-grained tag set provides the best results for Arabic dependency parsing when gold tags are known, while a much smaller tag set is preferred in the automatic setting.

### 4.2 Representation and Modeling: Incorporating Morphological Information

Many of the studies presented here explore the use of feature representation of morphological information for the purpose of syntactic parsing (Ambati et al., 2010a; Ambati et al., 2010b; Bengoetxea and Gojenola, 2010; Goldberg and Elhadad, 2010; Marton et al., 2010; Tsarfaty and Sima'an, 2010). Clear trends among the contributions emerge concerning the *kind* of morphological information that helps statistical parsing. Morphological CASE is shown to be beneficial across the board. It is shown to help for parsing Basque, Hebrew, Hindi and to some extent Arabic.[3] Morphological DEFINITENESS and STATE are beneficial for Hebrew and Arabic when explicitly represented in the model. STATE, ASPECT and MOOD are beneficial for Hindi, but only marginally beneficial for Arabic. CASE and SUBORDINATION-TYPE are the most beneficial features for Basque transition-based dependency parsing.

A closer view into the results mentioned in the previous paragraph suggests that, beyond the kind of information that is being used, the way in which morphological information is represented and used by the model has substantial ramification as to whether or not it leads to performance improvements. The so-called "agreement features" GENDER, NUMBER, PERSON, provide for an interesting case study in this respect. When included directly as

[3]For Arabic, CASE is useful when gold morphology information is available, but substantially hurt results when it is not.

machine learning features, agreement features benefit dependency parsing for Arabic (Marton et al., 2010), but not Hindi (dependency) (Ambati et al., 2010a; Ambati et al., 2010b) or Hebrew (Goldberg and Elhadad, 2010). When represented as simple splits of non-terminal symbols, agreement information does not help constituency-based parsing performance for Hebrew (Tsarfaty and Sima'an, 2010). However, when agreement patterns are directly represented on dependency arcs, they contribute an improvement for Hebrew dependency parsing (Goldberg and Elhadad, 2010). When agreement is encoded at the realization level inside a Relational-Realizational model (Tsarfaty and Sima'an, 2008), agreement features improve the state-of-the-art for Hebrew parsing (Tsarfaty and Sima'an, 2010).

One of the advantages of the latter study is that morphological information which is expressed at the level of words gets interpreted elsewhere, on functional elements higher up the constituency tree. In dependency parsing, similar cases may arise, that is, morphological information might not be as useful on the form on which it is expressed, but would be more useful at a different position where it could influence the correct attachment of the main verb to other elements. Interesting patterns of that sort occur in Basque, where the SUBORDINATIONTYPE morpheme attaches to the auxiliary verb, though it mainly influences attachments to the main verb.

Bengoetxea and Gojenola (2010) attempted two different ways to address this, one using a transformation segmenting the relevant morpheme and attaching it to the main verb instead, and another by propagating the morpheme along arcs, through a "stacking" process, to where it is relevant. Both ways led to performance improvements. The idea of a segmentation transformation imposes non-trivial pre-processing, but it may be that automatically learning the propagation of morphological features is a promising direction for future investigation.

Another, albeit indirect, way to include morphological information in the parsing model is using so-called latent information or some mechanism of clustering. The general idea is the following: when morphological information is added to standard terminal or non-terminal symbols, it imposes restrictions on the distribution of these no-longer-equivalent elements. Learning latent information does not represent morphological information directly, but presumably, the distributional restrictions can be automatically learned along with the splits of labels symbols in models such as (Petrov et al., 2006). For Korean (Chung et al., 2010), latent information contributes significant improvements. One can further do the opposite, namely, merging terminals symbols for the purpose of obtaining an abstraction over morphological features. When such clustering uses a morphological signature of some sort, it is shown to significantly improve constituency-based parsing for French (Candito and Seddah, 2010).

### 4.3 Representation and Modeling: Free Word Order and Flexible Constituency Structure

Off-the-shelf parsing tools are found in abundance for English. One problematic aspect of using them to parse MRLs lies in the fact that these tools focus on the statistical modeling of *configurational* information. These models often condition on the position of words relative to one another (*e.g.* in transition-based dependency parsing) or on the distance between words inside constituents (*e.g.* in Head-Driven parsing). Many of the contributions to the workshop show that working around existing implementations may be insufficient, and we may have to come up with more radical solutions.

Several studies present results that support the conjecture that when free word-order is explicitly taken into account, morphological information is more likely to contribute to parsing accuracy. The Relational-Realizational model used in (Tsarfaty and Sima'an, 2010) allows for reordering of constituents at a configuration layer, which is independent of the realization patterns learned from the data (*vis-à-vis* case marking and agreement). The easy-first algorithm of (Goldberg and Elhadad, 2010) which allows for significant flexibility in the order of attachment, allows the model to benefit from agreement patterns over dependency arcs that are easier to detect and attach first. The use of larger subtrees in (Chung et al., 2010) for parsing Korean, within a Bayesian framework, allows the model to learn distributions that take more elements into account, and thus learn the different distributions associated with morphologically marked elements in constituency structures, to improve performance.

In addition to free word order, MRLs show higher degree of freedom in extraposition. Both of these phenomena can result in discontinuous structures. In constituency-based treebanks, this is either annotated as additional information which has to be recovered somehow (traces in the case of the PTB, complex edge labels in the German TüBa-D/Z), or as discontinuous phrase structures, which cannot be handled with current PCFG models. Maier (2010) suggests the use of Linear Context-Free Rewriting Systems (LCFRSs) in order to make discontinuous structure transparent to the parsing process and yet preserve familiar notions from constituency.

Dependency representation uses non-projective dependencies to reflect discontinuities, which is problematic to parse with models that assume projectivity. Different ways have been proposed to deal with non-projectivity (Nivre and Nilsson, 2005; McDonald et al., 2005; McDonald and Pereira, 2006; Nivre, 2009). Bengoetxea and Gojenola (2010) discuss non-projective dependencies in Basque and show that the pseudo-projective transformation of (Nivre and Nilsson, 2005) improves accuracy for dependency parsing of Basque. Moreover, they show that in combination with other transformations, it improves the utility of these other ones, too.

### 4.4 Estimation and Smoothing: Coping with Lexical Sparsity

Morphological word form variation augments the vocabulary size and thus worsens the problem of lexical data sparseness. Words occurring with medium-frequency receive less reliable estimates, and the number of rare/unknown words is increased. One way to cope with the one of both aspects of this problem is through *clustering*, that is, providing an abstract representation over word forms that reflects their shared morphological and morphosyntactic aspects. This was done, for instance, in previous work on parsing German. Versley and Rehbein (2009) cluster words according to linear context features. These clusters include valency information added to verbs and morphological features such as case and number added to pre-terminal nodes. The clusters are then integrated as features in a discriminative parsing model to cope with unknown words. Their discriminative model thus obtains state-of-the-art results on parsing German.

Several contribution address similar challenges. For constituency-based generative parsers, the simple technique of replacing word forms with more abstract symbols is investigated by (Seddah et al., 2010; Candito and Seddah, 2010). For French, replacing each word form by its predicted part-of-speech and lemma pair results in a slight performance improvement (Seddah et al., 2010). When words are clustered, even according to a very local linear-context similarity measure, measured over a large raw corpus, and when word clusters are used in place of word forms, the gain in performance is even higher (Candito and Seddah, 2010). In both cases, the technique provides more reliable estimates for in-vocabulary words, since a given lemma or cluster appear more frequently. It also increases the known vocabulary. For instance, if a plural form is unseen in the training set but the corresponding singular form is known, then in a setting of using lemmas in terminal symbols, both forms are known.

For dependency parsing, Marton et al. (2010) investigates the use of morphological features that involve some semantic abstraction over Arabic forms. The use of undiacritized lemmas is shown to improve performance. Attia et al. (2010) specifically address the handling of unknown words in the latent-variable parsing model. Here again, the technique that is investigated is to project unknown words to more general symbols using morphological clues. A study on three languages, English, French and Arabic, shows that this method helps in all cases, but that the greatest improvement is obtained for Arabic, which has the richest morphology among three.

## 5 Where we're at

It is clear from the present overview that we are yet to obtain a complete understanding concerning which models effectively parse MRLs, how to annotate treebanks for MRLs and, importantly, how to evaluate parsing performance across types of languages and treebanks. These foundational issues are crucial for deriving more conclusive recommendations as to the kind of models and morphological features that can lead to advancing the state-of-the-art for parsing MRLs. One way to target such an understanding would be to encourage the investigation of particular tasks, individually or in the context of shared tasks, that are tailored to treat those problematic aspects of MRLs that we surveyed here.

So far, constituency-based parsers have been assessed based on their performance on the PTB (and to some extent, across German treebanks (Kübler, 2008)) whereas comparison across languages was rendered opaque due to data set differences and representation idiosyncrasies. It would be interesting to investigate such a cross-linguistic comparison of parsers in the context of a shared task on constituency-based statistical parsing, in additional to dependency-based ones as reported in (Nivre et al., 2007a). Standardizing data sets for a large number of languages with different characteristics, would require us, as a community, to aim for constituency-representation guidelines that can represent the shared aspects of structures in different languages, while at the same time allowing differences between them to be reflected in the model.

Furthermore, it would be a good idea to introduce parsing tasks, for either constituent-based or dependency-based setups, which consider raw text as input, rather than morphologically segmented and analyzed text. Addressing the parsing problem while facing the morphological disambiguation challenge in its full-blown complexity would be illuminating and educating for at least two reasons: firstly, it would give us a better idea of what is the state-of-the-art for parsing MRLs in realistic scenarios. Secondly, it might lead to profound insights about the potentially successful ways to use morphology inside a parser, which may differ from the insights concerning the use of morphology in the less realistic parsing scenarios, where gold morphological information is given.

Finally, to be able to perceive where we stand with respect to parsing MRLs and how models fare against one another across languages, it would be crucial to arrive at evaluation metrics that capture information that is shared among the different representations, for instance, functional information concerning predicate-argument relations. Using the different kinds of measures in the context of cross-framework tasks will help us understand the utility of the different evaluation metrics that have been proposed and to arrive at a clearer picture of what it is that we wish to compare, and how we can faithfully do so across models, languages and treebanks.

## 6 Conclusion

This paper presents the synthesis of 11 contributions to the first workshop on statistical parsing for morphologically rich languages. We have shown that architectural, representational, and estimation issues associated with parsing MRLs are found to be challenging across languages and parsing frameworks. The use of morphological information in the non gold-tagged input scenario is found to cause substantial differences in parsing performance, and in the kind of morphological features that lead to performance improvements.

Whether or not morphological features help parsing also depends on the kind of model in which they are embedded, and the different ways they are treated within. Furthermore, sound statistical estimation methods for morphologically rich, complex lexica, turn out to be crucial for obtaining good parsing accuracy when using general-purpose models and algorithms. In the future we hope to gain better understanding of the common pitfalls in, and novel solutions for, parsing morphologically ambiguous input, and to arrive at principled guidelines for selecting the model and features to include when parsing different kinds of languages. Such insights may be gained, among other things, in the context of more morphologically-aware shared parsing tasks.

## Acknowledgements

The program committee would like to thank NAACL for hosting the workshop and SIGPARSE for their sponsorship. We further thank INRIA Alpage team for their generous sponsorship. We are finally grateful to our reviewers and authors for their dedicated work and individual contributions.

## References

Bharat Ram Ambati, Samar Husain, Sambhav Jain, Dipti Misra Sharma, and Rajeev Sangal. 2010a. Two methods to incorporate local morphosyntactic features in Hindi dependency parsing. In *Proceedings of the NAACL/HLT Workshop on Statistical Parsing of Morphologically Rich Languages (SPMRL 2010)*, Los Angeles, CA.

Bharat Ram Ambati, Samar Husain, Joakim Nivre, and Rajeev Sangal. 2010b. On the role of morphosyntactic features in Hindi dependency parsing. In *Proceedings of the NAACL/HLT Workshop on Statistical Parsing of Morphologically Rich Languages (SPMRL 2010)*, Los Angeles, CA.

Abhishek Arun and Frank Keller. 2005. Lexicalization in crosslinguistic probabilistic parsing: The case of French. In *Proceedings of the 43rd Annual Meeting of the Association for Computational Linguistics*, pages 306–313, Ann Arbor, MI.

Mohammed Attia, Jennifer Foster, Deirdre Hogan, Joseph Le Roux, Lamia Tounsi, and Josef van Genabith. 2010. Handling unknown words in statistical latent-variable parsing models for Arabic, English and French. In *Proceedings of the NAACL/HLT Workshop on Statistical Parsing of Morphologically Rich Languages (SPMRL 2010)*, Los Angeles, CA.

Kepa Bengoetxea and Koldo Gojenola. 2010. Application of different techniques to dependency parsing of Basque. In *Proceedings of the NAACL/HLT Workshop on Statistical Parsing of Morphologically Rich Languages (SPMRL 2010)*, Los Angeles, CA.

Daniel M. Bikel. 2002. Design of a multi-lingual, parallel-processing statistical parsing engine. In *Proceedings of the Second International Conference on Human Language Technology Research*, pages 178–182. Morgan Kaufmann Publishers Inc. San Francisco, CA, USA.

E. Black, S. Abney, D. Flickinger, C. Gdaniec, R. Grishman, P. Harrison, D. Hindle, R. Ingria, F. Jelinek, J. Klavans, M. Liberman, M. Marcus, S. Roukos, B. Santorini, and T. Strzalkowski. 1991. A procedure for quantitatively comparing the syntactic coverage of English grammars. In *Proceedings of the DARPA Speech and Natural Language Workshop*, pages 306–311, San Mateo (CA). Morgan Kaufman.

Rens Bod. 2003. An efficient implementation of a new DOP model. In *Proceedings of the tenth conference on European chapter of the Association for Computational Linguistics*, pages 19–26, Budapest, Hungary.

Joan Bresnan. 2001. *Lexical-Functional Syntax*. Blackwell, Oxford.

Sabine Buchholz and Erwin Marsi. 2006. CoNLL-X shared task on multilingual dependency parsing. In *Proceedings of the Tenth Conference on Computational Language Learning (CoNLL)*, pages 149–164, New York, NY.

Marie Candito and Djamé Seddah. 2010. Parsing word clusters. In *Proceedings of the NAACL/HLT Workshop on Statistical Parsing of Morphologically Rich Languages (SPMRL 2010)*, Los Angeles, CA.

Xavier Carreras, Michael Collins, and Terry Koo. 2008. TAG, dynamic programming, and the perceptron for efficient, feature-rich parsing. In *Proceedings of the Twelfth Conference on Computational Natural Language Learning (CoNLL)*, pages 9–16, Manchester, UK.

Eugene Charniak and Mark Johnson. 2005. Course-to-fine n-best-parsing and maxent discriminative reranking. In *Proceedings of the 43rd Annual Meeting of the ACL*, pages 173–180, Barcelona, Spain, June.

Eugene Charniak. 2000. A maximum-entropy-inspired parser. In *Proceedings of the 1st Annual Meeting of the North American Chapter of the ACL (NAACL)*, Seattle.

David Chiang. 2000. Statistical parsing with an automatically-extracted Tree Adjoining Grammar. In *Proceedings of the 38th Annual Meeting on Association for Computational Linguistics*, pages 456–463, Hong Kong. Association for Computational Linguistics Morristown, NJ, USA.

Tagyoung Chung, Matt Post, and Daniel Gildea. 2010. Factors affecting the accuracy of Korean parsing. In *Proceedings of the NAACL/HLT Workshop on Statistical Parsing of Morphologically Rich Languages (SPMRL 2010)*, Los Angeles, CA.

Michael Collins, Jan Hajič, Lance Ramshaw, and Christoph Tillmann. 1999. A statistical parser for Czech. In *Proceedings of the 37th Annual Meeting of the ACL*, volume 37, pages 505–512, College Park, MD.

Michael Collins. 1997. Three Generative, Lexicalized Models for Statistical Parsing. In *Proceedings of the 35th Annual Meeting of the Association for Computational Linguistics*, pages 16–23, Madrid, Spain.

Anna Corazza, Alberto Lavelli, Giogio Satta, and Roberto Zanoli. 2004. Analyzing an Italian treebank with state-of-the-art statistical parsers. In *Proceedings of the Third Third Workshop on Treebanks and Linguistic Theories (TLT 2004)*, Tübingen, Germany.

Brooke Cowan and Michael Collins. 2005. Morphology and reranking for the statistical parsing of Spanish. In *in Proceedins of EMNLP*.

Benoit Crabbé and Marie Candito. 2008. Expériences d'analyse syntaxique statistique du français. In *Actes de la 15ème Conférence sur le Traitement Automatique des Langues Naturelles (TALN'08)*, pages 45–54, Avignon, France.

Amit Dubey and Frank Keller. 2003. Probabilistic parsing for German using sister-head dependencies. In *In Proceedings of the 41st Annual Meeting of the Association for Computational Linguistics*, pages 96–103, Ann Arbor, MI.

Amit Dubey. 2005. What to do when lexicalization fails: parsing German with suffix analysis and smoothing. In *43rd Annual Meeting of the Association for Computational Linguistics*.

Jenny Rose Finkel, Alex Kleeman, and Christopher D. Manning. 2008. Efficient, feature-based, conditional random field parsing. In *Proceedings of ACL*.

Yoav Goldberg and Michael Elhadad. 2010. Easy-first dependency parsing of Modern Hebrew. In *Proceedings of the NAACL/HLT Workshop on Statistical Parsing of Morphologically Rich Languages (SPMRL 2010)*, Los Angeles, CA.

Yoav Goldberg and Reut Tsarfaty. 2008. A single framework for joint morphological segmentation and syntactic parsing. In *Proceedings of the 46nd Annual Meeting of the Association for Computational Linguistics*.

Yoav Goldberg, Reut Tsarfaty, Meni Adler, and Michael Elhadad. 2009. Enhancing unlexicalized parsing performance using a wide coverage lexicon, fuzzy tag-set mapping, and em-hmm-based lexical probabilities. In *Proceedings of the 12th Conference of the European Chapter of the Association for Computational Linguistics*, pages 327–335.

Kenneth L. Hale. 1983. Warlpiri and the grammar of non-configurational languages. *Natural Language and Linguistic Theory*, 1(1).

Erhard W. Hinrichs, Sandra Kübler, and Karin Naumann. 2005. A unified representation for morphological, syntactic, semantic, and referential annotations. In *Proceedings of the ACL Workshop on Frontiers in Corpus Annotation II: Pie in the Sky*, pages 13–20, Ann Arbor, MI.

Liang Huang. 2008. Forest reranking: Discriminative parsing with non-local features. In *Proceedings of ACL*.

Dan Klein and Christopher D. Manning. 2003. Accurate unlexicalized parsing. In *Proceedings of ACL*, pages 423–430.

Sandra Kübler, Erhard W. Hinrichs, and Wolfgang Maier. 2006. Is it really that difficult to parse German? In *Proceedings of the 2006 Conference on Empirical Methods in Natural Language Processing*, pages 111–119, Sydney, Australia, July. Association for Computational Linguistics.

Sandra Kübler. 2008. The PaGe 2008 shared task on parsing German. In *Proceedings of the Workshop on Parsing German*, pages 55–63. Association for Computational Linguistics.

Seth Kulick, Ryan Gabbard, and Mitchell Marcus. 2006. Parsing the Arabic treebank: Analysis and improvements. In *Proceedings of TLT*.

Dekang Lin. 1995. A dependency-based method for evaluating broad-coverage parsers. In *International Joint Conference on Artificial Intelligence*, pages 1420–1425, Montreal.

Mohamed Maamouri, Ann Bies, Tim Buckwalter, and Wigdan Mekki. 2004. The Penn Arabic treebank: Building a large-scale annotated Arabic corpus. In *Proceedings of NEMLAR International Conference on Arabic Language Resources and Tools*.

Mohamed Maamouri, Ann Bies, and Seth Kulick. 2008. Enhanced annotation and parsing of the Arabic treebank. In *Proceedings of INFOS*.

David M. Magerman. 1995. Statistical decision-tree models for parsing. In *Proceedings of the 33rd Annual Meeting on Association for Computational Linguistics*, pages 276–283, Cambridge, MA.

Wolfgang Maier. 2010. Direct parsing of discontinuous constituents in german. In *Proceedings of the NAACL/HLT Workshop on Statistical Parsing of Morphologically Rich Languages (SPMRL 2010)*, Los Angeles, CA.

Mitchell Marcus, Beatrice Santorini, and Mary Ann Marcinkiewicz. 1993. Building a large annotated corpus of English: The Penn Treebank. *Computational Linguistics*, 19(2):313–330.

Yuval Marton, Nizar Habash, and Owen Rambow. 2010. Improving Arabic dependency parsing with lexical and inflectional morphological features. In *Proceedings of the NAACL/HLT Workshop on Statistical Parsing of Morphologically Rich Languages (SPMRL 2010)*, Los Angeles, CA.

Ryan T. McDonald and Fernando C. N. Pereira. 2006. Online learning of approximate dependency parsing algorithms. In *Proc. of EACL'06*.

Ryan T. McDonald, Koby Crammer, and Fernando C. N. Pereira. 2005. Online large-margin training of dependency parsers. In *Proc. of ACL'05*, Ann Arbor, USA.

Igor Mel'čuk. 1988. *Dependency Syntax: Theory and Practice*. State University of New York Press.

Marianne Mithun. 1992. Is basic word order universal? In Doris L. Payne, editor, *Pragmatics of Word Order Flexibility*. John Benjamins, Amsterdam.

Joakim Nivre and Jens Nilsson. 2005. Pseudo-projective dependency parsing. In *Proceedings of the 43rd Annual Meeting of the Association for Computational Linguistics (ACL)*, Ann Arbor, MI.

Joakim Nivre, Johan Hall, Sandra Kübler, Ryan McDonald, Jens Nilsson, Sebastian Riedel, and Deniz Yuret. 2007a. The CoNLL 2007 shared task on dependency parsing. In *Proceedings of the CoNLL Shared Task Session of EMNLP-CoNLL 2007*, pages 915–932, Prague, Czech Republic, June. Association for Computational Linguistics.

Joakim Nivre, Johan Hall, Sandra Kübler, Ryan McDonald, Jens Nilsson, Sebastian Riedel, and Deniz Yuret. 2007b. The CoNLL 2007 shared task on dependency parsing. In *Proceedings of the CoNLL Shared Task Session of EMNLP-CoNLL 2007*, pages 915–932.

Joakim Nivre, Johan Hall, Jens Nilsson, Atanas Chanev, Gülşen Eryiğit, Sandra Kübler, Svetoslav Marinov, and Erwin Marsi. 2007c. MaltParser: A language-independent system for data-driven dependency parsing. *Natural Language Engineering*, 13(2):95–135.

Joakim Nivre. 2009. Non-projective dependency parsing in expected linear time. In *Proceedings of the Joint Conference of the 47th Annual Meeting of the ACL and the 4th International Joint Conference on Natural Language Processing of the AFNLP*.

Slav Petrov and Dan Klein. 2007. Improved inference for unlexicalized parsing. In *Human Language Technologies 2007: The Conference of the North American Chapter of the Association for Computational Linguistics; Proceedings of the Main Conference*.

Slav Petrov, Leon Barrett, Romain Thibaux, and Dan Klein. 2006. Learning accurate, compact, and interpretable tree annotation. In *Proceedings of the 21st International Conference on Computational Linguistics and 44th Annual Meeting of the Association for Computational Linguistics*, Sydney, Australia, July. Association for Computational Linguistics.

Ines Rehbein and Josef van Genabith. 2007. Treebank annotation schemes and parser evaluation for German. In *Proceedings of the 2007 Joint Conference on Empirical Methods in Natural Language Processing and Computational Natural Language Learning (EMNLP-CoNLL)*, Prague, Czech Republic.

Geoffrey Sampson and Anna Babarczy. 2003. A test of the leaf-ancestor metric for parse accuracy. *Natural Language Engineering*, 9(04):365–380.

Natalie Schluter and Josef van Genabith. 2007. Preparing, restructuring, and augmenting a French Treebank: Lexicalised parsers or coherent treebanks? In *Proc. of PACLING 07*, Melbourne, Australia.

Djamé Seddah, Marie Candito, and Benoit Crabbé. 2009. Cross parser evaluation and tagset variation: A French Treebank study. In *Proceedings of the 11th Internation Conference on Parsing Technologies (IWPT'09)*, pages 150–161, Paris, France, October. Association for Computational Linguistics.

Djamé Seddah, Grzegorz Chrupała, Ozlem Cetinoglu, Josef van Genabith, and Marie Candito. 2010. Lemmatization and statistical lexicalized parsing of morphologically-rich languages. In *Proceedings of the NAACL/HLT Workshop on Statistical Parsing of Morphologically Rich Languages (SPMRL 2010)*, Los Angeles, CA.

Wojciech Skut, Thorsten Brants, Brigitte Krenn, and Hans Uszkoreit. 1998. A linguistically interpreted corpus of German newspaper texts. In *ESSLLI Workshop on Recent Advances in Corpus Annotation*, Saarbrücken, Germany.

Reut Tsarfaty and Khalil Sima'an. 2007. Three-dimensional parametrization for parsing morphologically rich languages. In *Proceedings of the 10th International Conference on Parsing Technologies (IWPT)*, pages 156–167.

Reut Tsarfaty and Khalil Sima'an. 2008. Relational-Realizational parsing. In *Proceedings of the 22nd International Conference on Computational Linguistics*, pages 889–896.

Reut Tsarfaty and Khalil Sima'an. 2010. Modeling morphosyntactic agreement in constituency-based parsing of Modern Hebrew. In *Proceedings of the NAACL/HLT Workshop on Statistical Parsing of Morphologically Rich Languages (SPMRL 2010)*, Los Angeles, CA.

Yannick Versley and Ines Rehbein. 2009. Scalable discriminative parsing for german. In *Proceedings of the 11th International Conference on Parsing Technologies (IWPT'09)*, pages 134–137, Paris, France, October. Association for Computational Linguistics.

# Improving Arabic Dependency Parsing with Lexical and Inflectional Morphological Features

**Yuval Marton, Nizar Habash** and **Owen Rambow**
Center for Computational Learning Systems (CCLS)
Columbia University
{ymarton,habash,rambow}@ccls.columbia.edu

## Abstract

We explore the contribution of different lexical and inflectional morphological features to dependency parsing of Arabic, a morphologically rich language. We experiment with all leading POS tagsets for Arabic, and introduce a few new sets. We show that training the parser using a simple regular expressive extension of an impoverished POS tagset with high prediction accuracy does better than using a highly informative POS tagset with only medium prediction accuracy, although the latter performs best on gold input. Using controlled experiments, we find that definiteness (or determiner presence), the so-called phi-features (person, number, gender), and undiacritzed lemma are most helpful for Arabic parsing on predicted input, while case and state are most helpful on gold.

## 1 Introduction

Parsers need to learn the syntax of the modeled language, in order to project structure on newly seen sentences. Parsing model design aims to come up with features that best help parsers to learn the syntax and choose among different parses. One aspect of syntax, which is often not explicitly modeled in parsing, involves morphological constraints on syntactic structure, such as agreement. In this paper, we explore the role of morphological features in parsing Modern Standard Arabic (MSA). For MSA, the space of possible morphological features is fairly large. We determine which morphological features help and why, and we determine the upper bound for their contribution to parsing quality.

We first present the corpus we use (§2), then relevant Arabic linguistic facts (§3); we survey related work (§4), describe our experiments (§5), and conclude with analysis of parsing error types (§6).

## 2 Corpus

We use the Columbia Arabic Treebank (CATiB) (Habash and Roth, 2009). Specifically, we use the portion converted from part 3 of the Penn Arabic Treebank (PATB) (Maamouri et al., 2004) to the CATiB format, which enriches the CATiB dependency trees with full PATB morphological information. CATiB's dependency representation is based on traditional Arabic grammar and emphasizes syntactic case relations. It has a reduced POS tagset (with six tags only), but a standard set of eight dependency relations: **SBJ** and **OBJ** for subject and (direct or indirect) object, respectively, (whether they appear pre- or post-verbally); **IDF** for the idafa (possessive) relation; **MOD** for most other modifications; and other less common relations that we will not discuss here. For more information, see (Habash and Roth, 2009). The CATiB treebank uses the word segmentation of the PATB.[1] It splits off several categories of orthographic clitics, but not the definite article ال *Al*. In all of the experiments reported in this paper, we use the gold segmentation. An example CATiB dependency tree is shown in Figure 1.[2]

## 3 Relevant Linguistic Concepts

**Morphemes**: At a shallow level, Arabic words can be described in terms of their morphemes. In addition to concatenative prefixes and suffixes, Ara-

[1] Tokenization involves further decisions on the segmented token forms, such as spelling normalization.

[2] All Arabic transliterations are presented in the HSB transliteration scheme (Habash et al., 2007).



*Proceedings of the NAACL HLT 2010 First Workshop on Statistical Parsing of Morphologically-Rich Languages*, pages 13–21,
Los Angeles, California, June 2010. ©2010 Association for Computational Linguistics

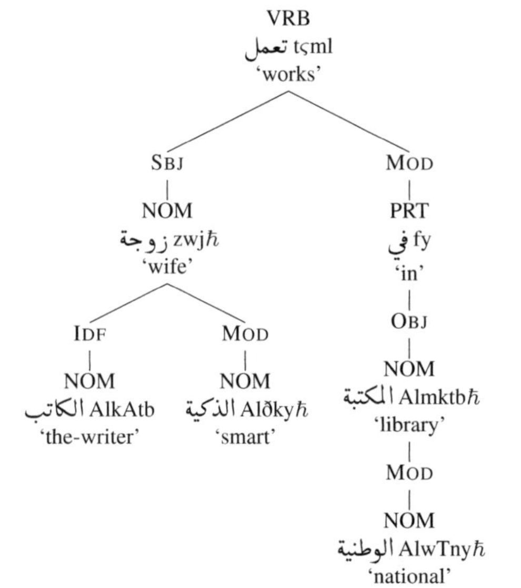


Figure 1: CATiB. تعمل زوجة الكاتب الذكية في المكتبة الوطنية *tςml zwjħ AlkAtb Alðkyħ fy Almktbħ AlwTnyħ* 'The writer's smart wife works at the national library.' (Annotation example)

bic has templatic morphemes called *root* and *pattern*. For example, the word يكاتبون *yu+kAtib+uwn* 'they correspond' has one prefix and one suffix, in addition to a stem composed of the root ك-ت-ب *k-t-b* 'writing related' and the pattern *1A2i3*. [3]

**Lexeme and Features**: At a deeper level, Arabic words can be described in terms of sets of inflectional and lexical morphological features. We first discuss lexical features. The set of word forms that only vary inflectionally among each other is called the *lexeme*. A *lemma* is a particular word form used to represent, or cite, the lexeme word set. For example, verb lemmas are third person masculine singular perfective. We explore using both diacritized lemma, and undiacritized lemma (*lmm*). Just as the lemma abstracts over inflectional morphology, the root abstracts over both inflectional and derivational morphology and thus provides a deeper level of lexical abstraction than the lemma. The pattern feature is the pattern of the lemma of the lexeme, not of the word form.

The inflectional morphological features[4] define the dimensions of Arabic inflectional morphology, or the space of variations of a particular word. PATB-tokenized words vary along nine dimensions: GENDER and NUMBER (for nominals and verbs); PERSON, ASPECT, VOICE and MOOD (for verbs); and CASE, STATE, and the attached definite article proclitic DET (for nominals). The inflectional features abstract away from the specifics of morpheme forms, since they can affect more than one morpheme in Arabic. For example, changing the value of the aspect feature in the example above from imperfective to perfective yields the word form كاتبوا *kAtab+uwA* 'they corresponded', which differs in terms of prefix, suffix and pattern.

Inflectional features interact with syntax in two ways. First, there are agreement features: two words in a sentence which are in a specific syntactic configuration have the same value for a specific set of features. In MSA, we have subject-verb agreement on PERSON, GENDER, and NUMBER (but NUMBER only if the subject precedes the verb), and we have noun-adjective agreement in PERSON, NUMBER, GENDER, and DET.[5] Second, morphology can show a specific syntactic configuration on a single word. In MSA, we have CASE and STATE marking. Different types of dependents have different CASE; for example, verbal subjects are always marked NOMINATIVE. CASE and STATE are rarely explicitly manifested in undiacritized MSA.

Lexical features do not participate in syntactic constraints on structure as inflectional features do. Instead, bilexical dependencies are used in parsing to model semantic relations which often are the only way to disambiguate among different possible syntactic structures; lexical features provide a way of reducing data sparseness through lexical abstraction. We compare the effect on parsing of different subsets of lexical and inflectional features. Our hypothesis is that the inflectional features involved in agreement and the lexical features help parsing.

**The core POS tagsets**: Words also have associated part-of-speech (POS) tags, e.g., "verb", which further abstract over morphologically and syntactically similar lexemes. Traditional Arabic grammars often describe a very general three-way distinction into verbs, nominals and particles. In comparison, the tagset of the Buckwalter Morphological Analyzer (Buckwalter, 2004) used in the PATB has a core POS set of 44 tags (before morphologi-

[3]The digits in the pattern correspond to the positions root radicals are inserted.

[4]The inflectional features we use in this paper are form-based (illusory) as opposed to functional features (Smrž, 2007). We plan to work with functional features in the future.

[5]We do not explicitly address here agreement phenomena that require more complex morpho-syntactic modeling. These include adjectival modifiers of irrational (non-human) plural nominals, and pre-nominal number modifiers.

cal extension). Henceforth, we refer to this tagset as CORE44. Cross-linguistically, a core set containing around 12 tags is often assumed, including: noun, proper noun, verb, adjective, adverb, preposition, particles, connectives, and punctuation. Henceforth, we reduce CORE44 to such a tagset, and dub it CORE12. The CATIB6 tagset can be viewed as a further reduction, with the exception that CATIB6 contains a passive voice tag; however, it constitutes only 0.5% of the tags in the training.

**Extended POS tagsets**: The notion of "POS tagset" in natural language processing usually does *not* refer to a core set. Instead, the Penn English Treebank (PTB) uses a set of 46 tags, including not only the core POS, but also the complete set of morphological features (this tagset is still fairly small since English is morphologically impoverished). In modern standard Arabic (MSA), the corresponding type of tagset (core POS extended with a complete description of morphology) would contain upwards of 2,000 tags, many of which are extremely rare (in our training corpus of about 300,000 words, we encounter only 430 of such POS tags with complete morphology). Therefore, researchers have proposed tagsets for MSA whose size is similar to that of the English PTB tagset, as this has proven to be a useful size computationally. These tagsets are hybrids in the sense that they are neither simply the core POS, nor the complete morphological tagset, but instead they choose certain morphological features to include along with the core POS tag.

The following are the various tagsets we compare in this paper: **(a)** the core POS tagsets CORE44 and the newly introduced CORE12; **(b)** CATiB treebank tagset (CATIB6) (Habash and Roth, 2009); and its newly introduced extension, CATIBEX, by greedy regular expressions indicating particular morphemes such as the prefix ال *Al+* or the suffix ون *+wn*.[6] **(c)** the PATB full tagset (BW), size ≈2000+ (Buckwalter, 2004); and two extensions of the PATB reduced tagset (PENN POS, a.k.a. RTS, size 24), both outperforming it: **(d)** Kulick et al. (2006)'s tagset (KULICK), size ≈43, one of whose most important extensions is the marking of the definite article clitic, and **(e)** Diab and BenAjiba (2010)'s EXTENDED RTS tagset (ERTS), which marks gender, number and definiteness, size ≈134; Besides using morphological information to extend POS tagsets, we explore using it in separate features in parsing models. Following this exploration, we also extend CORE12, producing **(f)** CORE12EX (see Section 5 for details).

[6] Inspired by a similar extension in Habash and Roth (2009).

## 4 Related Work

Much work has been done on the use of morphological features for parsing of morphologically rich languages. Collins et al. (1999) report that an optimal tagset for parsing Czech consists of a basic POS tag plus a CASE feature (when applicable). This tagset (size 58) outperforms the basic Czech POS tagset (size 13) and the complete tagset (size ≈3000+). They also report that the use of gender, number and person features did not yield any improvements. We get similar results for CASE in the gold experimental setting but not when using predicted POS tags (POS tagger output). This may be a result of CASE tagging having a lower error rate in Czech (5.0%) (Hajič and Vidová-Hladká, 1998) compared to Arabic (≈14.0%, see Table 3). Similarly, Cowan and Collins (2005) report that the use of a subset of Spanish morphological features (number for adjectives, determiners, nouns, pronouns, and verbs; and mode for verbs) outperforms other combinations. Our approach is comparable to their work in terms of its systematic exploration of the space of morphological features. We also find that the number feature helps for Arabic. Looking at Hebrew, a Semitic language related to Arabic, Tsarfaty and Sima'an (2007) report that extending POS and phrase structure tags with definiteness information helps unlexicalized PCFG parsing.

As for work on Arabic, results have been reported on PATB (Kulick et al., 2006; Diab, 2007), the Prague Dependency Treebank (PADT) (Buchholz and Marsi, 2006; Nivre, 2008) and the Columbia Arabic Treebank (CATiB) (Habash and Roth, 2009).

Besides the work we describe in §3, Nivre (2008) reports experiments on Arabic parsing using his MaltParser (Nivre et al., 2007), trained on the PADT. His results are not directly comparable to ours because of the different treebanks representations and tokenization used, even though all our experiments reported here were performed using the MaltParser. Our results agree with previous published work on Arabic and Hebrew in that marking the definite article is helpful for parsing. However, we go beyond previous work in that we also extend this morphologically enhanced feature set to include additional lexical and inflectional morphological features. Previous work with MaltParser in Russian, Turkish and Hindi showed gains with case but not with agreement features (Nivre et al., 2008; Eryigit et al., 2008; Nivre, 2009). Our work is the first to show gains using agreement in MaltParser and in Arabic dependency parsing.

## 5 Experiments

### 5.1 Experimental Space

We examined a large space of settings including the following: **(a)** the contribution of POS tagsets to the parsing quality, as a function of the amount of information encoded in the tagset; **(b)** parsing performance on gold vs. predicted POS and morphological feature values for all models; **(c)** prediction accuracy of each POS tagset and morphological feature; **(d)** the contribution of numerous morphological features in a controlled fashion; and **(e)** the contribution of certain feature and POS tagset combinations. All results are reported mainly in terms of labeled attachment accuracy (parent word and the dependency relation to it). Unlabeled attachment accuracy and label accuracy are also given, space permitting.

### 5.2 Parser

For all experiments reported here we used the syntactic dependency parser MaltParser v1.3 (Nivre, 2003; Nivre, 2008; Kübler et al., 2009) – a transition-based parser with an input buffer and a stack, using SVM classifiers to predict the next state in the parse derivation. All experiments were done using the Nivre "eager" algorithm.[7] We trained the parser on the training portion of PATB part 3 (Maamouri et al., 2004). We used the same split as in Zitouni et al. (2006) for dev/test, and kept the test unseen during training.

There are five default *attributes*, in the MaltParser terminology, for each token in the text: word ID (ordinal position in the sentence), word form, POS tag, head (parent word ID), and deprel (the dependency relation between the current word and its parent). There are default *MaltParser features* (in the machine learning sense),[8] which are the values of functions over these attributes, serving as input to the MaltParser internal classifiers. The most commonly used feature functions are the top of the input buffer (next word to process, denoted buf[0]), or top of the stack (denoted stk[0]); following items on buffer or stack are also accessible (buf[1], buf[2], stk[1], etc.). Hence MaltParser features are defined as POS tag at top of the stack, word form at top of the buffer, etc. Kübler et al. (2009) describe a "typical" MaltParser model configuration of attributes and features.[9] Starting with it, in a series of initial controlled experiments, we settled on using buf[0], buf[1], stk[0], stk[1] for the wordform, and buf[0], buf[1], buf[2], buf[3], stk[0], stk[1], stk[2] for the POS tag. For features of all new MaltParser-attributes (discussed later), we used buf[0] and stk[0]. We did not change the features for the deprel. This new MaltParser configuration resulted in gains of 0.3-1.1% in labeled attachment accuracy (depending on the POS tagset) over the default MaltParser configuration. We also experimented with using normalized word forms (*Alif Maqsura* conversion to *Ya*, and hamza removal from each *Alif*) as is common in parsing and statistical machine translation literature. This resulted in a small decrease in performance (0.1-0.2% in labeled attachment accuracy). We settled on using the non-normalized word form. All experiments reported below were conducted using this new configuration.

### 5.3 Parsing quality as a function of POS tag richness

We turn first to the contribution of POS information to parsing quality, as a function of the amount of information encoded in the POS tagset. A first rough estimation for the amount of information is the actual tagset size, as it appears in the training data. For this purpose we compared POS tagsets based on, or closely inspired by, previously published work. These sets are typically morphologically-enriched (marking the existence of a determiner in the word, person, gender, number, etc.). The num-

[7]Nivre (2008) reports that non-projective and pseudo-projective algorithms outperform the "eager" projective algorithm in MaltParser; however, our training data did not contain any non-projective dependencies, so there was no point in using these algorithms. The Nivre "standard" algorithm is also reported to do better on Arabic, but in a preliminary experimentation, it did slightly worse than the "eager" one. This could be due to high percentage of right branching (left headed structures) in our Arabic training set, an observation already noted in Nivre (2008).

[8]The terms "feature" and "attribute" are over loaded in the literature. We use them in the linguistic sense, unless specifically noted otherwise, e.g., "MaltParser feature(s)".

[9]It is slightly different from the default configuration.

ber of tag types occurring in the training data follow each tagset in parentheses: BW (430 tags), ERTS (134 tags), KULICK (32 tags), and the smallest POS tagset published: CATIB6 (6 tags). In optimal conditions (using gold POS tags), the richest tagset (BW) is indeed the best performer (84.02%), and the poorest (CATIB6) is the worst (81.04%). Mid-size tagsets are in the high 82%, with the notable exception of KULICK, which does better than ERTS, in spite of having 1/4 the tagset size; moreover, it is the best performer in unlabeled attachment accuracy (85.98%), in spite of being less than tenth the size of BW. Our extended mid-size tagset, CATIBEX, was a mid-level performer as expected.

In order to control the level of morphological and lexical information in the POS tagset, we used the above-mentioned additional tagsets: CORE44 (40 tags), and CORE12 (12 tags). Both were also mid-size mid-level performers (in spite of containing no morphological extension), with CORE12 doing slightly better. See Table 1 columns 2-4.

### 5.4 Predicted POS tags

So far we discussed optimal (gold) conditions. But in practice, POS tags are annotated by automatic taggers, so parsers get *predicted* POS tags as input, as opposed to gold (human annotated) tags. The more informative the tagset, the less accurate the tag prediction might be, so the effect on overall parsing quality is unclear. Therefore, we repeated the experiments above with POS tags predicted by the Morphological Analysis and Disambiguation for Arabic (MADA) toolkit (Habash and Rambow, 2005). See Table 1, columns 5-7. It turned out that BW, the best gold performer, with lowest POS prediction accuracy (81.8%), suffered the biggest drop (11.38%) and was the worst performer with predicted tags. The simplest tagset, CATIB6, and its extension, CATIBEX, benefited from the highest POS prediction accuracy (97.7%), and their performance suffered the least. CATIBEX was the best performer with predicted POS tags. Performance drop and POS prediction accuracy are given in columns 8 and 9, respectively. Next, we augmented the parsing models with inflectional and lexical morphological features.

### 5.5 Inflectional features

Experimenting with inflectional morphological features is especially important in Arabic parsing, since Arabic is morphologically rich. In order to further explore the contribution of inflectional and lexical morphological information in a controlled manner, we focused on the best performing core POS tagset, CORE12 as baseline; using three different setups, we added nine morphological features, extracted from MADA: DET, PERSON, ASPECT, VOICE, MOOD, GENDER, NUMBER, STATE, and CASE. In setup ***All***, we augmented the baseline model with all nine MADA features (as nine additional MaltParser attributes); in setup ***Sep***, we augmented the baseline model with each of the MADA features, one at a time, separately; and in setup ***Greedy***, we combined them in a greedy heuristic (since the entire feature space is too vast to exhaust): starting with the most gainful feature from *Sep*, adding the next most gainful feature, keeping it as additional MaltParser attribute if it helped, or discarding it otherwise, and repeating this heuristics through the least gainful feature. We also augmented the same baseline CORE12 model with a manually constructed list of surface affixes (e.g., *Al+, +wn, ħ*) as additional MaltParser attributes (LINGNGRAMS). This list was also in the base of the CATIBEX extension; it is linguistically informed, yet represents a simple (albeit shallow) alternative to morphological analysis. Results are given in Table 2.

Somewhat surprisingly, setup *All* hurts performance on the predicted input. This can be explained if one examines the prediction accuracy of each feature (Table 3). Features which are not predicted with very high accuracy, such as CASE (86.3%), can dominate the negative contribution, even though they are principle top contributors in optimal (gold) conditions (see discussion below). The determiner feature (DET), followed by the STATE (construct state, *idafa*) feature, were top individual contributors in setup *Sep*. Adding DET and all the so-called phi-features (PERSON, NUMBER, GENDER) in the *Greedy* setup, yielded 1.43% gain over the CORE12 baseline. Adding LINGNGRAMS yielded a 1.19% gain over the CORE12 baseline.

We repeated the same setups (*All*, *Sep*, and *Greedy*) with gold POS tags, to examine the contribution of the morphological features in optimal conditions. Here CASE, followed by STATE and DET, were the top contributors. Performance of CASE is the notable difference from the predicted conditions above. Surprisingly, only CASE and STATE helped in the *Greedy* setup, although one might expect that the phi features help too. (See lower half of Table 2).

Table 1: Parsing performance with each POS tagset, on gold and predicted input. labeled = labeled attachment accuracy (dependency + relation). unlabeled = unlabeled attachment accuracy (dependency only). label acc = relation label prediction accuracy. labeled diff = difference between labeled attachment accuracy on gold and predicted input. POS acc = POS tag prediction accuracy.

| tagset | gold labeled | gold unlabled | gold label acc. | predicted labeled | predicted unlabled | predicted label acc. | gold-pred. labeled diff. | POS acc. | tagset size |
|---|---|---|---|---|---|---|---|---|---|
| CATIB6 | 81.04 | 83.66 | 92.59 | 78.31 | 82.03 | 90.55 | **-2.73** | **97.7** | 6 |
| CATIBEX | 82.52 | 84.97 | 93.40 | **79.74** | **83.30** | **91.44** | -2.78 | **97.7** | 44 |
| CORE12 | 82.92 | 85.40 | 93.52 | 78.68 | 82.48 | 90.63 | -4.24 | 96.3 | 12 |
| CORE44 | 82.71 | 85.17 | 93.28 | 78.39 | 82.16 | 90.36 | -4.32 | 96.1 | 40 |
| ERTS | 82.97 | 85.23 | 93.76 | 78.93 | 82.56 | 90.96 | -4.04 | 95.5 | 134 |
| KULICK | 83.60 | **85.98** | 94.01 | 79.39 | 83.15 | 91.14 | -4.21 | 95.7 | 32 |
| BW | **84.02** | 85.77 | **94.83** | 72.64 | 77.91 | 86.46 | -11.38 | 81.8 | 430 |

Table 2: CORE12 POS tagset with morphological features. Left half: Using predicted POS tags. In it: Top part: Adding all nine features to CORE12. Second part: Adding each feature separately, comparing difference from CORE12+madafeats, predicted (second part). Third part: Greedily adding best features from third part, predicted; difference from previous successful greedy step. Bottom part: Surface affixes (leading and trailing character n-grams). Right half: Left half repeated with gold tags.

| set -up | predicted POS and features: CORE12+... | labeled | diff. | unlabeled | gold POS and features: CORE12+... | labeled | diff. | unlabeled |
|---|---|---|---|---|---|---|---|---|
| *All* | (baseline repeated) | 78.68 | – | 82.48 | (baseline repeated) | 82.92 | – | 85.40 |
| | +madafeats | 77.91 | -0.77 | 82.14 | +madafeats | 85.15 | 2.23 | 86.61 |
| *Sep* | +DET | **79.82** | **1.14** | 83.18 | +CASE | **84.61** | **1.69** | 86.30 |
| | +STATE | 79.34 | 0.66 | 82.85 | +STATE | 84.15 | 1.23 | 86.38 |
| | +GENDER | 78.75 | 0.07 | 82.35 | +DET | 83.96 | 1.04 | 86.21 |
| | +PERSON | 78.74 | 0.06 | 82.45 | +NUMBER | 83.08 | 0.16 | 85.50 |
| | +NUMBER | 78.66 | -0.02 | 82.39 | +PERSON | 83.07 | 0.15 | 85.41 |
| | +VOICE | 78.64 | -0.04 | 82.41 | +VOICE | 83.05 | 0.13 | 85.42 |
| | +ASPECT | 78.60 | -0.08 | 82.39 | +MOOD | 83.05 | 0.13 | 85.47 |
| | +MOOD | 78.54 | -0.14 | 82.35 | +ASPECT | 83.01 | 0.09 | 85.43 |
| | +CASE | 75.81 | -2.87 | 80.24 | +GENDER | 82.96 | 0.04 | 85.24 |
| *Greedy* | +DET+STATE | 79.42 | -0.40 | 82.84 | +CASE+STATE | **85.37** | **0.76** | 86.88 |
| | +DET+GENDER | 79.90 | 0.08 | 83.20 | +CASE+STATE+DET | 85.18 | -0.19 | 86.66 |
| | +DET+GENDER+PERSON | 79.94 | 0.04 | 83.21 | +CASE+STATE+NUMBER | 85.36 | -0.01 | 86.87 |
| | +DET+PHI | **80.11** | **0.17** | 83.29 | +CASE+STATE+PERSON | 85.27 | -0.10 | 86.76 |
| | +DET+PHI+VOICE | 79.96 | -0.15 | 83.18 | +CASE+STATE+VOICE | 85.25 | -0.12 | 86.76 |
| | +DET+PHI+ASPECT | 80.01 | -0.10 | 83.20 | +CASE+STATE+MOOD | 85.23 | -0.14 | 86.72 |
| | +DET+PHI+MOOD | 80.03 | -0.08 | 83.21 | +CASE+STATE+ASPECT | 85.23 | -0.14 | 86.78 |
| | — | | | | +CASE+STATE+GENDER | 85.26 | -0.11 | 86.75 |
| | +NGRAMSLING | **79.87** | **1.19** | 83.21 | +NGRAMSLING | **84.02** | **1.10** | 86.16 |

### 5.6 Lexical features

Next, we experimented with adding morphological features involving semantic abstraction to some degree: the diacritized LEMMA (abstracting away from inflectional information, and indicating active/passive voice due to diacritization information), the undiacritized lemma (LMM), the ROOT (further abstraction indicating "core" predicate or action), and the PATTERN (a generally complementary abstraction, often indicating causation and reflexiveness). We experimented with the same setups as above: *All*, *Sep*, and *Greedy*. Adding all four features yielded a minor gain in setup *All*. LMM was the best single contributor (1.05%), closely followed by ROOT (1.03%) in *Sep*. CORE12+LMM+ROOT+LEMMA was the best greedy combination (79.05%) in setup *Greedy*. See Table 4.

### 5.7 Putting it all together

We further explored whether morphological data should be added to an Arabic parsing model as stand-alone machine learning features, or should they be used to enhance and extend a POS tagset. We created a new POS tagset, CORE12EX, size 81(see bottom of Table 3), by extending the CORE12 tagset with the features that most improved the

CORE12 baseline: DET and the phi features. But CORE12EX did worse than its non-extended (but feature-enhanced) counterpart, CORE12+DET+PHI. Another variant, CORE12EX+DET+PHI, which used both the extended tagset and the additional DET and phi features, did not improve over CORE12+DET+PHI either.

Following the results in Table 2, we added the affix features NGRAMSLING (which proved to help the CORE12 baseline) to the best augmented CORE12+DET+PHI model, dubbing the new model CORE12+DET+PHI+NGRAMSLING, but performance dropped here too. We greedily augmented CORE12+DET+PHI with lexical features, and found that the undiacritzed lemma (LMM) improved performance on predicted input (80.23%). In order to test whether these findings hold with other tagsets, we added the winning features (DET+PHI, with and without LMM) to the best POS tagset in predicted conditions, CATIBEX. Both variants yielded gains, with CATIBEX+DET+PHI+LMM achieving 80.45% accuracy, the best result on predicted input.

### 5.8 Validating Results on Unseen Test Set

Once experiments on the development set (PATB3-DEV) were done, we ran the best performing models on a previously unseen test set – the test split of part 3 of the PATB (PATB3-TEST). Table 6 shows that the same trends held on this set too, with even greater relative gains, up to 1.77% absolute gains.

Table 3: Feature prediction accuracy and set sizes. * = The set includes a "N/A" value.

| feature | acc | set size |
|---|---|---|
| normalized word form (A,Y) | 99.3 | 29737 |
| non-normalized word form | 98.9 | 29980 |
| NGRAMSLING preffix | 100.0 | 8 |
| NGRAMSLING suffix | 100.0 | 20 |
| DET | 99.6 | 3* |
| PERSON | 99.1 | 4* |
| ASPECT | 99.1 | 5* |
| VOICE | 98.9 | 4* |
| MOOD | 98.6 | 5* |
| GENDER | 99.3 | 3* |
| NUMBER | 99.5 | 4* |
| STATE | 95.6 | 4* |
| CASE | 86.3 | 5* |
| ROOT | 98.4 | 9646 |
| PATTERN | 97.0 | 338 |
| LEMMA (diacritized) | 96.7 | 16837 |
| LMM (undiacritized lemma) | 98.3 | 15305 |
| CORE12EX | 96.0 | 81 |

Table 4: Lexical morpho-semantic features. Top part: Adding each feature separately; difference from CORE12, predicted. Bottom part: Greedily adding best features from previous part, predicted; difference from previous successful greedy step.

| | POS tagset | labeled | diff. | unlab. | label |
|---|---|---|---|---|---|
| *All* | CORE12 (repeated) | 78.68 | – | 82.48 | 90.63 |
| | CORE12+LMM+ROOT +LEMMA+PATTERN | 78.85 | 0.17 | 82.46 | 90.82 |
| *Sep* | CORE12+lmm | 78.96 | 1.05 | 82.54 | 90.80 |
| | CORE12+ROOT | 78.94 | 1.03 | 82.64 | 90.72 |
| | CORE12+LEMMA | 78.80 | 0.89 | 82.42 | 90.71 |
| | CORE12+PATTERN | 78.59 | 0.68 | 82.39 | 90.60 |
| *Greedy* | CORE12+LMM+ROOT | 79.04 | 0.08 | 82.63 | 90.86 |
| | CORE12+LMM+ROOT +LEMMA | **79.05** | 0.01 | 82.63 | 90.87 |
| | CORE12+LMM+ROOT +PATTERN | 78.93 | -0.11 | 82.58 | 90.82 |

Table 6: Results on PATB3-TEST for models which performed best on PATB3-DEV – predicted input.

| POS tagset | labeled | diff. | unlab. | label |
|---|---|---|---|---|
| CORE12 | 77.29 | – | 81.04 | 90.05 |
| CORE12+DET+PHI | 78.57 | 1.28 | 81.66 | 91.09 |
| CORE12+DET+PHI+LMM | **79.06** | **1.77** | 82.07 | 91.37 |

## 6 Error Analysis

For selected feature sets, we look at the overall error reduction with respect to the CORE12 baseline, and see what dependency relations particularly profit from that feature combination: What dependencies achieve error reductions greater than the average error reduction for that feature set over the whole corpus. We investigate dependencies by labels, and for **MOD** we also investigate by the POS label of the dependent node (so **MOD-P** means a preposition node attached to a governing node using a **MOD** arc).

DET: As expected, it particularly helps **IDF** and **MOD-N**. The error reduction for **IDF** is 19.3%!

STATE: Contrary to naïve expectations, STATE does not help **IDF**, but instead *increases* error by 9.4%. This is presumably because the feature does not actually predict construct state except when construct state is marked explicitly, but this is rare.

DET+PHI: The phi features are the only subject-verb agreement features, and they are additional agreement features (in addition to definiteness) for noun-noun modification. Indeed, relative to just adding DET, we see the strongest increases in these two dependencies, with an additional average in-

Table 5: Putting it all together

| POS tagset | inp.qual. | labeled | diff. | unlabeled | label Acc. |
|---|---|---|---|---|---|
| CORE12+DET+PHI (repeated) | predicted | **80.11** | 0.17 | 83.29 | 91.82 |
| CORE12+DET+PHI | gold | 84.20 | -0.95 | 86.23 | 94.49 |
| CORE12EX | predicted | 78.89 | -1.22 | 82.38 | 91.17 |
| CORE12EX | gold | 83.06 | 0.14 | 85.26 | 93.80 |
| CORE12EX+DET+PHI | predicted | 79.19 | -0.92 | 82.52 | 91.39 |
| CORE12+DET+PHI+NGRAMSLING | predicted | 79.77 | -0.34 | 83.03 | 91.66 |
| CORE12+DET+PHI+LMM | predicted | **80.23** | 0.12 | 83.34 | 91.94 |
| CORE12+DET+PHI+LMM+ROOT | predicted | 80.10 | -0.13 | 83.25 | 91.84 |
| CORE12+DET+PHI+LMM+PATTERN | predicted | 80.03 | -0.20 | 83.15 | 91.77 |
| CATIBEX+DET+PHI | predicted | 80.00 | 0.26 | 83.29 | 91.81 |
| CATIBEX+DET+PHI+LMM | predicted | **80.45** | 0.71 | 83.65 | 92.03 |

crease for **IDF** (presumably because certain N-N modifications are rejected in favor of **IDF**s). All other dependencies remain at the same level as with only DET.

LMM, ROOT, LEMMA: These features abstract over the word form and thus allow generalizations in bilexical dependecies, which in parsing stand in for semantic modeling. The strongest boost from these features comes from **MOD-N** and **MOD-P**, which is as expected since these dependencies are highly ambiguous, and **MOD-P** is never helped by the morphological features.

DET+PHI+LMM: This feature combination yields gains on all main dependency types (**SBJ, OBJ, IDF, MOD-N, MOD-P, MOD-V**). But the contribution from the inflectional and lexical features are unfortunately not additive. We also compare the improvement contributed just by LMM as compared to DET and PHI. This improvement is quite small, but we see that **MOD-N** does not improve (in fact, it gets worse – presumably because there are too many features), while **MOD-P** (which is not helped by the morphological features) does improve. Oddly, **OBJ** also improves, for which we have no explanation.

When we turn to our best-performing configuration, CATIBEX with the added DET, phi features (PERSON, NUMBER, GENDER), and LMM, we see that this configuration improves over CORE12 with the same features for two dependency types only: **SBJ** and **MOD-N** These are exactly the two types for which agreement features are useful, and both the features DET+PHI and the CATIBEX POS tagset represent information for agreement. The question arises why this information is not redundant. We speculate that the fact that we are learning different classifiers for different POS tags helps MaltParser learn attachment decisions which are specific to types of dependent node morphology.

In summary, our best performing configuration yields an error reduction of 8.3% over the core POS tag (CORE12). **SBJ** errors are reduced by 13.3%, **IDF** errors by 17.7%, and **MOD-N** errors by 14.9%. Error reduction for **OBJ**, **MOD-P**, and **MOD-V** are all less than 4%. We note that the remaining **MOD-P** errors make up 6.2% of all dependency relations, roughly one third of remaining errors.

## 7 Conclusions and Future Work

We explored the contribution of different inflectional and lexical features to dependency parsing of Arabic, under gold and predicted POS conditions. While more informative features (e.g., richer POS tags) yield better parsing quality in gold conditions, they are hard to predict, and as such they might not contribute to – and even hurt – the parsing quality under predicted conditions. We find that definiteness (DET), phi-features (PERSON, NUMBER, GENDER), and undiacritzed lemma (LMM) are most helpful for Arabic parsing on predicted input, while CASE and STATE are most helpful on gold.

In the future we plan to improve CASE prediction accuracy; produce high accuracy supertag features, modeling active and passive valency; and use other parsers (e.g., McDonald and Pereira, 2006).

## Acknowledgments

This work was supported by the DARPA GALE program, contract HR0011-08-C-0110. We thank Joakim Nivre for his useful remarks, and Ryan Roth for his help with CATiB conversion and MADA.

## References


Sabine Buchholz and Erwin Marsi. 2006. CoNLL-X shared task on multilingual dependency parsing. In *Proceedings of Computational Natural Language Learning (CoNLL)*, pages 149–164.

Timothy A. Buckwalter. 2004. Buckwalter Arabic Morphological Analyzer Version 2.0. Linguistic Data Consortium, University of Pennsylvania, 2002. LDC Cat alog No.: LDC2004L02, ISBN 1-58563-324-0.

Michael Collins, Jan Hajic, Lance Ramshaw, and Christoph Tillmann. 1999. A statistical parser for czech. In *Proceedings of the 37th Annual Meeting of the the Association for Computational Linguistics (ACL)*, College Park, Maryland, USA, June.

Brooke Cowan and Michael Collins. 2005. Morphology and reranking for the statistical parsing of spanish. In *Proceedings of Human Language Technology (HLT) and the Conference on Empirical Methods in Natural Language Processing (EMNLP)*, pages 795–802.

Mona Diab and Yassine BenAjiba. 2010. From raw text to base phrase chunks: The new generation of AMIRA Tools for the processing of Modern Standard Arabic. In *(to appear)*. Spring LNCS, Special Jubilee edition.

Mona Diab. 2007. Towards an optimal pos tag set for modern standard arabic processing. In *Proceedings of Recent Advances in Natural Language Processing (RANLP)*, Borovets, Bulgaria.

Gülsen Eryigit, Joakim Nivre, and Kemal Oflazer. 2008. Dependency parsing of turkish. *Computational Linguistics*, 34(3):357–389.

Nizar Habash and Owen Rambow. 2005. Arabic Tokenization, Part-of-Speech Tagging and Morphological Disambiguation in One Fell Swoop. In *Proceedings of the 43rd Annual Meeting of the the Association for Computational Linguistics (ACL)*, Ann Arbor, Michigan, June.

Nizar Habash and Ryan Roth. 2009. Catib: The columbia arabic treebank. In *Proceedings of the ACL-IJCNLP 2009 Conference Short Papers*, pages 221–224, Suntec, Singapore, August.

Nizar Habash, Abdelhadi Soudi, and Tim Buckwalter. 2007. On Arabic Transliteration. In A. van den Bosch and A. Soudi, editors, *Arabic Computational Morphology: Knowledge-based and Empirical Methods*. Springer.

Jan Hajič and Barbora Vidová-Hladká. 1998. Tagging Inflective Languages: Prediction of Morphological Categories for a Rich, Structured Tagset. In *Proceedings of the International Conference on Computational Linguistics (COLING)- the Association for Computational Linguistics (ACL)*, pages 483–490.

Sandra Kübler, Ryan McDonald, and Joakim Nivre. 2009. *Dependency Parsing*. Synthesis Lectures on Human Language Technologies. Morgan and Claypool Publishers.

Seth Kulick, Ryan Gabbard, and Mitch Marcus. 2006. Parsing the Arabic Treebank: Analysis and improvements. In *Proceedings of the Treebanks and Linguistic Theories Conference*, pages 31–42, Prague, Czech Republic.

Mohamed Maamouri, Ann Bies, Timothy A. Buckwalter, and Wigdan Mekki. 2004. The Penn Arabic Treebank: Building a Large-Scale Annotated Arabic Corpus. In *Proceedings of the NEMLAR Conference on Arabic Language Resources and Tools*, pages 102–109, Cairo, Egypt.

Ryan McDonald and Fernando Pereira. 2006. Online learning of approximate dependency parsing algorithms. In *Proceedings of the 11th Conference of the the European Chapter of the Association for Computational Linguistics (EACL)*.

Joakim Nivre, Johan Hall, Jens Nilsson, Atanas Chanev, Gulsen Eryigit, Sandra Kubler, Svetoslav Marinov, and Erwin Marsi. 2007. MaltParser: A language-independent system for data-driven dependency parsing. *Natural Language Engineering*, 13(2):95–135.

Joakim Nivre, Igor M. Boguslavsky, and Leonid K. Iomdin. 2008. Parsing the SynTagRus Treebank of Russian. In *Proceedings of the 22nd International Conference on Computational Linguistics (COLING)*, pages 641–648.

Joakim Nivre. 2003. An efficient algorithm for projective dependency parsing. In *Proceedings of the 8th International Conference on Parsing Technologies (IWPT)*, pages 149–160, Nancy, France.

Joakim Nivre. 2008. Algorithms for Deterministic Incremental Dependency Parsing. *Computational Linguistics*, 34(4).

Joakim Nivre. 2009. Parsing Indian languages with MaltParser. In *Proceedings of the ICON09 NLP Tools Contest: Indian Language Dependency Parsing*, pages 12–18.

Otakar Smrž. 2007. *Functional Arabic Morphology. Formal System and Implementation*. Ph.D. thesis, Charles University, Prague.

Reut Tsarfaty and Khalil Sima'an. 2007. Three-dimensional parametrization for parsing morphologically rich languages. In *Proceedings of the 10th International Conference on Parsing Technologies (IWPT)*, pages 156–167, Morristown, NJ, USA.

Imed Zitouni, Jeffrey S. Sorensen, and Ruhi Sarikaya. 2006. Maximum Entropy Based Restoration of Arabic Diacritics. In *Proceedings of the 21st International Conference on Computational Linguistics (COLING) and the 44th Annual Meeting of the the Association for Computational Linguistics (ACL)*, pages 577–584, Sydney, Australia.

# Two methods to incorporate local morphosyntactic features in Hindi dependency parsing

**Bharat Ram Ambati, Samar Husain, Sambhav Jain, Dipti Misra Sharma and Rajeev Sangal**
Language Technologies Research Centre, IIIT-Hyderabad, India - 500032.
{ambati,samar}@research.iiit.ac.in, sambhav-jain@students.iiit.ac.in,{dipti,sangal}@mail.iiit.ac.in

## Abstract

In this paper we explore two strategies to incorporate local morphosyntactic features in Hindi dependency parsing. These features are obtained using a shallow parser. We first explore which information provided by the shallow parser is most beneficial and show that local morphosyntactic features in the form of chunk type, head/non-head information, chunk boundary information, distance to the end of the chunk and suffix concatenation are very crucial in Hindi dependency parsing. We then investigate the best way to incorporate this information during dependency parsing. Further, we compare the results of various experiments based on various criterions and do some error analysis. All the experiments were done with two data-driven parsers, MaltParser and MSTParser, on a part of multi-layered and multi-representational Hindi Treebank which is under development. This paper is also the first attempt at complete sentence level parsing for Hindi.

## 1 Introduction

The dependency parsing community has since a few years shown considerable interest in parsing morphologically rich languages with flexible word order. This is partly due to the increasing availability of dependency treebanks for such languages, but it is also motivated by the observation that the performance obtained for these languages have not been very high (Nivre et al., 2007a). Attempts at handling various non-configurational aspects in these languages have pointed towards shortcomings in traditional parsing methodologies (Tsarfaty and Sima'an, 2008; Eryigit et al., 2008; Seddah et al., 2009; Husain et al., 2009; Gadde et al., 2010). Among other things, it has been pointed out that the use of language specific features may play a crucial role in improving the overall parsing performance. Different languages tend to encode syntactically relevant information in different ways, and it has been hypothesized that the integration of morphological and syntactic information could be a key to better accuracy. However, it has also been noted that incorporating these language specific features in parsing is not always straightforward and many intuitive features do not always work in expected ways.

In this paper we explore various strategies to incorporate local morphosyntactic features in Hindi dependency parsing. These features are obtained using a shallow parser. We conducted experiments with two data-driven parsers, MaltParser (Nivre et al., 2007b) and MSTParser (McDonald et al., 2006). We first explore which information provided by the shallow parser is most beneficial and show that local morphosyntactic features in the form of chunk type, head/non-head information, chunk boundary information, distance to the end of the chunk and suffix concatenation are very crucial in Hindi dependency parsing. We then investigate the best way to incorporate this information during dependency parsing. All the experiments were done on a part of multi-layered and multi-representational Hindi Treebank (Bhatt et al., 2009)[1].

The shallow parser performs three tasks, (a) it gives the POS tags for each lexical item, (b) provides morphological features for each lexical item, and (c) performs chunking. A chunk is a minimal (non-recursive) phrase consisting of correlated, inseparable words/entities, such that the intra-chunk dependencies are not distorted (Bharati et

[1] This Treebank is still under development. There are currently 27k tokens with complete sentence level annotation.



*Proceedings of the NAACL HLT 2010 First Workshop on Statistical Parsing of Morphologically-Rich Languages*, pages 22–30,
Los Angeles, California, June 2010. ©2010 Association for Computational Linguistics

al., 2006). Together, a group of lexical items with some POS tag and morphological features within a chunk can be utilized to automatically compute local morphosyntactic information. For example, such information can represent the postposition/case-marking in the case of noun chunks, or it may represent the tense, aspect and modality (TAM) information in the case of verb chunks. In the experiments conducted for this paper such local information is automatically computed and incorporated as a feature to the head of a chunk. In general, local morphosyntactic features correspond to all the parsing relevant local linguistic features that can be utilized using the notion of chunk. Previously, there have been some attempts at using chunk information in dependency parsing. Attardi and Dell'Orletta (2008) used chunking information in parsing English. They got an increase of 0.35% in labeled attachment accuracy and 0.47% in unlabeled attachment accuracy over the state-of-the-art dependency parser.

Among the three components (a-c, above), the parsing accuracy obtained using the POS feature is taken as baseline. We follow this by experiments where we explore how each of morph and chunk features help in improving dependency parsing accuracy. In particular, we find that local morphosyntactic features are the most crucial. These experiments are discussed in section 2. In section 3 we will then see an alternative way to incorporate the best features obtained in section 2. In all the parsing experiments discussed in section 2 and 3, at each step we explore all possible features and extract the best set of features. Best features of one experiment are used when we go to the next set of experiments. For example, when we explore the effect of chunk information, all the relevant morph information from previous set of experiments is taken into account.

This paper is also the first attempt at complete sentence level parsing for Hindi. Due to the availability of dependency treebank for Hindi (Begum et al., 2008), there have been some previous attempts at Hindi data-driven dependency parsing (Bharati et al., 2008; Mannem et al., 2009; Husain et al., 2009). Recently in ICON-09 NLP Tools Contest (Husain, 2009; and the references therein), rule-based, constraint based, statistical and hybrid approaches were explored for dependency parsing. Previously, constraint based approaches to Indian language (IL) dependency parsing have also been explored (Bharati et al., 1993, 1995, 2009b, 2009c). All these attempts, however, were finding inter-chunk dependency relations, given gold-standard POS and chunk tags. Unlike these previous parsers, the dependencies in this work are between lexical items, i.e. the dependency tree is complete.

The paper is arranged as follows, in section 2 and 3, we discuss the parsing experiments. In section 4, we describe the data and parser settings. Section 5 gives the results and discusses some related issues. General discussion and possible future work is mentioned in section 6. We conclude the paper in section 7.

## 2 Getting the best linguistic features

As mentioned earlier, a shallow parser consists of three main components, (a) POS tagger, (b) morphological analyzer and (c) chunker. In this section we systematically explore what is the effect of each of these components. We'll see in section 2.3 that the best features of a-c can be used to compute local morphosyntactic features that, as the results show, are extremely useful.

### 2.1 Using POS as feature (PaF):

In this experiment we only use the POS tag information of individual words during dependency parsing. First a raw sentence is POS-tagged. This POS-tagged sentence is then given to a parser to predict the dependency relations. Figure 1, shows the steps involved in this approach for (1).

(1) raama ne eka seba khaayaa
'Ram' ERG 'one' 'apple' 'ate'
'Ram ate an apple'

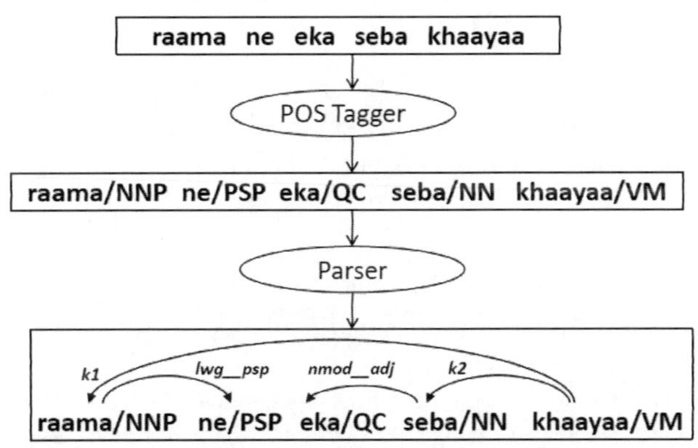


Figure 1: Dependency parsing using only POS information from a shallow parser.

In (1) above, 'NN', 'PSP', 'QC', 'NN' and 'VM' are the POS tags[2] for *raama, ne, eka, seba* and *khaayaa* respectively. This information is provided as a feature to the parser. The result of this experiment forms our baseline accuracy.

### 2.2 Using Morph as feature (MaF):

In addition to POS information, in this experiment we also use the morph information for each token. This morphological information is provided as a feature to the parser. Morph has the following information

- Root: Root form of the word
- Category: Course grained POS
- Gender: Masculine/Feminine/Neuter
- Number: Singular/Plural
- Person: First/Second/Third person
- Case: Oblique/Direct case
- Suffix: Suffix of the word

Take *raama* in (1), its morph information comprises of root = '*raama*', category = 'noun' gender = 'masculine', number = 'singular', person = 'third', case = 'direct', suffix = '0'. Similarly, *khaayaa* ('ate') has the following morph information. root = '*khaa*', category = 'verb' gender = 'masculine', numer = 'singular', person = 'third', case = 'direct', suffix = 'yaa'.

Through a series of experiments, the most crucial morph features were selected. Root, case and suffix turn out to be the most important features. Results are discussed in section 5.

### 2.3 Using local morphosyntax as feature (LMSaF)

Along with POS and the most useful morph features (root, case and suffix), in this experiment we also use local morphosyntactic features that reflect various chunk level information. These features are:

- Type of the chunk
- Head/non-head of the chunk
- Chunk boundary information
- Distance to the end of the chunk
- Suffix concatenation

In example 1 (see section 2.1), there are two noun chunks and one verb chunk. *raama* and *seba* are the heads of the noun chunks. *khaayaa* is the head of the verb chunk. We follow standard IOB[3] notation for chunk boundary. *raama*, *eka* and *khaayaa* are at the beginning (B) of their respective chunks. *ne* and *seba* are inside (I) their respective chunks. *raama* is at distance 1 from the end of the chunk and *ne* is at a distance 0 from the end of the chunk.

Once we have a chunk and morph feature like suffix, we can perform suffix concatenation automatically. A group of lexical items with some POS tags and suffix information within a chunk can be utilized to automatically compute this feature. This feature can, for example, represent the postposition/case-marking in the case of noun chunk, or it may represent the tense, aspect and modality (TAM) information in the case of verb chunks. Note that, this feature becomes part of the lexical item that is the head of a chunk. Take (2) as a case in point:

(2) [NP raama/NNP ne/PSP] [NP seba/NN]
'Ram' ERG 'apple'
[VGF khaa/VM liyaa/VAUX]
'eat' 'PRFT'
'Ram ate an apple'

The suffix concatenation feature for *khaa,* which is the head of the VGF chunk, will be '0+yaa' and is formed by concatenating the suffix of the main verb with that of its auxiliary. Similarly, the suffix concatenation feature for *raama,* which is head of the NP chunk, will be '0+ne'. This feature turns out to be very important. This is because in Hindi (and many other Indian languages) there is a direct correlation between the TAM markers and the case that appears on some nominals (Bharati et al., 1995). In (2), for example, *khaa liyaa* together gives the past perfective aspect for the verb *khaanaa* 'to eat'. Since, Hindi is split ergative, the subject of the transitive verb takes an ergative case marker when the verb is past perfective. Similar

[2] NN: Common noun, PSP: Post position, QC: Cardinal, VM: Verb. A list of complete POS tags can be found here: http://ltrc.iiit.ac.in/MachineTrans/research/tb/POS-Tag-List.pdf. The POS/chunk tag scheme followed in the Treebank is described in Bharati et al. (2006).

[3] Inside, Outside, Beginning of the chunk.

correlation between the case markers and TAM exist in many other cases.

## 3 An alternative approach to use best features: A 2-stage setup (2stage)

So far we have been using various information such as POS, chunk, etc. as features. Rather than using them as features and doing parsing at one go, we can alternatively follow a 2-stage setup. In particular, we divide the task of parsing into:

- Intra-chunk dependency parsing
- Inter-chunk dependency parsing

We still use POS, best morphological features (case, suffix, root) information as regular features during parsing. But unlike LMSaF mentioned in section 2.3, where we gave local morphosyntactic information as a feature, we divided the task of parsing into sub-tasks. A similar approach was also proposed by Bharati et al. (2009c). During intra-chunk dependency parsing, we try to find the dependency relations of the words within a chunk. Following which, chunk heads of each chunk within a sentence are extracted. On these chunk heads we run an inter-chunk dependency parser. For each chunk head, in addition to POS tag, useful morphological features, any useful intra-chunk information in the form of lexical item, suffix concatenation, dependency relation are also given as a feature.

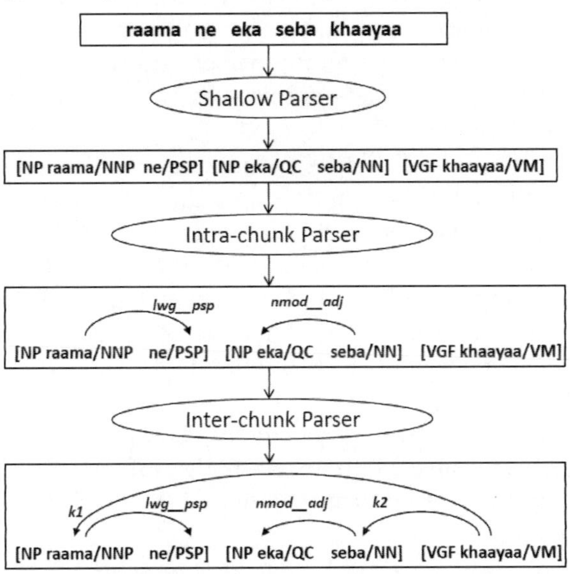


Figure 2: Dependency parsing using chunk information: 2-stage approach.

Figure 2 shows the steps involved in this approach for (1). There are two noun chunks and one verb chunk in this sentence. *raama* and *seba* are the heads of the noun chunks. *khaaya* is the head of the verb chunk. The intra-chunk parser attaches *ne* to *raama* and *eka* to *seba* with dependency labels 'lwg__psp' and 'nmod__adj'[4] respectively. Heads of each chunk along with its POS, morphological features, local morphosyntactic features and intra-chunk features are extracted and given to inter-chunk parser. Using this information the inter-chunk dependency parser marks the dependency relations between chunk heads. *khaaya* becomes the root of the dependency tree. *raama* and *seba* are attached to *khaaya* with dependency labels 'k1' and 'k2'[5] respectively.

## 4 Experimental Setup

In this section we describe the data and the parser settings used for our experiments.

### 4.1 Data

For our experiments we took 1228 dependency annotated sentences (27k tokens), which have complete sentence level annotation from the new multi-layered and multi-representational Hindi Treebank (Bhatt et al., 2009). This treebank is still under development. Average length of these sentences is 22 tokens/sentence and 10 chunks/sentence. We divided the data into two sets, 1000 sentences for training and 228 sentences for testing.

### 4.2 Parsers and settings

All experiments were performed using two data-driven parsers, MaltParser[6] (Nivre et al., 2007b), and MSTParser[7] (McDonald et al., 2006).

[4] nmod__adj is an intra-chunk label for quantifier-noun modification. lwg__psp is the label for post-position marker. Details of the labels can be seen in the intra-chunk guidelines http://ltrc.iiit.ac.in/MachineTrans/research/tb/IntraChunk-Dependency-Annotation-Guidelines.pdf

[5] k1 (karta) and k2 (karma) are syntactico-semantic labels which have some properties of both grammatical roles and thematic roles. k1 behaves similar to subject and agent. k2 behaves similar to object and patient (Bharati et al., 1995; Vaidya et al., 2009). For complete tagset, see (Bharati et al., 2009).

[6] Malt Version 1.3.1

[7] MST Version 0.4b

| | Malt | | | | | | MST+MaxEnt | | | | | |
|---|---|---|---|---|---|---|---|---|---|---|---|---|
| | Cross-validation | | | Test-set | | | Cross-validation | | | Test-set | | |
| | *UAS* | *LAS* | *LS* | *UAS* | *LAS* | *LS* | *UAS* | *LAS* | *LS* | *UAS* | *LAS* | *LS* |
| PaF | 89.4 | 78.2 | 80.5 | 90.4 | 80.1 | 82.4 | 86.3 | 75.1 | 77.9 | 87.9 | 77.0 | 79.3 |
| MaF | 89.6 | 80.5 | 83.1 | 90.4 | 81.7 | 84.1 | 89.1 | 79.2 | 82.5 | 90.0 | 80.9 | 83.9 |
| LMSaF | 91.5 | 82.7 | 84.7 | 91.8 | 84.0 | 86.2 | 90.8 | 79.8 | 82.0 | 92.0 | 81.8 | 83.8 |
| 2stage | **91.8** | **83.3** | **85.3** | **92.4** | **84.4** | **86.3** | **92.1** | **82.2** | **84.3** | **92.7** | **84.0** | **86.2** |

Table 1: Results of all the four approaches using gold-standard shallow parser information.

Malt is a classifier based shift/reduce parser. It provides option for six parsing algorithms, namely, arc-eager, arc-standard, convington projective, covington non-projective, stack projective, stack eager and stack lazy. The parser also provides option for libsvm and liblinear learning model. It uses graph transformation to handle non-projective trees (Nivre and Nilsson, 2005). MST uses Chu-Liu-Edmonds (Chu and Liu, 1965; Edmonds, 1967) Maximum Spanning Tree algorithm for non-projective parsing and Eisner's algorithm for projective parsing (Eisner, 1996). It uses online large margin learning as the learning algorithm (McDonald et al., 2005). In this paper, we use MST only for unlabeled dependency tree and use a separate maximum entropy model[8] (MaxEnt) for labeling. Various combination of features such as node, its parent, siblings and children were tried out before arriving at the best results.

As the training data size is small we did 5-fold cross validation on the training data for tuning the parameters of the parsers and for feature selection. Best settings obtained using cross-validated data are applied on test set. We present the results both on cross validated data and on test data.

For the Malt Parser, arc-eager algorithm gave better performance over others in all the approaches. Libsvm consistently gave better performance over liblinear in all the experiments. For SVM settings, we tried out different combinations of best SVM settings of the same parser on different languages in CoNLL-2007 shared task (Hall et al., 2007) and applied the best settings. For feature model, apart from trying best feature settings of the same parser on different languages in CoNLL-2007 shared task (Hall et al., 2007), we also tried out different combinations of linguistically intuitive features and applied the best feature model. The best feature model is same as the feature model used in Ambati et al. (2009a), which is the best performing system in the ICON-2009 NLP Tools Contest (Husain, 2009).

For the MSTParser, non-projective algorithm, order=2 and training-k=5 gave best results in all the approaches. For the MaxEnt, apart from some general useful features, we experimented considering different combinations of features of node, parent, siblings, and children of the node.

## 5 Results and Analysis

All the experiments discussed in section 2 and 3 were performed considering both gold-standard shallow parser information and automatic shallow parser[9] information. Automatic shallow parser uses a rule based system for morph analysis, a CRF+TBL based POS-tagger and chunker. The tagger and chunker are 93% and 87% accurate respectively. These accuracies are obtained after using the approach of PVS and Gali, (2007) on larger training data. In addition, while using automatic shallow parser information to get the results, we also explored using both gold-standard and automatic information during training. As expected, using automatic shallow parser information for training gave better performance than using gold while training.

Table 1 and Table 2 shows the results of the four experiments using gold-standard and automatic shallow parser information respectively. We evaluated our experiments based on unlabeled attachment score (UAS), labeled attachment score (LAS) and labeled score (LS) (Nivre et al., 2007a). Best LAS on test data is 84.4% (with 2stage) and 75.4% (with LMSaF) using gold and automatic shallow parser information respectively. These results are obtained using MaltParser. In the following subsection we discuss the results based on different criterion.

[8] http://maxent.sourceforge.net/

[9] http://ltrc.iiit.ac.in/analyzer/hindi/

| | Malt | | | | | | MST+MaxEnt | | | | | |
|---|---|---|---|---|---|---|---|---|---|---|---|---|
| | Cross-validation | | | Test-set | | | Cross-validation | | | Test-set | | |
| | *UAS* | *LAS* | *LS* | *UAS* | *LAS* | *LS* | *UAS* | *LAS* | *LS* | *UAS* | *LAS* | *LS* |
| PaF | 82.2 | 69.3 | 73.4 | 84.6 | 72.9 | 76.5 | 79.4 | 66.5 | 70.7 | 81.6 | 69.4 | 73.1 |
| MaF | 82.5 | 71.6 | 76.1 | 84.0 | 73.6 | 77.6 | 82.3 | 70.4 | 75.4 | 83.4 | 72.7 | 77.3 |
| LMSaF | **83.2** | **73.0** | **77.0** | **85.5** | **75.4** | **78.9** | **82.6** | **71.3** | **76.1** | **85.0** | **73.4** | **77.3** |
| 2stage | 79.0 | 69.5 | 75.6 | 79.6 | 71.1 | 76.8 | 78.8 | 66.6 | 72.6 | 80.1 | 69.7 | 75.4 |

Table 2: Results of all the four experiments using automatic shallow parser information.

POS tags provide very basic linguistic information in the form of broad grained categories. The best LAS for PaF while using gold and automatic tagger were 80.1% and 72.9% respectively. The morph information in the form of case, suffix and root information proved to be the most important features. But surprisingly, gender, number and person features didn't help. Agreement patterns in Hindi are not straightforward. For example, the verb agrees with k2 if the k1 has a post-position; it may also sometimes take the default features. In a passive sentence, the verb agrees only with k2. The agreement problem worsens when there is coordination or when there is a complex verb. It is understandable then that the parser is unable to learn the selective agreement pattern which needs to be followed.

LMSaF on the other hand encode richer information and capture some local linguistic patterns. The first four features in LMSaF (chunk type, chunk boundary, head/non-head of chunk and distance to the end of chunk) were found to be useful consistently. The fifth feature, in the form of suffix concatenation, gave us the biggest jump, and captures the correlation between the TAM markers of the verbs and the case markers on the nominals.

### 5.1 Feature comparison: PaF, MaF vs. LMSaF

Dependency labels can be classified as two types based on their nature, namely, inter-chunk dependency labels and intra-chunk labels. Inter-chunk dependency labels are syntacto-semantic in nature. Whereas intra-chunk dependency labels are purely syntactic in nature.

Figure 3, shows the f-measure for top six inter-chunk and intra-chunk dependency labels for PaF, MaF, and LMSaF using Maltparser on test data using automatic shallow parser information. The first six labels (k1, k2, pof, r6, ccof, and k7p) are the top six inter-chunk labels and the next six labels (lwg__psp, lwg__aux, lwg__cont, rsym, nmod__adj, and pof__cn) are the top six intra-chunk labels. First six labels (inter-chunk) correspond to 28.41% and next six labels (intra-chunk) correspond to 48.81% of the total labels in the test data. The figure shows that with POS information alone, f-measure for top four intra-chunk labels reached more than 90% accuracy. The accuracy increases marginally with the addition of morph and local morphosytactic features. The results corroborates with our intuition that intra-chunk dependencies are mostly syntactic. For example, consider an intra-chunk label 'lwg__psp'. This is the label for postposition marker. A post-position marker succeeding a noun is attached to that noun with the label 'lwg__psp'. POS tag for post-position marker is PSP. So, if a NN (common noun) or a NNP (proper noun) is followed by a PSP (post-position marker), then the PSP will be attached to the preceding NN/NNP with the dependency label 'lwg_psp'. As a result, providing POS information itself gave an f-measure of 98.3% for 'lwg_psp'. With morph and local morphosytactic features, this got increased to 98.4%. However, f-measure for some labels like 'nmod__adj' is around 80% only. 'nmod__adj' is the label for adjective-noun, quantifier-noun modifications. Low accuracy for these labels is mainly due to two reasons. One is POS tag errors. And the other is attachment errors due to genuine ambiguities such as compounding.

For inter-chunk labels (first six columns in the figure 3), there is considerable improvement in the f-measure using morph and local morphosytactic features. As mentioned, local morphosyntactic features provide local linguistic information. For example, consider the case of verbs. At POS level, there are only two tags 'VM' and 'VAUX' for main verbs and auxiliary verbs respectively (Bharati et al., 2006). Information about finite/non-finiteness is not present in the POS tag. But, at chunk level there are four different chunk tags for

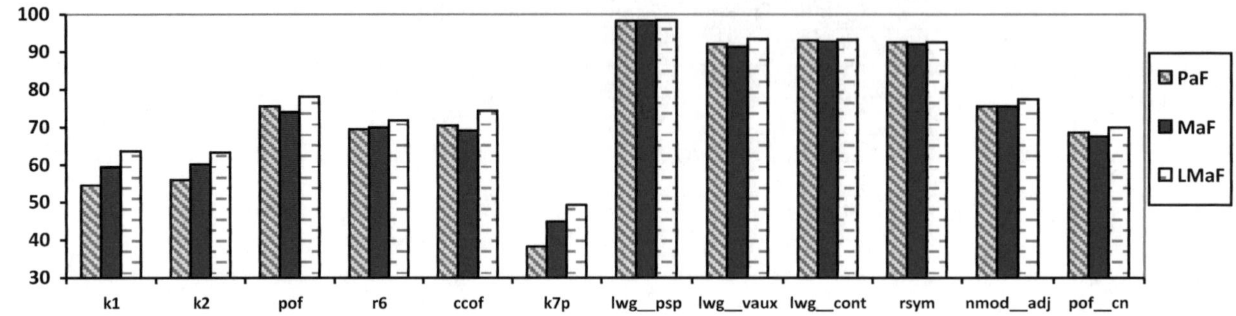


Figure 3: F-measure of top 6, inter-chunk and intra-chunk labels for PaF, MaF and LMSaF approaches using Maltparser on test data using automatic shallow parser information.

verbs, namely VGF, VGNF, VGINF and VGNN. They are respectively, finite, non-finite, infinitival and gerundial chunk tags. The difference in the verbal chunk tag is a good cue for helping the parser in identifying different syntactic behavior of these verbs. Moreover, a finite verb can become the root of the sentence, whereas a non-finite or infinitival verb can't. Thus, providing chunk information also helped in improving the correct identification of the root of the sentence.

Similar to Prague Treebank (Hajicova, 1998), coordinating conjuncts are heads in the treebank that we use. The relation between a conjunct and its children is shown using 'ccof' label. A coordinating conjuct takes children of similar type only. For example, a coordinating conjuct can have two finite verbs or two non-finite verbs as its children, but not a finite verb and a non-finite verb. Such instances are also handled more effectively if chunk information is incorporated. The largest increase in performance, however, was due to the 'suffix concatenation' feature. Significant improvement in the core inter-chunk dependency labels (such as k1, k2, k4, etc.) due to this feature is the main reason for the overall improvement in the parsing accuracy. As mentioned earlier, this is because this feature captures the correlation between the TAM markers of the verbs and the case markers on the nominals.

### 5.2 Approach comparison: LMSaF vs. 2stage

Both LMSaF and 2stage use chunk information. In LMSaF, chunk information is given as a feature whereas in 2stage, sentence parsing is divided into intra-chunk and inter-chunk parsing. Both the approaches have their pros and cons. In LMSaF as everything is done in a single stage there is much richer context to learn from. In 2stage, we can provide features specific to each stage which can't be done in a single stage approach (McDonald et al., 2006). But in 2stage, as we are dividing the task, accuracy of the division and the error propagation might pose a problem. This is reflected in the results where the 2-stage performs better than the single stage while using gold standard information, but lags behind considerably when the features are automatically computed.

During intra-chunk parsing in the 2stage setup, we tried out using both a rule-based approach and a statistical approach (using MaltParser). The rule based system performed slightly better (0.1% LAS) than statistical when gold chunks are considered. But, with automatic chunks, the statistical approach outperformed rule-based system with a difference of 7% in LAS. This is not surprising because, the rules used are very robust and mostly based on POS and chunk information. Due to errors induced by the automatic POS tagger and chunker, the rule-based system couldn't perform well. Consider a small example chunk given below.

| | | |
|---|---|---|
| (( | | NP |
| meraa | 'my' | PRP |
| bhaaii | 'brother' | NN |
| )) | | |

As per the Hindi chunking guidelines (Bharati et al., 2006), *meraa* and *bhaaii* should be in two separate chunks. And as per Hindi dependency annotation guidelines (Bharati et al., 2009), *meraa* is attached to *bhaaii* with a dependency label 'r6'[10]. When the chunker wrongly chunks them in a single

[10] 'r6' is the dependency label for genitive relation.

chunk, intra-chunk parser will assign the dependency relation for *meraa*. Rule based system can never assign 'r6' relation to *meraa* as it is an inter-chunk label and the rules used cannot handle such cases. But in a statistical system, if we train the parser using automatic chunks instead of gold chunks, the system can potentially assign 'r6' label.

### 5.3 Parser comparison: MST vs. Malt

In all the experiments, results of MaltParser are consistently better than MST+MaxEnt. We know that Maltparser is good at short distance labeling and MST is good at long distance labeling (McDonald and Nivre, 2007). The root of the sentence is better identified by MSTParser than MaltParser. Our results also confirm this. MST+MaxEnt and Malt could identify the root of the sentence with an f-measure of 89.7% and 72.3% respectively. Presence of more short distance labels helped Malt to outperform MST. Figure 5, shows the f-measure relative to dependency length for both the parsers on test data using automatic shallow parser information for LMSaF.

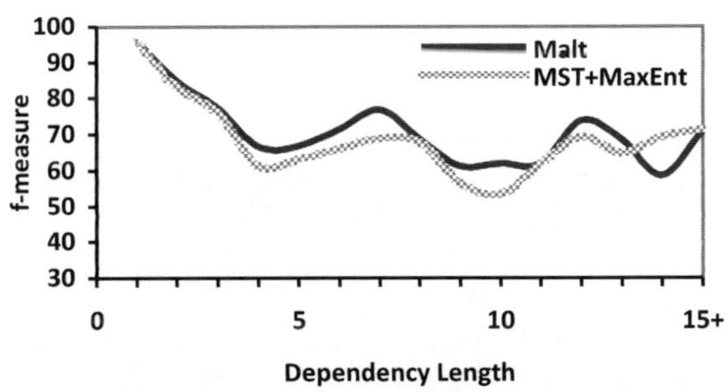


Figure 5: Dependency arc f-measure relative to dependency length.

## 6 Discussion and Future Work

We systematically explored the effect of various linguistic features in Hindi dependency parsing. Results show that POS, case, suffix, root, along with local morphosyntactic features help dependency parsing. We then described 2 methods to incorporate such features during the parsing process. These methods can be thought as different paradigms of modularity. For practical reasons (i.e. given the POS tagger/chunker accuracies), it is wiser to use this information as features rather than dividing the task into two stages.

As mentioned earlier, this is the first attempt at complete sentence level parsing for Hindi. So, we cannot compare our results with previous attempts at Hindi dependency parsing, due to, (a) The data used here is different and (b) we produce complete sentence parses rather than chunk level parses.

As mentioned in section 5.1, accuracies of intra-chunk dependencies are very high compared to inter-chunk dependencies. Inter-chunk dependencies are syntacto-semantic in nature. The parser depends on surface syntactic cues to identify such relations. But syntactic information alone is always not sufficient, either due to unavailability or due to ambiguity. In such cases, providing some semantic information can help in improving the inter-chunk dependency accuracy. There have been attempts at using minimal semantic information in dependency parsing for Hindi (Bharati et al., 2008). Recently, Ambati et al. (2009b) used six semantic features namely, human, non-human, in-animate, time, place, and abstract for Hindi dependency parsing. Using gold-standard semantic features, they showed considerable improvement in the core inter-chunk dependency accuracy. Some attempts at using clause information in dependency parsing for Hindi (Gadde et al., 2010) have also been made. These attempts were at inter-chunk dependency parsing using gold-standard POS tags and chunks. We plan to see their effect in complete sentence parsing using automatic shallow parser information also.

## 7 Conclusion

In this paper we explored two strategies to incorporate local morphosyntactic features in Hindi dependency parsing. These features were obtained using a shallow parser. We first explored which information provided by the shallow parser is useful and showed that local morphosyntactic features in the form of chunk type, head/non-head info, chunk boundary info, distance to the end of the chunk and suffix concatenation are very crucial for Hindi dependency parsing. We then investigated the best way to incorporate this information during dependency parsing. Further, we compared the results of various experiments based on various criterions and did some error analysis. This paper was also the first attempt at complete sentence level parsing for Hindi.

## References


B. R. Ambati, P. Gadde, and K. Jindal. 2009a. Experiments in Indian Language Dependency Parsing. In *Proc of the ICON09 NLP Tools Contest: Indian Language Dependency Parsing*, pp 32-37.

B. R. Ambati, P. Gade, C. GSK and S. Husain. 2009b. Effect of Minimal Semantics on Dependency Parsing. In *Proc of RANLP09 student paper workshop.*

G. Attardi and F. Dell'Orletta. 2008. Chunking and Dependency Parsing. In *Proc of LREC Workshop on Partial Parsing: Between Chunking and Deep Parsing.* Marrakech, Morocco.

R. Begum, S. Husain, A. Dhwaj, D. Sharma, L. Bai, and R. Sangal. 2008. Dependency annotation scheme for Indian languages. In *Proc of IJCNLP-2008.*

A. Bharati, V. Chaitanya and R. Sangal. 1995. *Natural Language Processing: A Paninian Perspective,* Prentice-Hall of India, New Delhi.

A. Bharati, S. Husain, B. Ambati, S. Jain, D. Sharma, and R. Sangal. 2008. Two semantic features make all the difference in parsing accuracy. In *Proc of ICON.*

A. Bharati, R. Sangal, D. M. Sharma and L. Bai. 2006. AnnCorra: Annotating Corpora Guidelines for POS and Chunk Annotation for Indian Languages. *Technical Report (TR-LTRC-31), LTRC, IIIT-Hyderabad.*

A. Bharati, D. M. Sharma, S. Husain, L. Bai, R. Begam and R. Sangal. 2009a. AnnCorra: TreeBanks for Indian Languages, Guidelines for Annotating Hindi TreeBank. http://ltrc.iiit.ac.in/MachineTrans/research/tb/DS-guidelines/DS-guidelines-ver2-28-05-09.pdf

A. Bharati, S. Husain, D. M. Sharma and R. Sangal. 2009b. Two stage constraint based hybrid approach to free word order language dependency parsing. *In Proc. of IWPT.*

A. Bharati, S. Husain, M. Vijay, K. Deepak, D. M. Sharma and R. Sangal. 2009c. Constraint Based Hybrid Approach to Parsing Indian Languages. *In Proc of PACLIC 23. Hong Kong. 2009.*

R. Bhatt, B. Narasimhan, M. Palmer, O. Rambow, D. M. Sharma and F. Xia. 2009. Multi-Representational and Multi-Layered Treebank for Hindi/Urdu. *In Proc. of the Third LAW at 47th ACL and 4th IJCNLP.*

Y.J. Chu and T.H. Liu. 1965. On the shortest arborescence of a directed graph. *Science Sinica*, 14:1396–1400.

J. Edmonds. 1967. Optimum branchings. *Journal of Research of the National Bureau of Standards*, 71B:233–240.

J. Eisner. 1996. Three new probabilistic models for dependency parsing: An exploration. In *Proc of COLING-96*, pp. 340–345.

G. Eryigit, J. Nivre, and K. Oflazer. 2008. Dependency Parsing of Turkish. *Computational Linguistics* 34(3), 357-389.

P. Gadde, K. Jindal, S. Husain, D. M. Sharma, and R. Sangal. 2010. Improving Data Driven Dependency Parsing using Clausal Information. In *Proc of NAACL-HLT 2010,* Los Angeles, CA.

E. Hajicova. 1998. Prague Dependency Treebank: From Analytic to Tectogrammatical Annotation. In *Proc of TSD'98.*

J. Hall, J. Nilsson, J. Nivre, G. Eryigit, B. Megyesi, M. Nilsson and M. Saers. 2007. Single Malt or Blended? A Study in Multilingual Parser Optimization. In *Proc of the CoNLL Shared Task Session of EMNLP-CoNLL 2007*, 933—939.

S. Husain. 2009. Dependency Parsers for Indian Languages. In *Proc of ICON09 NLP Tools Contest: Indian Language Dependency Parsing.* Hyderabad, India.

S. Husain, P. Gadde, B. Ambati, D. M. Sharma and R. Sangal. 2009. A modular cascaded approach to complete parsing. In *Proc. of the COLIPS IALP.*

P. Mannem, A. Abhilash and A. Bharati. 2009. LTAG-spinal Treebank and Parser for Hindi. In *Proc of International Conference on NLP, Hyderabad. 2009.*

R. McDonald, K. Crammer, and F. Pereira. 2005. Online large-margin training of dependency parsers. In *Proc of ACL.* pp. 91–98.

R. McDonald, K. Lerman, and F. Pereira. 2006. Multilingual dependency analysis with a two-stage discriminative parser. In *Proc of the Tenth (CoNLL-X)*, pp. 216–220.

R. McDonald and J. Nivre. 2007. Characterizing the errors of data-driven dependency parsing models. In *Proc. of EMNLP-CoNLL.*

J. Nivre, J. Hall, S. Kubler, R. McDonald, J. Nilsson, S. Riedel and D. Yuret. 2007a. The CoNLL 2007 Shared Task on Dependency Parsing. In *Proc of EMNLP/CoNLL-2007.*

J. Nivre, J. Hall, J. Nilsson, A. Chanev, G. Eryigit, S. Kübler, S. Marinov and E Marsi. 2007b. *MaltParser: A language-independent system for data-driven dependency parsing. Natural Language Engineering*, 13(2), 95-135.

J. Nivre and J. Nilsson. 2005. Pseudo-projective dependency parsing. In *Proc. of ACL-2005*, pp. 99–106.

Avinesh PVS and K. Gali. 2007. Part-Of-Speech Tagging and Chunking Using Conditional Random Fields and Transformation Based Learning. *In Proc of the SPSAL workshop during IJCAI '07.*

D. Seddah, M. Candito and B. Crabbé. 2009. Cross parser evaluation: a French Treebanks study. In *Proc. of IWPT,* 150-161.

R. Tsarfaty and K. Sima'an. 2008. Relational-Realizational Parsing. In *Proc. of CoLing,* 889-896.

A. Vaidya, S. Husain, P. Mannem, and D. M. Sharma. 2009. A karaka-based dependency annotation scheme for English. In *Proc. of CICLing,* 41-52.

# Application of Different Techniques to Dependency Parsing of Basque

**Kepa Bengoetxea**
IXA NLP Group
University of the Basque Country
Technical School of Engineering, Bilbao,
Plaza La Casilla 3, 48012, Bilbao
kepa.bengoetxea@ehu.es

**Koldo Gojenola**
IXA NLP Group
University of the Basque Country
Technical School of Engineering, Bilbao,
Plaza La Casilla 3, 48012, Bilbao
koldo.gojenola@ehu.es

## Abstract

We present a set of experiments on dependency parsing of the Basque Dependency Treebank (BDT). The present work has examined several directions that try to explore the rich set of morphosyntactic features in the BDT: i) experimenting the impact of morphological features, ii) application of dependency tree transformations, iii) application of a two-stage parsing scheme (stacking), and iv) combinations of the individual experiments. All the tests were conducted using MaltParser (Nivre et al., 2007a), a freely available and state of the art dependency parser generator.

## 1 Introduction

This paper presents several experiments performed on dependency parsing of the Basque Dependency Treebank (BDT, Aduriz et al., 2003). Basque can be briefly described as a morphologically rich language with free constituent order of the main sentence elements with respect to the main verb.

This work has been developed in the context of dependency parsing exemplified by the CoNLL Shared Task on Dependency Parsing in years 2006 and 2007 (Nivre et al., 2007b), where several systems competed analyzing data from a typologically varied range of 19 languages. The treebanks for all languages were standardized using a previously agreed CoNLL-X format (see Figure 1). An early version of the BDT (BDT I) was one of the evaluated treebanks, which will allow a comparison with our results. One of the conclusions of the CoNLL 2007 workshop (Nivre et al., 2007a) was that there is a class of languages, those that combine a relatively free word order with a high degree of inflection, that obtained the worst scores. This asks for the development of new methods and algorithms that will help to reach the parsing performance of the more studied languages, as English.

In this work, we will take the opportunity of having a new fresh version of the BDT, (BDT II henceforth), which is the result of an extension (three times bigger than the original one), and its redesign (see section 3.2). Using MaltParser, a freely available and state of the art dependency parser for all the experiments (Nivre et al., 2007a), this paper will concentrate on the application of different techniques to the task of parsing this new treebank, with the objective of giving a snapshot that can show the expected gains of each technique, together with some of their combinations. Some of the techniques have already been evaluated with other languages/treebanks or BDT I, while others have been adapted or extended to deal with specific aspects of the Basque language or the Basque Treebank. We will test the following:

- Impact of rich morphology. Although many systems performed feature engineering on the BDT at CoNLL 2007, providing a strong baseline, we will take a step further to improve parsing accuracy taking into account the effect of specific morphosyntactic features.
- Application of dependency-tree transformations. Nilsson et al. (2007) showed that they can increase parsing accuracy across languages/treebanks. We have performed similar experiments adapted to the specific properties of Basque and the BDT.
- Several works have tested the effect of using a two-stage parser (Nivre and McDonald, 2008; Martins et al., 2008), where the second parser takes advantage of features obtained by the first one. Similarly, we will experiment the



*Proceedings of the NAACL HLT 2010 First Workshop on Statistical Parsing of Morphologically-Rich Languages*, pages 31–39,
Los Angeles, California, June 2010. ©2010 Association for Computational Linguistics

| Index | Word | Lemma | Category | Subcategory | Features | Head | Dependency |
|---|---|---|---|---|---|---|---|
| 1 | etorri | etorri | V | V | _ | 3 | coord |
| 2 | dela | izan | AUXV | AUXV | REL:CMP\|SUBJ:3S | 1 | auxmod |
| 3 | eta | eta | CONJ | CONJ | _ | 6 | ccomp_obj |
| 4 | joan | joan | V | V | _ | 3 | coord |
| 5 | dela | izan | AUXV | AUXV | REL:CMP\|SUBJ:3S | 4 | auxmod |
| 6 | esan | esan | V | V | _ | 0 | ROOT |
| 7 | zien | *edun | AUXV | AUXV | SUBJ:3S\|OBJ:3P | 6 | auxmod |
| 8 | mutilak | mutil | NOUN | NOUN_C | CASE:ERG\|NUM:S | 6 | ncsubj |
| 9 | . | . | PUNT | PUNT_PUNT | _ | 8 | PUNC |

Figure 1: Example of a BDT sentence in the CoNLL-X format

(V = main verb, AUXV = auxiliary verb, CONJ = conjunction, REL = subordinated clause, CMP = completive, ccomp_obj = clausal complement object, ERG = ergative, SUBJ:3S: subject in 3rd person sing., OBJ:3P: object in 3rd person pl, coord = coordination, auxmod = auxiliary, ncsubj = non-clausal subject, ncmod = non-clausal modifier).

addition of new features to the input of the second-stage parser, in the form of morphosyntactic features propagated through the first parser's dependency tree and also as the addition of contextual features (such as category or dependency relation of parent, grandparent, and descendants).

- Combinations of the individual experiments.

The rest of the paper is organized as follows. After presenting related work in section 2, section 3 describes the main resources used in this work. Next, section 4 will examine the details of the different experiments to be performed, while section 5 will evaluate their results. Finally, the last section outlines our main conclusions.

## 2 Related work

Until recently, many works on treebank parsing have been mostly dedicated to languages with poor morphology, as exemplified by the Penn English Treebank. As the availability of treebanks for typologically different languages has increased, there has been a growing interest towards research on extending the by now standard algorithms and methods to the new languages and treebanks (Tsarfaty et al., 2009). For example, Collins et al. (1999) adapted Collins' parser to Czech, a highly-inflected language. Cowan and Collins (2005) apply the same parser to Spanish, concluding that the inclusion of morphological information improves the analyzer. Eryiğit et al. (2008) experiment the use of several types of morphosyntactic information in Turkish, showing how the richest the information improves precision. They also show that using morphemes as the unit of analysis (instead of words) gets better results, as a result of the agglutinative nature of Turkish, where each wordform contains several morphemes that can be individually relevant for parsing. Goldberg and Tsarfaty (2008) concluded that an integrated model of morphological disambiguation and syntactic parsing in Hebrew Treebank parsing improves the results of a pipelined approach. This is in accord with our experiment of dividing words into morphemes and transforming the tree accordingly (see section 4.2).

Since the early times of treebank-based parsing systems, a lot of effort has been devoted to aspects of preprocessing trees in order to improve the results (Collins, 1999). When applied to dependency parsing, several works (Nilsson et al., 2007; Bengoetxea and Gojenola, 2009a) have concentrated on modifying the structure of the dependency tree, changing its original shape. For example, Nilsson et al. (2007) present the application of pseudoprojective, verbal group and coordination transformations to several languages/treebanks using MaltParser, showing that they improve the results.

Another interesting research direction has examined the application of a two-stage parser, where the second parser tries to improve upon the result of a first parser. For example, Nivre and McDonald (2008) present the combination of two state of the art dependency parsers feeding each another, showing that there is a significant improvement over the simple parsers. This experiment can be seen as an instance of *stacked learning,* which was also tested on dependency parsing of several languages in (Martins et al., 2008) with significant improvements over the base parser.

## 3 Resources

This section will describe the main resources that have been used in the experiments. First, subsection 3.1 will describe the Basque Dependency Treebank, which has increased its size from 55,469 tokens in its original version to more than 150,000, while subsection 3.2 will present the main characteristics of MaltParser, a state of the art and data-driven dependency parser.

### 3.1 The Basque Dependency Treebank

Basque can be described as an agglutinative language that presents a high power to generate inflected word-forms, with free constituent order of sentence elements with respect to the main verb. The BDT can be considered a pure dependency treebank from its original design, due mainly to the syntactic characteristics of Basque.

```
(1) Etorri  dela    eta joan  dela     esan  zien mutilak
    come  that-has and go  that-has tell  did  boy-the
    The boy told them that he has come and gone
```

Figure 1 contains an example of a sentence (1), annotated in the CoNLL-X format. The text is organized in eight tab-separated columns: word-number, form, lemma, category, subcategory, morphological features, and the dependency relation (headword + dependency). The information in Figure 1 has been simplified due to space reasons, as typically the *Features* column will contain many *morphosyntactic*[1] features (case, number, type of subordinated sentence, …), which are relevant for parsing. The first version of the Basque Dependency Treebank contained 55,469 tokens forming 3,700 sentences (Aduriz et al., 2003). This treebank was used as one of the evaluated treebanks in the CoNLL 2007 Shared Task on Dependency Parsing (Nivre et al., 2007b). Our work will make use of the second version of the BDT (BDT II), which is the consequence of a process of extension and redesign of the original requirements:

- The new version contains 150,000 tokens (11,225 sentences), a three-fold increase.
- The new design considered that all the dependency arcs would connect sentence tokens. In contrast, the original annotation contained empty nodes, especially when dealing with ellipsis and some kinds of coordination. As a result, the number of non-projective arcs diminished from 2.9% in the original treebank to 1.3% in the new version.
- The annotation follows a stand-off markup approach, inspired on TEI-P4 (Artola et al., 2005). There was a conversion process from a set of interconnected XML files to the CoNLL-X format of the present experiments.

Although the different characteristics and size of the two treebank versions do not allow a strict comparison, our preliminary experiments showed that the results on both treebanks were similar regarding our main evaluation criterion (Labeled Attachment Score, or LAS). In the rest of the paper we will only use the new BDT II.

### 3.2 MaltParser

MaltParser (Nivre et al. 2007a) is a state of the art dependency parser that has been successfully applied to typologically different languages and treebanks. While several variants of the base parser have been implemented, we will use one of its standard versions (MaltParser version 1.3). The parser obtains deterministically a dependency tree in linear-time in a single pass over the input using two main data structures: a stack of partially analyzed items and the remaining input sequence. To determine the best action at each parsing step, the parser uses history-based feature models and discriminative machine learning. In all the following experiments, we will make use of a SVM classifier. The specification of the configuration used for learning can in principle include any kind of column in Figure 1 (such as word-form, lemma, category, subcategory or morphological features), together with a feature function. This means that a learning model can be described as a series of (*column, function*) pairs, where *column* represents the name of a column in Figure 1, and *function* makes reference to the parser's main data structures. For example, the two pairs (Word, Stack[0]), and (Word, Stack[1]) represent two features that correspond to the word-forms on top and next to top elements of the stack, respectively, while (POSTAG, Input[0]) represents the POS category of the first token in the remaining input sequence.

## 4 Experiments

The following subsections will present three types of techniques that will be tested with the aim of

[1] We will use the term *morphosyntactic* to name the set of features attached to each word-form, which by the agglutinative nature of Basque correspond to both morphology and syntax.

improving the results of the syntactic analyzer. Subsection 4.1 presents the process of fine-tuning the rich set of available morphosyntactic features. Then, 4.2 will describe the application of three types of tree transformations, while subsection 4.3 will examine the application of propagating syntactic features through a first-stage dependency tree, a process that can also be seen as an application of stacked learning, as tested in (Nivre and McDonald, 2008; Martins et al., 2008)

### 4.1 Feature engineering

The original CoNLL-X format uses 10 different columns (see Figure 1[2]), grouping the full set of morphosyntactic features in a single column. We will experiment the effect of individual features, following two steps:

- First, we tested the effect of incorporating each individual lexical feature, concluding that there were two features that individually gave significant performance increases. They were syntactic case, which is relevant for marking a word's syntactic function (or, equivalently, the type of dependency relation), and subordination type (REL henceforth). This REL feature appears in verb-ending morphemes that specify a type of subordinated sentence, such as in relative, completive, or indirect interrogative clauses. The feature is, therefore, relevant for establishing the main structure of a sentence, helping to delimit main and subordinated clauses, and it is also crucial for determining the dependency relation between the subordinated sentence and the main verb (head).
- Then, we separated these features in two independent columns, grouping the remaining features under the *Features* column. This way, Maltparser's learning specification can be more fine-grained, in terms of three morphosyntactic feature sets (CASE, REL and the rest, see Table 2).

This will allow us testing learning models with different configurations for each column, instead of treating the full set of features as a whole. So, we will have the possibility of experimenting with richer contexts (that is, advancing the Stack and/or Input[3] functions for each feature).

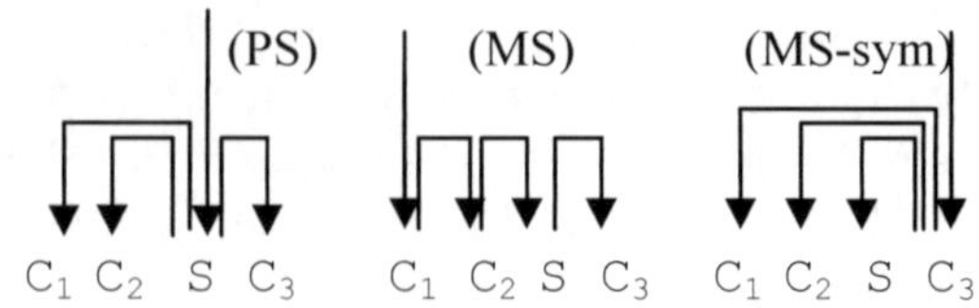


Figure 2. Dependency structures for coordination.

### 4.2 Tree transformations

Tree transformations have long been applied with the objective of improving parsing results (Collins, 1999; Nilsson et al., 2007). The general process consists of the following steps:

- Apply tree transformations to the treebank
- Train the system on the modified treebank
- Apply the parser to the test set
- Apply the inverse transformations
- Evaluate the result on the original treebank

We will test three different tree transformations, which had already been applied to the Treebank (BDT I) (Bengoetxea and Gojenola, 2009a):

- Projectivization ($T_P$). This is a language independent transformation already tested in several languages (Nivre and Nilsson, 2005). This transformation is totally language independent, and can be considered a standard transformation. Its performance on the first version of BDT had been already tested (Hall et al., 2007), giving significant improvements This is in accordance with BDT I having a 2.9% of non-projective arcs.
- Coordination ($T_C$). The transformation on coordinated sentences can be considered general (Nilsson et al., 2007) but it is also language dependent, as it depends on the specific configurations present in each language, mainly the set of coordination conjunctions and the types of elements that can be coordinated, together with their morphosyntactic properties (such as head initial or final). Coordination in BDT (both versions) is annotated in the so called Prague Style (PS, see Figure 2), where the conjunction is taken as the head, and the

[2] As a matter of fact, Figure 1 only shows 8 columns, although the CoNLL-X format includes two additional columns for the projective head (PHEAD) and projective dependency relation (PDEPREL), which have not been used in our work.

[3] Maltparser allows a rich set of functions to be specified for each column. In our experiments we mainly used the Stack and Input functions, which allow the inspection of the contents of the top elements of the Stack (Stack[0], Stack[1], …) or the currently unanalyzed input sequence (Input[0], Input [1], …).

conjuncts depend on it. Nilsson et al. (2007) advocate the Mel´cuk style (MS) for parsing Czech, taking the first conjunct as the head, and creating a chain where each element depends on the preceding one. Basque is a head final language, where many important syntactic features, like case or subordinating morphemes are located at the end of constituents. For that reason, Bengoetxea and Gojenola (2009a) proposed MS-sym, a symmetric variation of MS in which the coordinated elements will be dependents of the last conjunct (which will be the head, see Figure 2).

- Transformation of subordinated sentences (TS). They are formed in Basque by attaching the corresponding morphemes to the auxiliary verbs. However, in BDT (I and II) the verbal elements are organized around the main verb (semantic head) while the syntactic head corresponds to the subordination morpheme, which appears usually attached to the auxiliary. Its main consequence is that the elements bearing the relevant information for parsing are situated far in the tree with respect to their head. In Figure 3, we see that the morpheme *–la*, indicating a subordinated completive sentence, appears down in the tree, and this could affect the correct attachment to the main verb (*esan*). Figure 4 shows the effect of transforming the original tree in Figure 3. The subordination morpheme (*-la*) is separated from the auxiliary verb (*da*), and is "promoted" as the syntactic head of the subordinated sentence. New arcs are created from the main verb (*etorri*) to the morpheme (which is now the head), and also a new dependency relation (SUB).

Overall, the projectivization transformation ($T_P$) is totally language-independent. $T_C$ (coordination) can be considered in the middle, as it depends on the general characteristics of the language. Finally, the transformation of subordinated sentences ($T_S$) is specific to the treebank and intrinsecally linked to the agglutinative nature of Basque. Bengoetxea and Gojenola (2009a) also found that the order of transformations can be relevant. Their best system, after applying all the transformations, obtained a 76.80% LAS on BDT I (2.24% improvement over a baseline of 74.52%) on the test set. We include these already evaluated transformations in the present work with two objectives in mind:

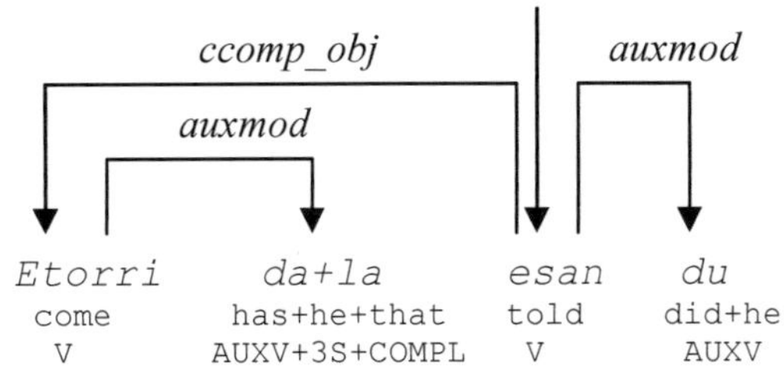

Figure 3. Dependency tree for the sentence *Etorri dela esan du* (He told that he would come).

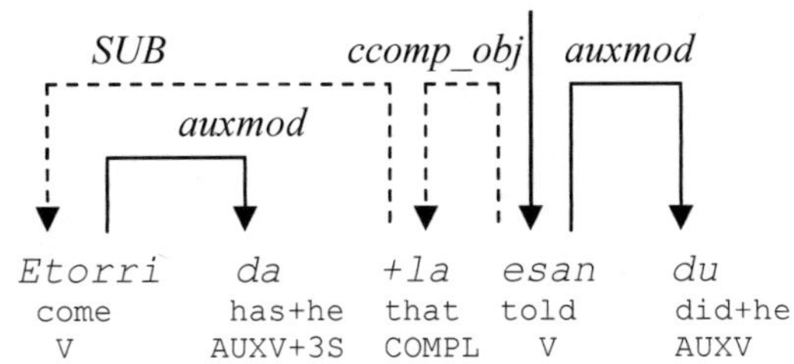

Figure 4. Effect of applying the transformation on subordinated sentences to the tree in Figure 3 (dotted lines represent the modified arcs).

- We want to test its effect on BDT II, 3 times larger than BDT I, and also with a lower proportion of non-projective arcs (1.3%).
- We are also interested in testing its combination with the rest of the techniques (see subsections 4.1 and 4.3).

### 4.3 Two-stage parsing (stacking)

Bengoetxea and Gojenola (2009b) tested the effect of propagating several morphosyntactic feature values after a first parsing phase, as in classical unification-based grammars, as a means of propagating linguistic information through syntax trees. They applied three types of feature propagation of the morphological feature values: a) from auxiliary verbs to the main verb (verb groups) b) propagation of case and number from post-modifiers to the head noun (noun phrases) c) from the last conjunct to the conjunction (coordination). This was done mainly because Basque is head final, and relevant features are located at the end of constituents.

Nivre and McDonald (2008) present an application of stacked learning to dependency parsing, in which a second predictor is trained to improve the performance of the first. Martins et al. (2008) specify the following steps:

- Split training data D into L partitions $D^1, \dots, D^L$.
- Train L instances of the level 0 parser in the following way: the l-th instance, $g^l$, is trained

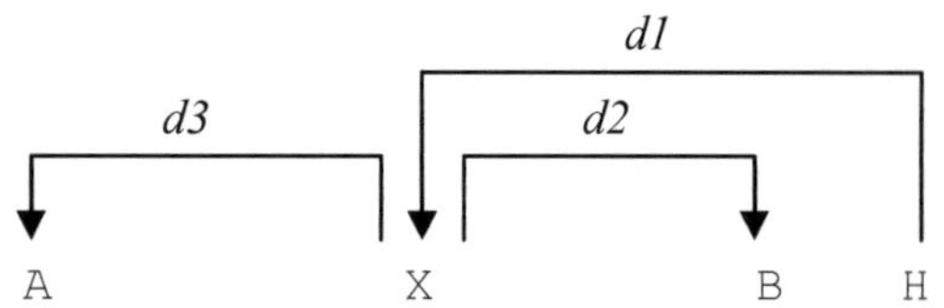


Figure 5. Stacked features. X can take several features from its descendants (dependency arcs d2 and d3) or his head (d1).

on $D^{-1} = D \setminus D^l$. Then use $g^l$ to output predictions for the (unseen) partition $D^l$. At the end, we have an augmented dataset $D^* = D$ + new set of stacked/propagated features.

- Train the level 0 parser g on the original training data D.
- Train the level 1 parser on the augmented training data $D^*$.

In our tests, it was enough with two partitions (L = 2), as experiments with L > 2 did not give any significant improvement. Figure 5 shows the types of information that can be added to each target element. The token X can take several kinds of information from its children (A and B) or his parent (H). The information that is propagated can vary, including part of speech, morphosyntactic features or the dependency relations between X and its children/parent. We can roughly classify the stacked features in two different sets:

- *Linguistic* features (feature passing), such as case or number, which are propagated applying linguistic principles, such as "*the syntactic case is propagated from the dependents towards the head of NPs and postpositional phrases*". The idea is to propagate several *morphosyntactic* features (case, number, …) from dependents to heads.
- *Parser* features. They will be based solely on different dependency tree configurations (see Figure 5), similarly to (Nivre and McDonald, 2008; Martins et al., 2008). Among them, we will test the inclusion of several features (dependency relation, category and morphosyntactic features) from the following: parent, grandparent, siblings, and children.

In the present work, we have devised the following experiments:

- We will test the effect of propagating *linguistic* features on the new BDT II. In contrast to (Bengoetxea and Gojenola, 2009b), who used the enriched *gold* data as $D^*$ directly, we will test Martins et al.'s proposal, in which the level 1 parser will be able to learn on the errors of the level 0 parser.
- We will extend these experiments with the use of different *parser* features (Nivre and McDonald, 2008; Martins et al., 2008).

### 4.4 Combination

Finally, we will combine the different techniques. An important point is to determine whether the techniques are independent (and accumulative) or it could also be that they can serve as alternative treatments to deal with the same phenomena.

## 5 Evaluation

BDT I was used at the CoNLL 2007 Shared Task, where many systems competed on it (Nivre et al., 2007b). We will use Labeled Attachment Score (LAS) as the evaluation measure: the percentage of correct arcs (both dependency relation and head) over all arcs, with respect to the gold standard. Table 1 shows the best CoNLL 2007 results on BDT I. The best system obtained a score of 76.94%, combining six variants of MaltParser, and competing with 19 systems. Carreras (2007) and Titov and Henderson (2007) obtained the second and third positions, respectively. We consider the last two lines in Table 1 as our baselines, which consist in applying a single MaltParser version (Hall et al., 2007), that obtained the fifth position at CoNLL 2007. Although Hall et al. (2007) applied the projectivization transformation ($T_P$), we will not use it in our baseline because we want to evaluate the effect of multiple techniques over a base parser. Although we could not use the subset of BDT II corresponding to BDT I, we run[4] a test with a set of sentences the size of BDT I. As could be ex-

| | | System | | LAS |
|---|---|---|---|---|
| BDT I | CoNLL 07 | Nivre et al. 2007b (MaltParser, combined) | | 76.94% |
| | | Carreras, 2007 | | 75.75% |
| | | Titov and Henderson, 2007 | | 75.49% |
| | | Hall et al., 2007 (MaltParser (single parser) + pseudoprojective transformation) | | 74.99% |
| | MaltParser (single parser) | | | 74.52% |
| BDT II | MaltParser (single parser) | | BDT I size | 74.83% |
| | | | Baseline | 77.08% |

Table 1. Top LAS scores for Basque dependency parsing.

[4] For space reasons, we do not specify details of the algorithm and the parameters. These data can be obtained, together with the BDT II data, from any of the authors.

| | | Stack[0] | Input[0] | Input[1] | Input[2] |
|---|---|---|---|---|---|
| 1 | **Features** | + | + | | |
| 2 | **CASE** | + | + | + | |
| | **REL** | + | + | + | + |
| | **Features (rest)** | + | + | | |

Table 2. Learning configurations for morphosyntactic features (1 = best model for the whole set of features. 2 = best model when specializing features).

pected, the three-fold increase in the new treebank gives a 2.35% improvement over BDT I.

For evaluation, we divided the treebank in three sets, corresponding to training, development, and test (80%, 10%, and 10%, respectively). All the experiments were done on the development set, leaving the best systems for the final test.

### 5.1 Single systems

Table 3 shows the results for the basic systems employing each of the techniques advanced in Section 4. As a first result, we see that a new step of reengineering MaltParser's learning configuration was rewarding (see row 2 in Table 3), as morphosyntactic features were more finely specified with respect to the most relevant features. Table 2 presents the baseline and the best learning model[5]. We see that advancing the input lookahead for CASE and REL gives an increase of 0.82 points.

Looking at the transformations (rows 3 to 7), the new Treebank BDT II obtains results similar to those described in (Bengoetxea and Gojenola, 2009a). As could be expected from the reduction of non-projective arcs (from 2.9% to 1.3%), the gains of $T_P$ are proportionally lower than in BDT I. Also, we can observe that $T_S$ alone worsens the baseline, but it gives the best results when combined with the rest (rows 6 and 7). This can be explained because $T_S$ creates new non-projective arcs, so it is effective only if $T_P$ is applied later. The transformation on coordination ($T_C$) alone does not get better results, but when combined with $T_P$ and $T_S$ gives the best results.

Applying feature propagation and stacking (see rows 9-17), we can see that most of the individual techniques (rows 9-14) give improvements over the baseline. When combining what we defined as *linguistic* features (those morphosyntactic features propagated by the application of three linguistic principles), we can see that their combination seems accumulative (row 15). The *parser* features also give a significant improvement individually (rows 12-14), but, when combined either among themselves (row 16) or with the linguistic features (row 17), their effect does not seem to be additive.

### 5.2 Combined systems

After getting significant improvements on the individual techniques and some of their combinations, we took a further step to integrate different techniques. An important aspect that must be taken into account is that the combination is not trivial all the times. For example, we have seen (section 5.1) that combinations of the three kinds of tree transformations must be defined having in mind the possible side-effects of any previous transformation. When combining different techniques, care must be taken to avoid any incompatibility. For that reason we only tested some possibilities. Rows 18-21 show some of the combined experiments. Combination of feature optimization with the pseudoprojective transformation yields an accumulative improvement (row 18). However, the combination of all the tree transformations with FO (row 19) does not accumulate. This can be due to the fact that feature optimization already *cancelled* the effect of the transformation on coordination and subordinated sentences, or otherwise it could also need a better exploration of their interleaved effect. Finally, row 21 shows that feature optimization, the pseudoprojective transformation and feature propagation are also accumulative, giving the best results. The relations among the rest of the transformations deserve future examination, as the results do not allow us to extract a precise conclusion.

## 6 Conclusions and future work

We studied several proposals for improving a baseline system for parsing the Basque Treebank. All the results were evaluated on the new version, BDT II, three times larger than the previous one. We have obtained the following main results:

- Using rich morphological features. We have extended previous works, giving a finer grained description of morphosyntactic features on the learner's configuration,

[5] This experiment was possible due to the fact that MaltParser's functionality was extended, allowing the specification of new columns/features, as the first versions of MaltParser only permitted a single column that included all the features.

| | | Row | System | LAS | |
|---|---|---|---|---|---|
| | Baseline | 1 | | 77.08% | |
| | Feature optimization | 2 | FO | *77.90% | (+0.82) |
| | Transformations | 3 | $T_P$ | **77.92% | (+0.84) |
| | | 4 | $T_S$ | 75.95% | (-1.13) |
| | | 5 | $T_C$ | 77.05% | (-0.03) |
| | | 6 | $T_S + T_P$ | **78.41% | (+1.33) |
| | | 7 | $T_S + T_C + T_P$ | **78.59% | (+1.51) |
| Single technique | Stacking | 9 | $S_{VG}$ | **77.68% | (+0.60) |
| | | 10 | $S_{NP}$ | 77.17% | (+0.09) |
| | | 11 | $S_C$ | 77.40% | (+0.32) |
| | | 12 | $S_P$ | *77.70% | (+0.62) |
| | | 13 | $S_{CH}$ | *77.80% | (+0.72) |
| | | 14 | $S_{GP}$ | 77.37% | (+0.29) |
| | | 15 | $S_{VG} + S_{NP} + S_C$ | **78.22% | (+1.14) |
| | | 16 | $S_P + S_{CH}$ | **77.96% | (+0.88) |
| | | 17 | $S_{VG} + S_{NP} + S_C + S_P + S_{CH}$ | **78.44% | (+1.36) |
| Combination | | 18 | $FO + T_P$ | **78.78% | (+1.70) |
| | | 19 | $FO + T_S + T_C + T_P$ | **78.47% | (+1.39) |
| | | 20 | $T_P + S_{VG} + S_{NP} + S_C$ | **78.56% | (+1.48) |
| | | 21 | $FO + T_P + S_{VG} + S_{NP} + S_C$ | **78.98% | (+1.90) |

Table 3. Evaluation results.

(FO: feature optimization; $T_P$ $T_C$ $T_S$: Pseudo-projective, Coordination and Subordinated sentence transformations;
$S_{VG}$, $S_{NP}$, $S_C$: Stacking (feature passing) on Verb Groups, NPs and Coordination;
$S_P$, $S_{CH}$, $S_{GP}$: Stacking (category, features and dependency) on Parent, CHildren and GrandParent;
*: statistically significant in McNemar's test, $p < 0.005$; **: statistically significant, $p < 0.001$)

showing that it can significantly improve the results. In particular, differentiating case and the type of subordinated sentence gives the best LAS increase (+0.82%).

- Tree transformations. We have replicated the set of tree transformations that were tested in the old treebank (Bengoetxea and Gojenola 2009a). Two of the transformations (projectivization and coordination) can be considered language independent, while the treatment of subordination morphemes is related to the morphological nature of Basque.
- Feature propagation. We have experimented the effect of a stacked learning scheme. Some of the stacked features were language-independent, as in (Nivre and McDonald. 2008), but we have also applied a generalization of the stacking mechanism to a morphologically rich language, as some of the stacked features are morphosyntactic features (such as case and number) which were propagated through a first stage dependency tree by the application of linguistic principles (noun phrases, verb groups and coordination).
- Combination of techniques. Although several of the combined approaches are accumulative with respect to the individual systems, some others do not give a improvement over the basic systems. A careful study must be conducted to investigate whether the approaches are exclusive or complementary. For example, the transformation on subordinated sentences and feature propagation on verbal groups seem to be attacking the same problem, i. e., the relations between main and subordinated sentences. In this respect, they can be viewed as alternative approaches to dealing with these phenomena.

The results show that the application of these techniques can give noticeable results, getting an overall improvement of 1.90% (from 77.08% until 78.98%), which can be roughly comparable to the effect of doubling the size of the treebank (see the last two lines of Table 1).

## Acknowledgements

This research was supported by the Department of Industry of the Basque Government (IE09-262) and the University of the Basque Country (GIU09/19). Thanks to Joakim Nivre and his team for their support using Maltparser and his fruitful suggestion about the use of stacked features.

## References


Itziar Aduriz, Maria Jesus Aranzabe, Jose Maria Arriola, Aitziber Atutxa, Arantza Diaz de Ilarraza, Aitzpea Garmendia and Maite Oronoz. 2003. Construction of a Basque dependency treebank. *Treebanks and Linguistic Theories*.

Xabier Artola, Arantza Díaz de Ilarraza, Nerea Ezeiza, Koldo Gojenola, Gorka Labaka, Aitor Sologaistoa, Aitor Soroa. 2005. A framework for representing and managing linguistic annotations based on typed feature structures. *Proceedings of the International Conference on Recent Advances in Natural Language Processing*, RANLP 2005.

Kepa Bengoetxea and Koldo Gojenola. 2009a. Exploring Treebank Transformations in Dependency Parsing. *Proceedings of the International Conference on Recent Advances in Natural Language Processing*, RANLP'2009.

Kepa Bengoetxea and Koldo Gojenola. 2009b. Application of feature propagation to dependency parsing. *Proceedings of the International Workshop on Parsing Technologies* (IWPT'2009).

Xavier Carreras. 2007. Experiments with a high-order projective dependency parser. In *Proceedings of the CoNLL 2007 Shared Task* (EMNLP-CoNLL).

Shay B. Cohen and Noah A. Smith. 2007. Joint Morphological and Syntactic Disambiguation. *In Proceedings of the CoNLL 2007 Shared Task.*

Michael Collins, Jan Hajic, Lance Ramshaw and Christoph Tillmann. 1999. *A Statistical Parser for Czech.* Proceedings of ACL.

Michael Collins. 1999. *Head-Driven Statistical Models for Natural Language Parsing.* PhD Dissertation, University of Pennsylvania..

Brooke Cowan and Michael Collins. 2005. Morphology and Reranking for the Statistical Parsing of Spanish. In *Proceedings of EMNLP 2005.*

Gülsen Eryiğit, Joakim Nivre and Kemal Oflazer. 2008. Dependency Parsing of Turkish. *Computational Linguistics*, Vol. 34 (3).

Yoav Goldberg and Reut Tsarfaty. 2008. A Single Generative Model for Joint Morphological Segmentation and Syntactic Parsing. *Proceedings of ACL-HLT* 2008, Colombus, Ohio, USA.

Johan Hall, Jens Nilsson, Joakim Nivre, Gülsen Eryigit, Beáta Megyesi, Mattias Nilsson and Markus Saers. 2007. Single Malt or Blended? A Study in Multilingual Parser Optimization. *Proceedings of the CoNLL Shared Task EMNLP-CoNLL.*

André F. T. Martins, Dipanjan Das, Noah A. Smith, Eric P. Xing. 2008. Stacking Dependency Parsing. *Proceedings of EMNLP-2008.*

Jens Nilsson, Joakim Nivre and Johan Hall. 2007. Generalizing Tree Transformations for Inductive Dependency Parsing. *Proceedings of the 45th Conference of the ACL.*

Joakim Nivre. 2006. *Inductive Dependency Parsing.* Springer.

Joakim Nivre, Johan Hall, Jens Nilsson, Chanev A., Gülsen Eryiğit, Sandra Kübler, Marinov S., and Edwin Marsi. 2007a. MaltParser: A language-independent system for data-driven dependency parsing. *Natural Language Engineering.*

Joakim Nivre, Johan Hall, Sandra Kübler, Ryan McDonald, Jens Nilsson, Sebastian Riedel and Deniz Yuret. 2007b. The CoNLL 2007 Shared Task on Dependency Parsing. *Proceedings of EMNLP-CoNLL.*

Joakim Nivre and Ryan McDonald. 2008. Integrating graph-based and transition-based dependency parsers. *Proceedings* of ACL-2008.

Ivan Titov and James Henderson. 2007. Fast and robust multilingual dependency parsing with a generative latent variable model. In *Proceedings of the CoNLL 2007 Shared Task* (EMNLP-CoNLL).

Reut Tsarfaty, Khalil Sima'an, and Remko Scha. 2009. An Alternative to Head-Driven Approaches for Parsing a (Relatively) Free Word-Order Language. *Proceedings of EMNLP.*

# Modeling Morphosyntactic Agreement in Constituency-Based Parsing of Modern Hebrew

**Reut Tsarfaty*** **and Khalil Sima'an**
Institute for Logic, Language and Computation
University of Amsterdam
{r.tsarfaty,k.simaan}@uva.nl

## Abstract

We show that naïve modeling of morphosyntactic agreement in a Constituency-Based (CB) statistical parsing model is worse than none, whereas a linguistically adequate way of modeling inflectional morphology in CB parsing leads to improved performance. In particular, we show that an extension of the Relational-Realizational (RR) model that incorporates agreement features is superior to CB models that treat morphosyntax as state-splits (SP), and that the RR model benefits more from inflectional features. We focus on parsing Hebrew and report the best result to date, $F_1$84.13 for parsing off of gold-tagged text, 5% error reduction from previous results.

## 1 Introduction

Agreement is defined by linguists as the systematic covariance of the grammatical properties of one linguistic element to reflect the semantic or formal properties of another (Corbett, 2001). Morphologically marked agreement features such as *gender, number* and *person* are used to realize grammatical relations between syntactic constituents, and such patterns are abundantly found in (less- or) non-configurational languages (Hale, 1983) where the order of words is known to be (relatively) free. Agreement features encompass information concerning the functional relations between constituents in the syntactic structure, but whether incorporating agreement features in a statistical parsing model leads to improved performance has so far remained an open question and saw contradictory results.

Taking Semitic languages as an example, it was shown that an SVM-based shallow parser (Goldberg et al., 2006) does not benefit from including agreement features for NP chunking in Hebrew. Phrase-structure based parsers for Arabic systematically discard morphological features from their label-set and never parametrize agreement explicitly (Maamouri et al., 2008). Models based on deep grammars such as CCG (Hockenmaier and Steedman, 2003) and HPSG (Miyao and Tsujii, 2008) could in principle use inflectional morphology, but they currently rely on functional information mainly. For formalisms that do incorporate morphology, generative models are may leak probability due to unification failures (Abney, 1997). Even results from dependency parsing remain inconclusive. It was shown for dependency parsing that case, definiteness and animacy features are useful to enhance parsing (e.g., (Øvrelid and Nivre, 2007)), agreement patterns are often excluded. When agreement features were included as features in dependency parser for Hebrew in (Goldberg and Elhadad, 2009) for Hebrew they obtained tiny-to-no improvement.

A question thus emerges whether there are any benefits in explicitly incorporating morphosyntactic agreement patterns into our models. This question is a manifestation of a greater issue, namely, whether it is beneficial to represent complex patterns of morphology in the statistical parsing model, or whether configurational information subsume the relevant patterns, as it is commonly assumed in constituency-based parsing. Here we claim that agreement features are useful for statistical parsing provided that they are represented and parametrized in a way that reflects their linguistic substance; to express functional information orthogonal to configuration.

*The first author is currently a researcher at the department of Linguistics and Philology at Uppsala University.



*Proceedings of the NAACL HLT 2010 First Workshop on Statistical Parsing of Morphologically-Rich Languages*, pages 40–48,
Los Angeles, California, June 2010. ©2010 Association for Computational Linguistics

We do so by extending the Relational-Realizational (RR) model we presented in (Tsarfaty and Sima'an, 2008) to explicitly encode agreement features in its native representation (RR-AGR). In the RR model, a joint distribution over grammatical relations is firstly articulated in the *projection* phase. The grammatical relations may be spelled out by positioning them with respect to one another in the *configuration* phase, through the use of morphology in the *realization* phase, or both. This paper shows that, for Hebrew, this RR-AGR strategy significantly outperforms a constituency-based model that treats agreement features as internally structured non-terminal state-splits (SP-AGR). As we accumulate morphological features, the performance gap between the RR and SP models becomes larger.

The best result we report for the RR-AGR model, $F_1$84.13, is the best result reported for Hebrew to date for parsing gold PoS-tagged segments, with 5% error reduction from previous results. This result is also significantly higher than all parsing results reported so far for Arabic, a Semitic language with similar morphosyntactic phenomena.[1] The RR approach is shown to be an adequate way to model complex morphosyntactic patterns for improving constituency based parsing of a morphologically rich, free word order language. Because the RR model is also proper and generative, it may also embed as a language model to enhance more complex NLP tasks, e.g., statistical Machine Translation.

## 2 The Data

The grammar of nonconfigurational languages allows for freedom in word ordering and discontinuities of syntactic constituents (Hale, 1983). Such languages do not rely on configurational information such as position and adjacency in marking grammatical relations such as *subject* and *object*, but instead they use word-level morphology. One way to encode grammatical relations in the form of words is by using morphological case, that is, explicitly marking an argument (e.g. nominative, accusative) with respect to its grammatical function. In (Tsarfaty et al., 2009) we showed that incorporating case indeed leads to improved performance for constituency-based, Relational-Realizational parsing of Hebrew.

A more involved way to morphologically encode grammatical relations is by making explicit reference to the properties of multiple linguistic elements. This is the general pattern of agreement, i.e.,

> "[A] systematic covariance between a semantic or a formal property of one element and a formal property of another." (Steele, adapted from (Corbett, 2001))

Describing agreement patterns involves explicit reference to the following four components; the element which determines the agreement properties is the **Controller** of the agreement, the element whose properties are determined by agreement is the **Target**, the syntactic environment in which the agreement occurs is the **Domain** of agreement, and the properties with respect to which they agree are agreement **Features** (Corbett, 2001). Agreement is an inherently asymmetrical relation. Combination of features displayed by controllers has to be accommodated by the inflectional features of the target, but there is no opposite requirement. Let us illustrate the formal description of agreement through Subject-Verb agreement familiar from English (1).

(1) a. Subject-Verb Agreement in English:
   Controller: NP
   Target: V
   Domain: S
   Features: *number, person*
 b. Example:
   i. They like the paper
   ii. *They likes the paper

The agreement target (the verb) in English has a rich enough inflectional paradigm that reflects the person and number features inherent in controllers — the nouns that realize subjects. (But nouns in English need not reflect, say, tense.) Had the subject been an NP, e.g., the phrase "the committee", the agreement pattern would have had to be determined by the features of the entire NP, and in English the features of the phrase would be determined by the lexical head "committee". The controller of the agreement (noun) does not coincide with the head of the lexical dependency (the verb), which means that the direction of morphological dependencies need not coincide with that of lexical dependencies.

[1] In (Maamouri et al., 2008), $F_1$78.1 for gold standard input.

**The Semitic Language Modern Hebrew** Modern Hebrew, (henceforth, Hebrew) is a Semitic language with a flexible word order and rich morphological structure. Hebrew nouns morphologically reflect their inherent *gender* and *number*. Pronouns also reflect *person* features. Hebrew verbs are inflected to reflect *gender, number, person* and *tense*. Adjectives are inflected to reflect the inherent properties of nouns, and both nouns and adjectives are inflected for *definiteness*. The Hebrew grammar uses this arsenal of properties to implement a wide variety of agreement patterns realizing grammatical relations.

**Agreement in Hebrew S Domains** Hebrew manifests different patterns of agreement in its S domain. Verbal predicates (the target) in matrix sentences (the domain) agree with their nominal subjects (the controller) on the agreement features *gender, number* and *person*. This occurs regardless of their configurational positions, as illustrated in (2b).

(2) a. Agreement in Verbal Sentences:
   Controller: NP
   Target: V
   Domain: S
   Features: *number, person, gender*

   b. i. דני נתן מתנה לדינה
      dani natan matana
      Dani.3MS gave.3MS present
      ledina
      to-Dina

      Dani gave a present to Dina (SVO)

   ii. מתנה נתן דני לדינה
      matana natan dani
      present gave.3MS Dani.3MS
      ledina
      to-Dina

      Dani gave a present to Dina (VI)

Subject-Predicate agreement relations are not only independent of surface positions, but are also orthogonal to the syntactic distributional type of the constituent realizing the predicate. Semitic languages allow for predicates to be realized as an NP, an ADJP or a PP clause (3b) lacking a verb altogether. (In the Hebrew treebank, such predicates are marked as PREDP). In all such cases, agreement feature-bundles realized as pronominals, which (Doron, 1986) calls Pron, are optionally placed after the subject. The position of Pron element with respect to the subject and predicate is fixed.[2] The role of these Pron elements is to indicate the argument-structure of a nominal sentence that is not projected by a verb. In the Hebrew treebank they are subsumed under predicative phrases (PREDPs). If a PREDP head is of type NP or ADJP it must be inflected to reflect the features of the subject controller, as is illustrated in examples (3b-i)–(3b-ii).

(3) a. Agreement in Nominal Sentences:
   Controller: NP
   Target: Pron
   Domain: S
   Features: *number, gender,person*

   b. i. דינה (היא) ציירת
      dina (hi) cayeret
      Dina.FS (Pron.3FS) painter.FS

      Dina is a painter

   ii. דינה (היא) מוכשרת
      Dina (hi) muchsheret
      Dina.FS (Pron.3FS) talented.FS

      Dina is talented

   iii. דינה (היא) בבית
      Dina (hi) babayit
      Dina.FS (Pron.3FS) in-the-house

      Dina is at home

   c. i. דינה ציירת *(היא) (hi)* dina cayeret
      (Pron.3FS)* Dina.FS painter.FS

The pronominal features *gender, number, person* are also a part the inflectional paradigm of the verb היה (be), which is extended to include tense features. These inflected elements are used as AUX which function as co-heads together with the main (nominal or verbal) predicate. AUX elements that take a nominal predicate as in (4b) agree with their subject, and so do auxiliaries that take a verbal complement, e.g., the modal verb in (4c). The nominal predicate in (4b) also agrees with the subject – and so does the modal verb in (4c). Agreement of AUX with the

[2] Doron (1986) shows that these Pron elements can not be considered the present tense supplements of AUX elements in Hebrew since their position with respect to the subject and predicate is fixed, whereas AUX can change position, see (4) below.

verbal or nominal predicates is again independent of their surface positions.

(4) a. Subject-AUX Agreement in Hebrew:
Controller: NP
Target: AUX
Domain: S
Features: *number, person, gender*

b. i. היא היתה בעבר ציירת

hi hayta be'avar
she.3FS was.3FS in-past
cayeret
painter.FS

She was a painter in the past

ii. בעבר היתה היא ציירת

be'avar hayta hi
in-past was.3FS she.3FS
cayeret
painter.FS

She was a painter in the past"

c. i. היא היתה אמורה להגיע

hi hayta amura
She.3FS was.3FS supposed.FS
lehagi'a
to-arrive

She was supposed to arrive

ii. היא אמורה היתה להגיע

hi amura hayta
She.3FS supposed.FS was.3FS
lehagi'a
to-arrive

She was supposed to arrive

**Agreement in Construct State Nouns** Semitic languages allow for the creation of noun compounds by phonologically marking their lexical head and adding a genitive complement. These constructions are called Construct-State Nouns (CSN) (Danon, 2008) and an example of a CSN is provided in (5a).[3]

(5) a. בת הצייר

bat ha-cayar
child.FS.CSN Def-painter.MS

The painter's daughter

[3]Also known as *iDaFa* constructions in Arabic.

In such cases, all the agreement features are taken from the head of the CSN, the noun 'daughter' in (5). Since CSNs may be embedded in other CSNs, the constructions may be arbitrarily long. When short or long, CSNs themselves may be modified by adjectives that agree with the CSN as a whole. This gives rise to multiple patterns of agreement within a single complex CSN. Consider, for instance, the modified CSN in (6a).

(6) a. בת הצייר המוכשרת

bat ha-cayar
child.FS.CSN Def-painter.MS
ha-muchsheret
Def-talented.FS

The talented daughter of the painter

The features Def, F, S of the adjective 'talented' agree with the inherent properties of the CSN head 'child.FS' and with the definiteness status of the embedded genitive Def-painter. This phenomenon is called by Danon (2008) definiteness-spreading, and what is important about such spreading is to observe that it is not always the case that all agreement features of a phrase are contributed by its lexical head.[4]

**Interim Summary** The challenges of modeling agreement inside constituency-based statistical models can be summarized as follows. The models are required to assign probability mass to alternating sequences of constituents while retaining equivalent feature distributions that capture agreement. Agreement is (i) orthogonal to the position of constituents (ii), orthogonal to their distributional types, and (iii) orthogonal to features' distributions among dominated subconstituents. Yet, from a functional point of view their contribution is entirely systematic.

## 3 The Models

The strong version of the well-known Lexicalist Hypothesis (LH) states that "syntactic rules cannot make reference to any aspect of word internal structure" (Chomsky, 1970). Anderson (1982) argues that syntactic processes operating within configurational structures can often manipulate, or have access to, formal and inherent properties of individual words. Anderson (1982) argues that a model

[4]Examples for non-overlapping contribution of features by multiple dependencies can be found in (Guthmann et al., 2009).

that is well-equipped to capture such phenomena is one that retains a relaxed version of the LH, that is, one in which syntactic processes do not make reference to aspects of word-internal structure *other than morphologically marked inflectional features*. What kind of parsing model would allow us to implement this relaxed version of the Lexicalist Hypothesis?

**The Morphosyntatctic State-Splits (SP) Model** One way to maintain a relaxed version of the LH in syntax is to assume a constituency-based representation in which the morphological features of words are percolated to the level of constituency in which they are syntactically relevant. This approach is characteristic of feature-based grammars (e.g., GPSG (Gazdar et al., 1985) and follow-up studies). These grammars assume a feature geometry that defines the internal structure of node labels in phrase-structure trees.[5]

Category-label state-splits can reflect the different morphosyntactic behavior of different non-terminals of the same type. Using such supervised, linguistically motivated, state-splits, based on the phrase-level marking of morphological information is one may build an efficient implementation of a PCFG-based parsing model that takes into account morphological features. State-split models were shown to obtain state-of-the-art performance with little computational effort. Supervised state-splits for constituency-based unlexicalized parsing in (Klein and Manning, 2003) in an accurate English parser. For the pair of Hebrew sentences (2b), the morphological state-split context-free representation of the domain S is as described at the top of figure 1.[6]

**The Relational-Realizational (RR) Model** A different way to implement a syntactic model that conform to the relaxed LH is by separating the inflectional features of surface words from their grammatical functions in the syntactic representation and letting the model learn systematic form-function correspondence patterns between them.

The Relational-Realizational (RR) model (Tsarfaty and Sima'an, 2008) takes such a 'separationalist' approach which is constituent-based. Grammatical relations are separated from their morphological or syntactic means of realization, which are in turn also distinguished. The easiest way to describe the RR model is via a three-phase generative process encompassing the *projection, configuration* and *realization* phases. In the *projection* phase, a clause-level syntactic category generates a Relational Network (RN), i.e., a set of grammatical function-labels representing the argument-structure of the clause. In the *configuration* phase, linear ordering is generated for the function-labels and optional realization slots are reserved for elements such as punctuation, auxiliaries and adjuncts. The *realization* phase spells out a rich morphosyntactic representation (MSR) — a syntactic label plus morphological features — realizing each grammatical function and each of the reserved slots. The process repeats as necessary until MSRs of pre-terminals are mapped to lexical items.

In (Tsarfaty et al., 2009) we have shown that the RR model makes beneficial use of morphological patterns involving case marking, but did not study the incorporation of inflectional agreement features such as *gender*. Since agreement features such as *gender, number* and case-related information such *accusativity, definiteness* are determined by non-overlapping subconstituents, it remains an open question whether an addition of agreement features into the model can be down in a linguistically adequate and statistically sound way, and whether or not they further improve performance.

We claim that the Relational-Realizational model of (Tsarfaty et al., 2009) has all the necessary ingredients to seamlessly migrate RR representations to ones that encode agreement explicitely. In order to explain how we do so let us recapitulate the empirical facts. Agreement is an asymmetric relation defined for a certain domain, in which the agreement properties of a target co-vary with the inherent properties of the controller. Consider the two sentences in (2b) in which the formal means to differentiate the subject from the object is by the pattern of an agreeing predicate. The RR representations of the domain S are given at the bottom of figure 1.

[5]While agreement patterns in feature-rich grammars give rise to re-entrancies that break context-freeness, GPSG shows that using feature-percolation we can get quite far in modeling morphosyntactic dependencies and retaining context-freeness.

[6]Horizontal markovization à la (Klein and Manning, 2003) would be self-defeating here. Markovization of constituents conditions inflectional features on configurational positions, which is inadequate for free word-order languages as Hebrew. This is already conjectured in the PhD thesis of Collins, and it is verified empirically for Hebrew in (Tsarfaty et al., 2009).

The agreement targets and agreement controllers are easy to recognize; controllers are the syntactic constituents that realize subjects, parametrized as $\mathbf{P}_{\text{realization}}(VB|PRD@S)$, and targets are the ones that realize predicates, parametrized as $\mathbf{P}_{\text{realization}}(NP|SBJ@S)$. Now, if we take the predicted labels of controllers and targets to include reference to inflectional features, we get the following parameterization of the realization parameters $\mathbf{P}_{\text{realization}}(VB\langle\text{FEATS}_i\rangle|PRD@S)$ and $\mathbf{P}_{\text{realization}}(NP\langle\text{FEATS}_j\rangle|SBJ@S)$ with $\langle\text{FEATS}_i\rangle$, $\langle\text{FEATS}_j\rangle$ the inflectional features indicated in their morphosyntactic representation. Now, we only need to make sure that $\langle\text{FEATS}_i\rangle$, $\langle\text{FEATS}_j\rangle$ indeed agree, *regardless of their position under S*.

We do so by explicitly marking the domain of agreement, the S category, with the features of the syntactically most prominent participant in the situation, the subject (this is where the non-symmetrical nature of agreement comes into play). The realization distributions take the following forms $\mathbf{P}_{\text{realization}}(VB\langle\text{FEATS}_j\rangle|PRD@S\langle\text{FEATS}_i\rangle)$ and $\mathbf{P}_{\text{realization}}(NP\langle\text{FEATS}_i\rangle|SBJ@S\langle\text{FEATS}_i\rangle)$. In the former, $NP\langle\text{FEATS}_i\rangle$ reflects the inherent features of the SBJ and in the latter $VB\langle\text{FEATS}_j\rangle$ reflects the agreement features of the PRD. Now, regardless of word order, and regardless of the internal structure of NPs, the parameters capturing agreement would be the same for examples (2b i-ii). The only parameters that differ are the configuration parameters (boxed), reflecting word-order alternation.

For the sake of completeness we include here also the SP vs. RR representation of S domains involving auxiliaries in figure 2. Here the sentences vary only in the position of the AUX element relative to the subject with which it agrees. Subjects, predicates, and slots that have been reserved for AUX elements, all reflect the same pattern of agreement through their conditioning on the rich representation of the domain.[7] More parameters that vary here (boxed) are AUX placement and realization parameters. Since Pron elements endow PREDPs with agreement features, agreement with verbless (nominal) predicates under S analogously follows.

[7]In Hebrew, even some adverbial modifiers reflect patterns of agreement, e.g., עודני (literally, "I am still", glossed 'still.1S'). This solution caters for all such patterns in which non-obligatory elements exhibit agreement.

## 4 Experiments

We aim to examine whether the explicit incorporation of agreement features helps Hebrew parsing, and if so, which of the two modeling strategies is better for utilizing the disambiguation cues provided by morphosyntactic agreement.

**Data** We use the Hebrew treebank v2.0 with the extended annotation of (Guthmann et al., 2009), which adds inflectional properties to non-terminal categories such as NP and VP. We head-annotate the corpus and systematically add the agreement features of Domains throughout the treebank. We further distinguish finite from non-finite verb forms, and cliticized from non-cliticized nouns, as in (Goldberg and Tsarfaty, 2008; Tsarfaty et al., 2009). On top of the treebank labels SBJ subject, OBJ object, COM complement and CNJ conjunction we add PRD predicates and IC infinitival complements.

**Procedure** We devised a procedure to read-off treebank grammars based on (i) GPSG-like, state-split context-free parameters (SP-AGR), and (ii) RR-AGR parameters in which context-free rules capture the *projection, configuration* and *realization* phases. In each model the multiplication provides the probability of the generation. We use relative frequency estimates and exhaustively parse gold pos-tagged input[8] using a general-purpose CKY parser. We use the same data split as in (Goldberg and Tsarfaty, 2008; Tsarfaty et al., 2009) (training on sentences 501-6000 and parsing sentences 1-500) and we convert all trees to the flat, coarse-grained, original treebank representation for the purpose of evaluation.

**Setup** We experiment with bare constituent labels, grand-parent decorated labels (gp), and labels decorated with grand-parent and head-tag labels (gp,hd). We use increasingly richer subsets of the {*gender, definiteness, accusativity*} set.[9]

[8]This choice to parse gold-tagged sentences is meant to alleviate the differences in the model's morphological disambiguation capacity. We want to evaluate the contribution of morphological features for syntactic disambiguation, and if the models will disambiguate the morphological analyses differently, the syntactic analysis will be assigned to different yields and the accuracy results would be strictly incomparable. But see (Goldberg and Tsarfaty, 2008) for a way to combine the two.

[9]We deliberately choose features that have non-overlapping behavior, to see whether their contribution is accumulative.

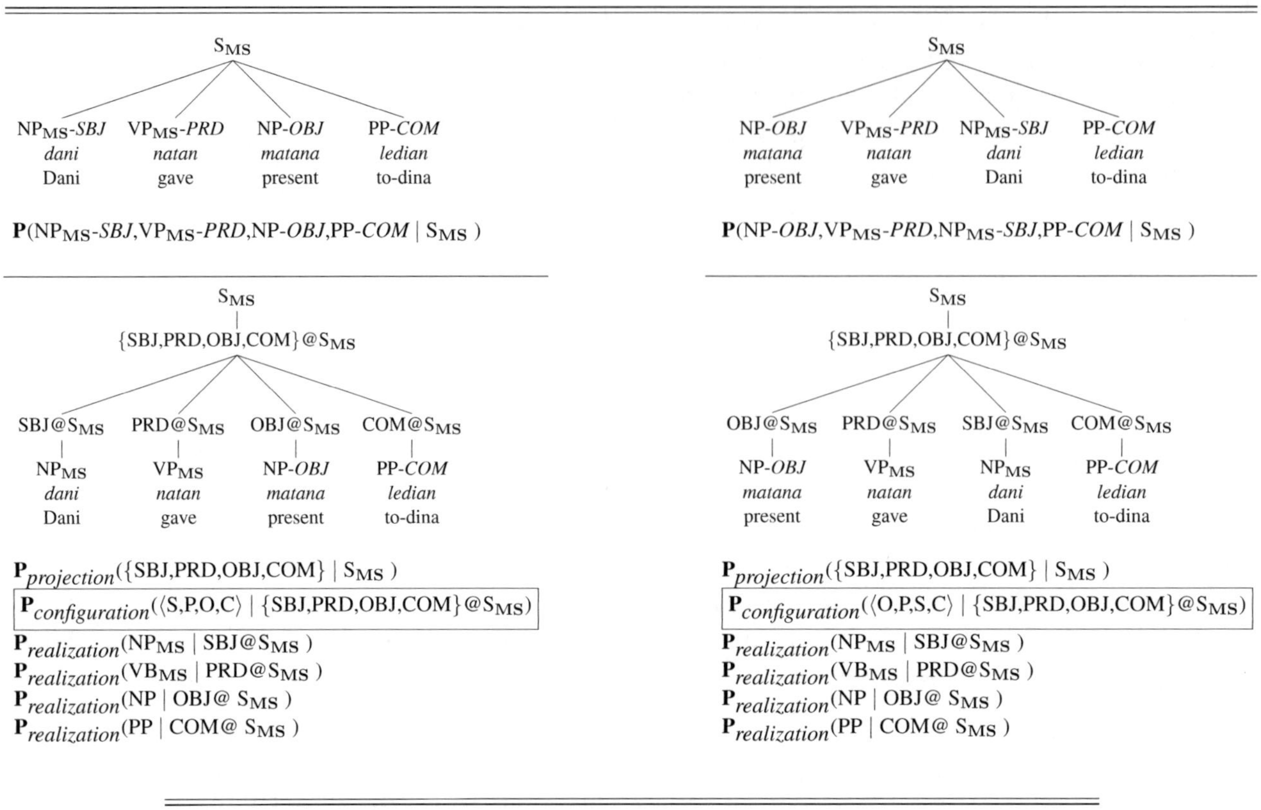


Figure 1: The SP-AGR (top) and RR-AGR representations of sentences (2b-i) (left) and (2b-ii).

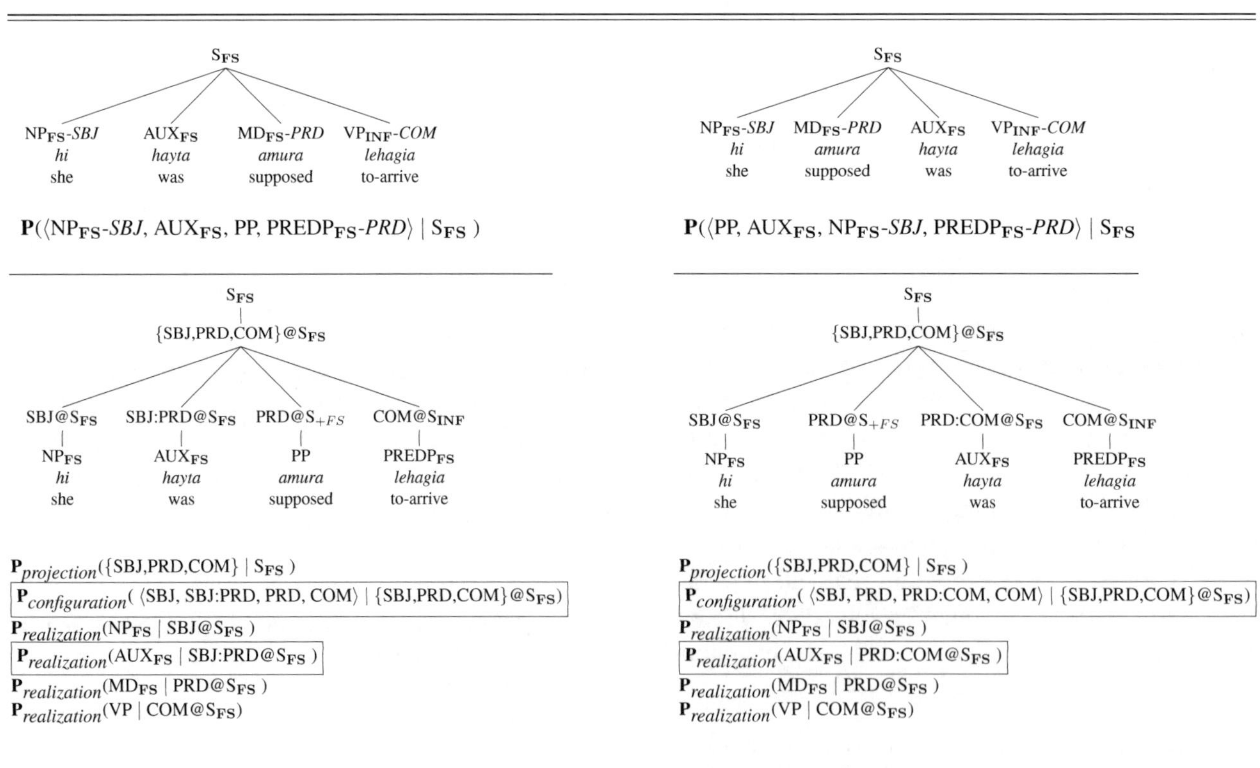


Figure 2: The SP-AGR (top) and RR-AGR representation of sentences (4c-i) (left) and (4c-ii).

| Model | ∅ | gender | def+acc | gender+def+acc |
|---|---|---|---|---|
| SP-AGR | 79.77 | 79.55 | 80.13 | 80.26 |
| | (3942) | (7594) | (4980) | (8933) |
| **RR-AGR** | 80.23 | 81.09 | 81.48 | **82.64** |
| | (3292) | (5686) | (3772) | **(6516)** |
| SP-AGR (gp) | 83.06 | 82.18 | 79.53 | 80.89 |
| | (5914) | (10765) | (12700) | (11028) |
| **RR-AGR (gp)** | 83.49 | 83.70 | 83.66 | **84.13** |
| | (6688) | (10063) | (12383) | **(12497)** |
| SP-AGR (gp,hd) | 76.61 | 64.07 | 75.12 | 61.69 |
| | (10081) | (16721) | (11681) | (18428) |
| **RR-AGR (gp,hd)** | **83.40** | 81.19 | 83.33 | 80.45 |
| | **(12497)** | (22979) | (13828) | (24934) |

Table 1: F-score (#params) measure for all models on the Hebrew treebank dev-set for Sentences Length $< 40$

## 5 Results and Discussion

Table 1 shows the standard F1 scores (and #parameters) for all models. Throughout, the RR-AGR model outperforms the SP-AGR models that use the same category set and the same morphological features as state splits. For RR-AGR and RR-AGR (gp) models, adding agreement features to case features improves performance. The accumulative contribution is significant. For SP-AGR and SP-AGR (gp) models, adding more features either remains at the same level of performance or becomes detrimental.

Since the SP/RR-AGR and SP/RR-AGR (gp) models are of comparable size for each feature-set, it is unlikely that the differences in performance are due to the lack of training data. A more reasonable explanation if that the RR parameters represent functional generalizations orthogonal to configuration for which statistical evidence is more easily found in the data. The robust realization distributions which cut across ordering alternatives can steer the disambiguation in the right direction.

The RR-AGR (gp) +gen+def+acc model yields the best result for parsing Hebrew to date (F1 84.13), improving upon our best model in (Tsarfaty et al., 2009) (F1 83.33, underlined) in a pos-tagged setting. For this setting, Arabic parsing results are F1 78.1. Given the similar morphosyntactic phenomena (agreement, MaSDaR, iDaFa) it would be interesting to see if the model enhances parsing for Arabic.

For (gp,hd) models (a configuration which was shown to give the best results in (Tsarfaty et al., 2009)) there is a significant decrease in accuracy with the gender feature, but there is a lesson to be learned. Firstly, while the RR-AGR (gp,hd) model shows moderate decrease with gender, the decrease in performance of SP-AGR (gp,hd) for the same feature-set is rather dramatic, which is consistent with the observation that the RR model is less vulnerable to sparseness and that it makes better use of the statistics of functional relations in the data.

Consulting the size of the different grammars, the combination of RR-AGR (gp, hd) with gender features indeed results in substantially larger grammars, and it is possible that at this point we indeed need to incorporate smoothing. At the same time there may be an alternative explanation for the decreased performance. It might be that the head-tag does not add informative cues beyond the contribution of the features which are spread inside the constituent, and are already specified. This is a reasonable hypothesis since *gender* in Hebrew always percolates through the head as opposed to *def/acc* that percolate from other forms. Incorporating head-tag in (Tsarfaty et al., 2009) might have led to improvement only due to the lack of agreement features which subsume the relevant pattern. This suggests that incorporating all co-heads and functional elements that contribute morphological features spread inside the constituent, is more adequate for modeling morphosyntax than focusing on the features of a single head.

## 6 Conclusion

We show that morphologically marked agreement features can significantly improve parsing performance if they are represented and parametrized in a way that reflects their linguistic substance: relating form-and-function in a non-linear fashion. We have so far dealt with the adequacy of representation and we plan to test whether more sophisticated estimation (e.g., split-merge-smooth estimation as in (Petrov et al., 2006)) can obtain further improvements from the explicit representation of agreement. At the same time, the state-of-the-art results we present render the RR model promising for further exploration with morphologically rich languages.

**Acknowledgements** The work of the first author has been funded by NWO, grant 017.001.271. We wish to thank Joakim Nivre and three anonymous reviewers for helpful comments on earlier drafts.

## References


Steven Abney. 1997. Stochastic attribute-value grammars. *Computational Linguistics*, 23(4):597–618.

Stephen R. Anderson. 1982. Where's morphology? *Linguistic Inquiry*.

Noam Chomsky. 1970. Remarks on nominalization. In R. Jacobs and P. Rosenbaum, editors, *Reading in English Transformational Grammar*. Waltham: Ginn.

Greville G. Corbett. 2001. Agreement: Terms and boundaries. In *SMG conference papers*.

Gabi Danon. 2008. Definiteness spreading in the hebrew construct-state. *Lingua*, 118(7):872–906.

Edit Doron. 1986. The pronominal "copula" as agreement clitic. *Syntax and Semantics*, (19):313–332.

Gerald Gazdar, Ewan Klein, Geoffrey K. Pullum, and Ivan A. Sag. 1985. *Generalised phrase structure grammar*. Blackwell, Oxford, England.

Yoav Goldberg and Michael Elhadad. 2009. Hebrew dependency parsing: Initial results. In *Proceedings of IWPT*.

Yoav Goldberg and Reut Tsarfaty. 2008. A single framework for joint morphological segmentation and syntactic parsing. In *Proceedings of ACL*.

Yoav Goldberg, Meni Adler, and Michael Elhadad. 2006. Noun phrase chunking in hebrew: Influence of lexical and morphological features. In *Proceedings of COLING-ACL*.

Nomie Guthmann, Yuval Krymolowski, Adi Milea, and Yoad Winter. 2009. Automatic annotation of morpho-syntactic dependencies in a Modern Hebrew treebank. In Frank Van Eynde, Anette Frank, Koenraad De Smedt, and Gertjan van Noord, editors, *Proceedings of TLT*.

Kenneth L. Hale. 1983. Warlpiri and the grammar of non-configurational languages. *Natural Language and Linguistic Theory*, 1(1).

Julia Hockenmaier and Mark Steedman. 2003. Parsing with generative models of predicate-argument structure. In *Proceedings of ACL*.

Dan Klein and Christopher D. Manning. 2003. Accurate unlexicalized parsing. In *Proceedings of ACL*.

Mohamed Maamouri, Ann Bies, and Seth Kulick. 2008. Enhanced annotation and parsing of the arabic treebank. In *Proceedings of INFOS*.

Yusuke Miyao and Jun'ichi Tsujii. 2008. Feature-forest models for probabilistic hpsg parsing. *Computational Linguistics*, 34(1):35–80.

Lilja Øvrelid and Joakim Nivre. 2007. Swedish dependency parsing with rich linguistic features. In *Proceeding of RANLP*.

Slav Petrov, Leon Barrett, Romain Thibaux, and Dan Klein. 2006. Learning accurate, compact, and interpretable tree annotation. In *Proceedings of ACL*.

Reut Tsarfaty and Khalil Sima'an. 2008. Relational-realizational parsing. In *Proceedings of CoLing*.

Reut Tsarfaty, Khalil Sima'an, and Remko Scha. 2009. An alternative to head-driven approaches for parsing a (relatively) free word order language. In *Proceedings of EMNLP*.

# Factors Affecting the Accuracy of Korean Parsing

**Tagyoung Chung**, **Matt Post** and **Daniel Gildea**
Department of Computer Science
University of Rochester
Rochester, NY 14627

## Abstract

We investigate parsing accuracy on the Korean Treebank 2.0 with a number of different grammars. Comparisons among these grammars and to their English counterparts suggest different aspects of Korean that contribute to parsing difficulty. Our results indicate that the coarseness of the Treebank's nonterminal set is a even greater problem than in the English Treebank. We also find that Korean's relatively free word order does not impact parsing results as much as one might expect, but in fact the prevalence of zero pronouns accounts for a large portion of the difference between Korean and English parsing scores.

## 1 Introduction

Korean is a head-final, agglutinative, and morphologically productive language. The language presents multiple challenges for syntactic parsing. Like some other head-final languages such as German, Japanese, and Hindi, Korean exhibits long-distance scrambling (Rambow and Lee, 1994; Kallmeyer and Yoon, 2004). Compound nouns are formed freely (Park et al., 2004), and verbs have well over 400 paradigmatic endings (Martin, 1992).

Korean Treebank 2.0 (LDC2006T09) (Han and Ryu, 2005) is a subset of a Korean newswire corpus (LDC2000T45) annotated with morphological and syntactic information. The corpus contains roughly 5K sentences, 132K words, and 14K unique morphemes. The syntactic bracketing rules are mostly the same as the previous version of the treebank (Han et al., 2001) and the phrase structure annotation schemes used are very similar to the ones used in Penn English treebank. The Korean Treebank is constructed over text that has been morphologically analyzed; not only is the text tokenized into morphemes, but all allomorphs are neutralized.

To our knowledge, there have been only a few papers focusing on syntactic parsing of Korean. Hermjakob (2000) implemented a shift-reduce parser for Korean trained on very limited (1K sentences) data, and Sarkar and Han (2002) used an earlier version of the Treebank to train a lexicalized tree adjoining grammar. In this paper, we conduct a range of experiments using the Korean Treebank 2.0 (hereafter, KTB) as our training data and provide analyses that reveal insights into parsing morphologically rich languages like Korean. We try to provide comparisons with English parsing using parsers trained on a similar amount of data wherever applicable.

## 2 Difficulties parsing Korean

There are several challenges in parsing Korean compared to languages like English. At the root of many of these challenges is the fact that it is highly inflected and morphologically productive. Effective morphological segmentation is essential to learning grammar rules that can generalize beyond the training data by limiting the number of out-of-vocabulary words. Fortunately, there are good techniques for doing so. The sentences in KTB have been segmented into basic morphological units.

Second, Korean is a pro-drop language: subjects and objects are dropped wherever they are pragmatically inferable, which is often possible given its rich morphology. Zero pronouns are a remarkably frequent phenomenon in general (Han, 2006), occuring



*Proceedings of the NAACL HLT 2010 First Workshop on Statistical Parsing of Morphologically-Rich Languages*, pages 49–57,
Los Angeles, California, June 2010. ©2010 Association for Computational Linguistics

an average of 1.8 times per sentence in the KTB. The standard approach in parsing English is to ignore NULL elements entirely by removing them (and recursively removing unary parents of empty nodes in a bottom-up fashion). This is less of a problem in English because these empty nodes are mostly trace elements that denote constituent movement. In the KTB, these elements are removed altogether and a crucial cue to grammatical inference is often lost. Later we will show the profound effect this has on parsing accuracy.

Third, word order in Korean is relatively free. This is also partly due to the richer morphology, since morphemes (rather than word order) are used to denote semantic roles of phrases. Consider the following example:

| | | | | |
|---|---|---|---|---|
| 존이 | 매리에게 | 책을 | 주었다 | . |
| John-NOM | Mary-DAT | book-ACC | give-PAST | . |

In the example, any permutation of the first three words produces a perfectly acceptable sentence. This freedom of word order could potentially result in a large number of rules, which could complicate analysis with new ambiguities. However, formal written Korean generally conforms to a canonical word order (SOV).

## 3 Initial experiments

There has been some work on Korean morphological analysis showing that common statistical methods such as maximum entropy modeling and conditional random fields perform quite well (Lee et al., 2000; Sarkar and Han, 2002; Han and Palmer, 2004; Lee and Rim, 2005). Most claim accuracy rate over 95%. In light of this, we focus on the parsing part of the problem utilizing morphology analysis already present in the data.

### 3.1 Setup

For our experiments we used all 5,010 sentences in the Korean Treebank (KTB), which are already segmented. Due to the small size of the corpus, we used ten-fold cross validation for all of our experiments, unless otherwise noted. Sentences were assigned to folds in blocks of one (i.e., fold 1 contained sentences 1, 11, 21, and so on.). Within each fold, 80% of the data was assigned to training, 10% to development, and 10% to testing. Each fold's vocabulary was set to all words occurring more than once in its training data, with a handful of count one tokens replacing unknown words based on properties of the word's surface form (all Korean words were placed in a single bin, and English words were binned following the rules of Petrov et al. (2006)). We report scores on the development set.

| model | F1 | $F1_{\leq 40}$ | types | tokens |
|---|---|---|---|---|
| Korean | 52.78 | 56.55 | 6.6K | 194K |
| English (§02–03) | 71.06 | 72.26 | 5.5K | 96K |
| English (§02–04) | 72.20 | 73.29 | 7.5K | 147K |
| English (§02–21) | 71.61 | 72.74 | 23K | 950K |

Table 1: Parser scores for Treebank PCFGs in Korean and English. For English, we vary the size of the training data to provide a better point of comparison against Korean. Types and tokens denote vocabulary sizes (which for Korean is the mean over the folds).

We report parser accuracy scores using the standard F1 metric, which balances precision and recall of the labeled constituents recovered by the parser: $2PR/(P+R)$. Throughout the paper, all evaluation occurs against gold standard trees that contain no NULL elements or nonterminal function tags or annotations, which in some cases requires the removal of those elements from parse trees output by the parser.

### 3.2 Treebank grammars

We begin by presenting in Table 1 scores for the standard Treebank grammar, obtained by reading a standard context-free grammar from the trees in the training data and setting rule probabilities to relative frequency (Charniak, 1996). For these initial experiments, we follow standard practice in English parsing and remove all (a) nonterminal function tags and (b) NULL elements from the parse trees before learning the grammar. For comparison purposes, we present scores from parsing the Wall Street Journal portion of the English Penn Treebank (PTB), using both the standard training set and subsets of it chosen to be similar in size to the KTB. All English scores are tested on section 22.

There are two interesting results in this table. First, Korean parsing accuracy is much lower than English parsing accuracy, and second, the accuracy difference does not appear to be due to a difference in the size of the training data, since reducing the size of the English training data did not affect accuracy scores very much.

Before attempting to explain this empirically, we note that Rehbein and van Genabith (2007) demonstrate that the F1 metric is biased towards parse trees with a high ratio of nonterminals to terminals, because mistakes made by the parser have a smaller effect on the overall evaluation score.[1] They recommend that F1 not be used for comparing parsing accuracy across different annotation schemes. The nonterminal to terminal ratio in the KTB and PTB are 0.40 and 0.45, respectively. It is a good idea to keep this bias in mind, but we believe that this small ratio difference is unlikely to account for the huge gap in scores displayed in Table 1.

The gap in parsing accuracy is unsurprising in light of the basic known difficulties parsing Korean, summarized earlier in the paper. Here we observe a number of features of the KTB that contribute to this difficulty.

**Sentence length** On average, KTB sentences are much longer than PTB sentences (23 words versus 48 words, respectively). Sentence-level F1 is inversely correlated with sentence length, and the relatively larger drop in F1 score going from column 3 to 2 in Table 1 is partially accounted for by the fact that column 3 represents 33% of the KTB sentences, but 92% of the English sentences.

**Flat annotation scheme** The KTB makes relatively frequent use of very flat and ambiguous rules. For example, consider the extreme cases of rule ambiguity in which the lefthand side nonterminal is present three or more times on its righthand side. There are only three instances of such "triple+-recursive" NPs among the ~40K trees in the training portion of the PTB, each occurring only once.

NP → NP NP NP , CC NP
NP → NP NP NP CC NP
NP → NP NP NP NP .

The KTB is an eighth of the size of this, but has fifteen instances of such NPs (listed here with their frequencies):

NP → NP NP NP NP (6)
NP → NP NP NP NP NP (3)
NP → NP NP NP NP NP NP (2)
NP → NP NP NP NP NP NP NP (2)
NP → SLQ NP NP NP SRQ PAD (1)
NP → SLQ NP NP NP NP SRQ PAN (1)

Similar rules are common for other nonterminals as well. Generally, flatter rules are easier to parse with because they contribute to parse trees with fewer nodes (and thus fewer independent decision points). However, the presence of a single nonterminal on both the left and righthand side of a rule means that the annotation scheme is failing to capture distributional differences which must be present.

**Nonterminal granularity** This brings us to a final point about the granularity of the nonterminals in the KTB. After removing function tags, there are only 43 nonterminal symbols in the KTB (33 of them preterminals), versus 72 English nonterminals (44 of them preterminals). Nonterminal granularity is a well-studied problem in English parsing, and there is a long, successful history of automatically refining English nonterminals to discover distributional differences. In light of this success, we speculate that the disparity in parsing performance might be explained by this disparity in the number of nonterminals. In the next section, we provide evidence that this is indeed the case.

## 4 Nonterminal granularity

There are many ways to refine the set of nonterminals in a Treebank. A simple approach suggested by Johnson (1998) is to simply annotate each node with its parent's label. The effect of this is to refine the distribution of each nonterminal over sequences of children according to its position in the sentence; for example, a VP beneath an SBAR node will have a different distribution over children than a VP beneath an S node. This simple technique alone produces a large improvement in English Treebank parsing. Klein and Manning (2003) expanded this idea with a series of experiments wherein they manually refined nonterminals to different degrees, which resulted in parsing accuracy rivaling that of bilexicalized parsing models of the time. More recently, Petrov et al. (2006) refined techniques originally proposed by Matsuzaki et al. (2005) and Prescher

[1]We thank one of our anonymous reviewers for bringing this to our attention.

| SBJ | subject with nominative case marker |
|---|---|
| OBJ | complement with accusative case marker |
| COMP | complement with adverbial postposition |
| ADV | NP that function as adverbial phrase |
| VOC | noun with vocative case maker |
| LV | NP coupled with "light" verb construction |

Table 2: Function tags in the Korean treebank

| model | F1 | $F1_{\leq 40}$ |
|---|---|---|
| Korean | | |
| coarse | 52.78 | 56.55 |
| w/ function tags | **56.18** | **60.21** |
| English (small) | | |
| coarse | **72.20** | **73.29** |
| w/ function tags | 70.50 | 71.78 |
| English (standard) | | |
| coarse | 71.61 | 72.74 |
| w/ function tags | **72.82** | **74.05** |

Table 3: Parser scores for Treebank PCFGs in Korean and English with and without function tags. The small English results were produced by training on §02–04.

(2005) for automatically learning latent annotations, resulting in state of the art parsing performance with cubic-time parsing algorithms.

We begin this section by conducting some simple experiments with the existing function tags, and then apply the latent annotation learning procedures of Petrov et al. (2006) to the KTB.

### 4.1 Function tags

The KTB has function tags that mark grammatical functions of NP and S nodes (Han et al., 2001), which we list all of them in Table 2. These function tags are principally grammatical markers. As mentioned above, the parsing scores for both English and Korean presented in Table 1 were produced with grammars stripped of their function tags. This is standard practice in English, where the existing tags are known not to help very much. Table 3 presents results of parsing with grammars with nonterminals that retain these function tags (we include results from Section 3 for comparison). Note that evaluation is done against the unannotated gold standard parse trees by removing the function tags after parsing with them.

The results for Korean are quite pronounced: we see a nearly seven-point improvement when retaining the existing tags. This very strongly suggests that the KTB nonterminals are too coarse when stripped of their function tags, and raises the question of whether further improvement might be gained from latent annotations.

The English scores allow us to make another point. Retaining the provided function tags results in a solid performance increase with the standard training corpus, but actually hurts performance when training on the small dataset. Note clearly that this does *not* suggest that parsing performance with the grammar from the small English data could not be improved with latent annotations (indeed, we will show that they can), but only that the given annotations do not help improve parsing accuracy. Taking the Korean and English accuracy results from this table together provides another piece of evidence that the Korean nonterminal set is too coarse.

### 4.2 Latent annotations

We applied the latent annotation learning procedures of Petrov et al.[2] to refine the nonterminals in the KTB. The trainer learns refinements over the coarse version of the KTB (with function tags removed). In this experiment, rather than doing 10-fold cross validation, we split the KTB into training, development, and test sets that roughly match the 80/10/10 splits of the folds:

| section | file IDs |
|---|---|
| training | 302000 to 316999 |
| development | 317000 to 317999 |
| testing | 320000 to 320999 |

This procedure results in grammars which can then be used to parse new sentences. Table 4 displays the parsing accuracy results for parsing with the grammar (after smoothing) at the end of each split-merge-smooth cycle.[3] The scores in this table show that, just as with the PTB, nonterminal refinement makes a huge difference in parser performance.

Again with the caveat that direct comparison of parsing scores across annotation schemes must be taken loosely, we note that the KTB parsing accuracy is still about 10 points lower than the best ac-

[2] http://code.google.com/p/berkeleyparser/

[3] As described in Petrov et al. (2006), to score a parse tree produced with a refined grammar, we can either take the Viterbi derivation or approximate a sum over derivations before projecting back to the coarse tree for scoring.

| | Viterbi | | max-sum | |
|---|---|---|---|---|
| **cycle** | **F1** | **F1$_{\leq 40}$** | **F1** | **F1$_{\leq 40}$** |
| 1 | 56.93 | 61.11 | 61.04 | 64.23 |
| 2 | 63.82 | 67.94 | 66.31 | 68.90 |
| 3 | 69.86 | 72.83 | 72.85 | 75.63 |
| 4 | 74.36 | 77.15 | 77.18 | 78.18 |
| 5 | 78.07 | 80.09 | 79.93 | 82.04 |
| 6 | 78.91 | 81.55 | 80.85 | 82.75 |

Table 4: Parsing accuracy on Korean test data from the grammars output by the Berkeley state-splitting grammar trainer. For comparison, parsing all sentences of §22 in the PTB with the same trainer scored 89.58 (max-sum parsing with five cycles) with the standard training corpus and 85.21 when trained on §2–4.

curacy scores produced in parsing the PTB which, in our experiments, were 89.58 (using max-sum to parse all sentences with the grammar obtained after five cycles of training).

An obvious suspect for the difference in parsing accuracy with latent grammars between English and Korean is the difference in training set sizes. This turns out not to be the case. We learned latent annotations on sections 2–4 of the PTB and again tested on section 22. The accuracy scores on the test set peak at 85.21 (max-sum, all sentences, five cycles of training). This is about five points lower than the English grammar trained on sections 2–21, but is still over four points higher than the KTB results.

In the next section, we turn to one of the theoretical difficulties with Korean parsing with which we began the paper.

## 5 NULL elements

Both the PTB and KTB include many NULL elements. For English, these elements are traces denoting constituent movement. In the KTB, there are many more kinds of NULL elements, in including trace markers, zero pronouns, relative clause reduction, verb deletions, verb ellipsis, and other unknown categories. Standard practice in English parsing is to remove NULL elements in order to avoid the complexity of parsing with $\epsilon$-productions. However, another approach to parsing that avoids such productions is to retain the NULL elements when reading the grammar; at test time, the parser is given sentences that contain markers denoting the empty elements. To evaluate, we remove these elements from the resulting parse trees output by the parser and compare against the stripped-down gold standard used in previous sections, in order to provide a fair point of comparison.

| **model** | **F1** | **F1$_{\leq 40}$** | **tokens** |
|---|---|---|---|
| English (standard training corpus) | | | |
| coarse | 71.61 | 72.74 | 950K |
| w/ function tags | 72.82 | 74.05 | 950K |
| w/ NULLs | **73.29** | **74.38** | 1,014K |
| Korean | | | |
| w/ verb ellipses | 52.85 | 56.52 | 3,200 |
| w/ traces | 55.88 | 59.42 | 3,868 |
| w/ r.c. markers | 56.74 | 59.87 | 3,794 |
| w/ zero pronouns | 57.56 | 61.17 | 4,101 |
| latent (5) w/ NULLs | 89.56 | 91.03 | 22,437 |

Table 5: Parser scores for Treebank PCFGs in English and Korean with NULL elements. *Tokens* denotes the number of words in the test data. The latent grammar was trained for five iterations.

Parsing in this manner helps us to answer the question of how much easier or more difficult parsing would be if the NULL elements were present. In this section, we present results from a variety of experiments parsing will NULL tokens in this manner. These results can be seen in Table 5. The first observation from this table is that in English, retaining NULL elements makes a few points difference.

The first four rows of the KTB portion of Table 5 contains results with retaining different classes of NULL elements, one at a time, according to the manner described above. Restoring deleted pronouns and relative clause markers has the largest effect, suggesting that the absence of these optional elements removes key cues needed for parsing.

In order to provide a more complete picture of the effect of empty elements, we train the Berkeley latent annotation system on a version of the KTB in which all empty elements are retained. The final row of Table 5 contains the score obtained when evaluating parse trees produced from parsing with the grammar after the fifth iteration (after which performance began to fall). With the empty elements, we have achieved accuracy scores that are on par with the best accuracy scores obtained parsing the English Treebank.

## 6 Tree substitution grammars

We have shown that coarse labels and the prevalence of NULL elements in Korean both contribute to parsing difficulty. We now turn to grammar formalisms that allow us to work with larger fragments of parse trees than the height-one rules of standard context-free grammars. Tree substitution grammars (TSGs) have been shown to improve upon the standard English Treebank grammar (Bod, 2001) in parser accuracy, and more recently, techniques for inferring TSG subtrees in a Bayesian framework have enabled learning more efficiently representable grammars, permitting some interesting analysis (O'Donnell et al., 2009; Cohn et al., 2009; Post and Gildea, 2009). In this section, we try parsing the KTB with TSGs. We experiment with different methods of learning TSGs to see whether they can reveal any insights into the difficulties parsing Korean.

### 6.1 Head rules

TSGs present some difficulties in learning and representation, but a simple extraction heuristic called a *spinal grammar* has been shown to be very useful (Chiang, 2000; Sangati and Zuidema, 2009; Post and Gildea, 2009). Spinal subtrees are extracted from a parse tree by using a set of head rules to maximally project each lexical item (a word or morpheme). Each node in the parse tree having a different head from its parent becomes the root of a new subtree, which induces a spinal TSG derivation in the parse tree (see Figure 1). A probabilistic grammar is derived by taking counts from these trees, smoothing them with counts of all depth-one rules from the same training set, and setting rule probabilities to relative frequency.

This heuristic requires a set of head rules, which we present in Table 6. As an evaluation of our rules, we list in Table 7 the accuracy results for parsing with spinal grammars extracted using the head rules we developed as well as with two head rule heuristics (head-left and head-right). As a point of comparison, we provide the same results for English, using the standard Magerman/Collins head rules for English (Magerman, 1995; Collins, 1997). Function tags were retained for Korean but not for English.

We observe a number of things from Table 7. First, the relative performance of the head-left and head-right spinal grammars between English and Korean capture the linguistic fact that English is predominantly head-first and Korean is predominantly head-final. In fact, head-finalness in Korean was so strong that our head rules consist of only a handful of exceptions to it. The default rule makes heads of postpositions (case and information clitics) such as dative case marker and topic marker. It is these words that often have dependencies with words in the rest of the sentence. The exceptions concern predicates that occur in the sentence-final position. As an example, predicates in Korean are composed of several morphemes, the final one of which indicates the mood of the sentence. However, this morpheme often does not require any inflection to reflect long-distance agreement with the rest of the sentence. Therefore, we choose the morpheme that would be considered the root of the phrase, which in Korean is the verbalization/adjectivization suffix, verb, adjective, auxiliary predicate, and copula (XSV, XSJ, VV, VJ, VX, CO). These items often include the information about valency of the predicate.

| NT | RC | rule |
|---|---|---|
| S | SFN | second rightmost child |
| VV | EFN | rightmost XSV |
| VX | EFN | rightmost VJ or CO |
| ADJP | EFN | rightmost VJ |
| CV | EFN | rightmost VV |
| LV | EFN | rightmost VV |
| NP | EFN | rightmost CO |
| VJ | EFN | rightmost XSV or XSJ |
| VP | EFN | rightmost VX, XSV, or VV |
| ⋆ | ⋆ | rightmost child |

Table 6: Head rules for the Korean Treebank. NT is the nonterminal whose head is being determined, RC identifies the label of its rightmost child. The default is to take the rightmost child as the head.

Second, in both languages, finer-grained specification of head rules results in performance above that of the heuristics (and in particular, the head-left heuristic for English and head-right heuristic for Korean). The relative improvements in the two languages are in line with each other: significant, but not nearly as large as the difference between the head-left and head-right heuristics.

Finally, we note that the test results together suggest that parsing with spinal grammars may be a

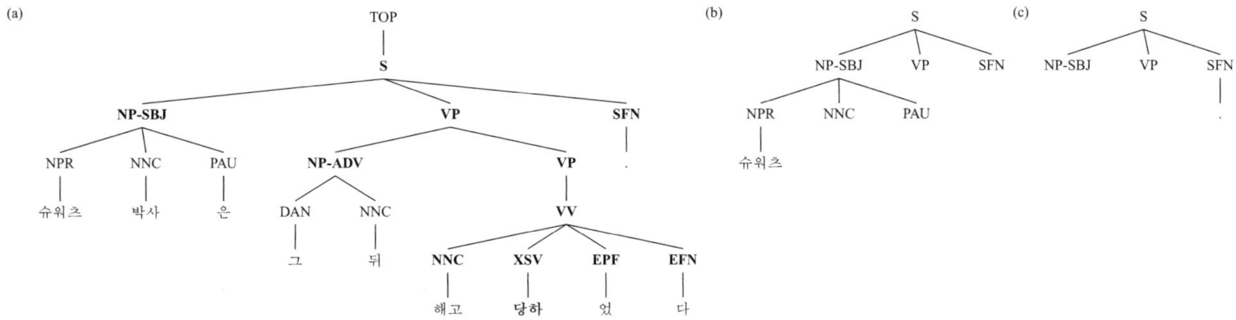


Figure 1: (a) A KTB parse tree; the bold nodes denote the top-level spinal subtree using our head selection rules. (b) The top-level spinal subtree using the head-left and (c) head-right extraction heuristics. A gloss of the sentence is *Doctor Schwartz was fired afterward.*

| model | F1 | $F1_{\leq 40}$ | size |
|---|---|---|---|
| Korean | | | |
| spinal (head left) | 59.49 | 63.33 | 49K |
| spinal (head right) | 66.05 | 69.96 | 29K |
| spinal (head rules) | 66.28 | 70.61 | 29K |
| English | | | |
| spinal (head left) | 77.92 | 78.94 | 158K |
| spinal (head right) | 72.73 | 74.09 | 172K |
| spinal (head rules) | 78.82 | 79.79 | 189K |

Table 7: Spinal grammar scores on the KTB and on PTB section 22.

good evaluation of a set of head selection rules.

### 6.2 Induced tree substitution grammars

Recent work in applying nonparametric machine learning techniques to TSG induction has shown that the resulting grammars improve upon standard English treebank grammars (O'Donnell et al., 2009; Cohn et al., 2009; Post and Gildea, 2009). These techniques use a Dirichlet Process prior over the subtree rewrites of each nonterminal (Ferguson, 1973); this defines a model of subtree generation that produces new subtrees in proportion to the number of times they have previously been generated. Inference under this model takes a treebank and uses Gibbs sampling to determine how to deconstruct a parse tree into a single TSG derivation. In this section, we apply these techniques to Korean.

This TSG induction requires one to specify a base measure, which assigns probabilities to subtrees being generated for the first time in the model. One base measure employed in previous work scored a subtree by multiplying together the probabilities of the height-one rules inside the subtree with a geometric distribution on the number of such rules. Since Korean is considered to be a free word-order language, we modified this base measure to treat the children of a height-one rule as a multiset (instead of a sequence). This has the effect of producing equivalence classes among the sets of children of each nonterminal, concentrating the mass on these classes instead of spreading it across their different instantiations.

To build the sampled grammars, we initialized the samplers from the best spinal grammar derivations and ran them for 100 iterations (once again, function tags were retained). We then took the state of the training data at every tenth iteration, smoothed together with the height-one rules from the standard Treebank. The best score on the development data for a sampled grammar was 68.93 (all sentences) and 73.29 (sentences with forty or fewer words): well above the standard Treebank scores from earlier sections and above the spinal heuristics, but well below the scores produced by the latent annotation learning procedures (a result that is consistent with English).

This performance increase reflects the results for English demonstrated in the above works. We see a large performance increase above the baseline Treebank grammar, and a few points above the best spinal grammar. One nice feature of these induced TSGs is that the rules learned lend themselves to analysis, which we turn to next.

### 6.3 Word order

In addition to the base measure mentioned above, we also experimented with the standard base mea-

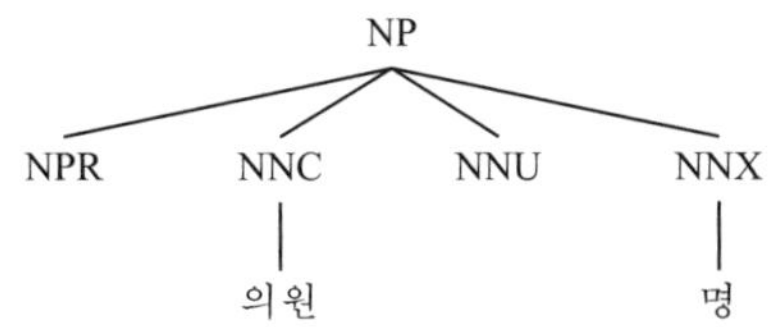


Figure 2: Example of a long distance dependency learned by TSG induction.

sure proposed by Cohn et al. and Post & Gildea, that treats the children of a nonterminal as a sequence. The grammars produced sampling under a model with this base measure were not substantively different from those of the unordered base measure. A partial explanation for this is that although Korean does permit a significant amount of reordering relative to English, the sentences in the KTB come from written newswire text, where word order is more standardized. Korean sentences are characterized as having a subject-object-verb (SOV) word order. There is some flexibility; OSV, in particular, is common in spoken Korean. In formal writing, though, SOV word order is overwhelmingly preferred. We see this reflected in the KTB, where SOV sentences are 63.5 times more numerous that OSV among sentences that have explicitly marked both the subject and the object. However, word order is not completely fixed even in the formal writing. NP-ADV is most likely to occur right before the VP it modifies, but can be moved earlier. For example,

$S \rightarrow$ NP-SBJ NP-ADV VP

is 2.4 times more frequent than the alternative with the order of the NPs reversed.

Furthermore, the notion of free(er) word order does not apply to all constituents. An example is nonterminals directly above preterminals. A Korean verb may have up to seven affixes; however, they always agglutinate in a fixed order.

### 6.4 Long distance dependencies

The TSG inference procedure can be thought of as discovering structural collocations in parse trees. The model prefers subtrees that are common in the data set and that comprise highly probable height-one rules. The parsing accuracy of these grammars is well below state of the art, but the grammars are smaller, and the subtrees learned can help us analyze the parse structure of the Treebank. One particular class of subtree is one that includes multiple lexical items with intervening nonterminals, which represent long distance dependencies that commonly co-occur. In Korean, a certain class of nouns must accompany a particular class of measure word (a morpheme) when counting the noun. In the example shown in Figure 2, (NNC 의원) (*members of assembly*) is followed by NNU, which expands to indicate ordinal, cardinal, and numeral nouns; NNU is in turn followed by (NNX 명), the politeness neutral measure word for counting people.

## 7 Summary & future work

In this paper, we addressed several difficult aspects of parsing Korean and showed that good parsing accuracy for Korean can be achieved despite the small size of the corpus.

Analysis of different parsing results from different grammatical formalisms yielded a number of useful observations. We found, for example, that the set of nonterminals in the KTB is not differentiated enough for accurate parsing; however, parsing accuracy improves substantially from latent annotations and state-splitting techniques that have been developed with English as a testbed. We found that freer word order may not be as important as might have been thought from basic a priori linguistic knowledge of Korean.

The prevalence of NULL elements in Korean is perhaps the most interesting difficulty in developing good parsing approaches for Korean; this is a key difference from English parsing that to our knowledge is not addressed by any available techniques. One potential approach is a special annotation of parents with deleted nodes in order to avoid conflating rewrite distributions. For example, $S \rightarrow VP$ is the most common rule in the Korean treebank after stripping away empty elements; however, this is a result of condensing the rule $S \rightarrow$ (NP-SBJ *pro*) VP and $S \rightarrow VP$, which presumably have different distributions. Another approach would be to attempt automatic recovery of empty elements as a pre-processing step.

**Acknowledgments** We thank the anonymous reviewers for their helpful comments. This work was supported by NSF grants IIS-0546554 and ITR-0428020.

## References


Rens Bod. 2001. What is the minimal set of fragments that achieves maximal parse accuracy? In *Proc. ACL*, Toulouse, France, July.

Eugene Charniak. 1996. Tree-bank grammars. In *Proc. of the National Conference on Artificial Intelligence*, pages 1031–1036.

David Chiang. 2000. Statistical parsing with an automatically-extracted tree adjoining grammar. In *Proc. ACL*, Hong Kong.

Trevor Cohn, Sharon Goldwater, and Phil Blunsom. 2009. Inducing compact but accurate tree-substitution grammars. In *Proc. NAACL*.

Michael Collins. 1997. Three penerative, lexicalised models for statistical parsing. In *Proc. ACL/EACL*.

Thomas S. Ferguson. 1973. A Bayesian analysis of some nonparametric problems. *Annals of Mathematical Statistics*, 1(2):209–230.

Chung-Hye Han and Martha Palmer. 2004. A morphological tagger for Korean: Statistical tagging combined with corpus-based morphological rule application. *Machine Translation*, 18(4):275–297.

Na-Rae Han and Shijong Ryu. 2005. Guidelines for Penn Korean Treebank version 2.0. Technical report, IRCS, University of Pennsylvania.

Chung-hye Han, Na-Rae Han, and Eon-Suk Ko. 2001. Bracketing guidelines for Penn Korean Treebank. Technical report, IRCS, University of Pennsylvania.

Na-Rae Han. 2006. *Korean zero pronouns: analysis and resolution*. Ph.D. thesis, University of Pennsylvania, Philadelphia, PA, USA.

Ulf Hermjakob. 2000. Rapid parser development: a machine learning approach for Korean. In *Proc. NAACL*, pages 118–123, May.

Mark Johnson. 1998. PCFG models of linguistic tree representations. *Computational Linguistics*, 24(4):613–632.

Laura Kallmeyer and SinWon Yoon. 2004. Tree-local MCTAG with shared nodes: Word order variation in German and Korean. In *Proc. TAG+7*, Vancouver, May.

Dan Klein and Chris Manning. 2003. Accurate unlexicalized parsing. In *Proc. ACL*.

Do-Gil Lee and Hae-Chang Rim. 2005. Probabilistic models for Korean morphological analysis. In *Companion to the Proceedings of the International Joint Conference on Natural Language Processing*, pages 197–202.

Sang-zoo Lee, Jun-ichi Tsujii, and Hae-Chang Rim. 2000. Hidden markov model-based Korean part-of-speech tagging considering high agglutinativity, word-spacing, and lexical correlativity. In *Proc. ACL*.

David M. Magerman. 1995. Statistical decision-tree models for parsing. In *Proc. ACL*.

Samuel E. Martin. 1992. *Reference Grammar of Korean: A Complete Guide to the Grammar and History of the Korean Language*. Tuttle Publishing.

Takuya Matsuzaki, Yusuke Miyao, and Jun'ichi Tsujii. 2005. Probabilistic CFG with latent annotations. In *Proc. ACL*, Ann Arbor, Michigan.

Timothy J. O'Donnell, Noah D. Goodman, and Joshua B. Tenenbaum. 2009. Fragment grammar: Exploring reuse in hierarchical generative processes. Technical report, MIT.

Seong-Bae Park, Jeong-Ho Chang, and Byoung-Tak Zhang. 2004. Korean compound noun decomposition using syllabic information only. In *Computational Linguistics and Intelligent Text Processing (CICLing)*, pages 146–157.

Slav Petrov, Leon Barrett, Romain Thibaux, and Dan Klein. 2006. Learning accurate, compact, and interpretable tree annotation. In *Proc. COLING/ACL*, Sydney, Australia, July.

Matt Post and Daniel Gildea. 2009. Bayesian learning of a tree substitution grammar. In *Proc. ACL*, Singapore, Singapore, August.

Detlef Prescher. 2005. Inducing head-driven PCFGs with latent heads: Refining a tree-bank grammar for parsing. *Machine Learning: ECML 2005*, pages 292–304.

Owen Rambow and Young-Suk Lee. 1994. Word order variation and tree-adjoining grammar. *Computational Intelligence*, 10:386–400.

Ines Rehbein and Josef van Genabith. 2007. Evaluating evaluation measures. In *Proceedings of the 16th Nordic Conference of Computational Linguistics (NODALIDA)*.

Federico Sangati and Willem Zuidema. 2009. Unsupervised methods for head assignments. In *Proc. EACL*.

Anoop Sarkar and Chung-hye Han. 2002. Statistical morphological tagging and parsing of Korean with an LTAG grammar. In *Proc. TAG+6*.

# Direct Parsing of Discontinuous Constituents in German

**Wolfgang Maier**
SFB 833, University of Tübingen
Nauklerstr. 35
72074 Tübingen, Germany
wmaier@sfs.uni-tuebingen.de

## Abstract

Discontinuities occur especially frequently in languages with a relatively free word order, such as German. Generally, due to the long-distance dependencies they induce, they lie beyond the expressivity of Probabilistic CFG, i.e., they cannot be directly reconstructed by a PCFG parser. In this paper, we use a parser for Probabilistic Linear Context-Free Rewriting Systems (PLCFRS), a formalism with high expressivity, to directly parse the German NeGra and TIGER treebanks. In both treebanks, discontinuities are annotated with crossing branches. Based on an evaluation using different metrics, we show that an output quality can be achieved which is comparable to the output quality of PCFG-based systems.

## 1 Introduction

Languages with a rather free word order, like German, display discontinuous constituents particularly frequently. In (1), the discontinuity is caused by an extraposed relative clause.

(1) wieder treffen alle Attribute zu, die auch
again match all attributes VPART which also
sonst immer passen
otherwise always fit
'Again, the same attributes as always apply.'

Another language with a rather free word order is Bulgarian. In (2), the discontinuity is caused by topicalization.

(2) Химикали$_1$ аз купувам само евтини t$_1$
Pens$_1$ I buy only expensive t$_1$
'As for pens, I only buy expensive ones.'

In most constituency treebanks, sentence annotation is restricted to having the shape of trees without crossing branches, and the non-local dependencies induced by the discontinuities are modeled by an additional mechanism. In the Penn Treebank (PTB) (Marcus et al., 1994), e.g., this mechanism is a combination of special labels and empty nodes, establishing implicit additional edges. In the German TüBa-D/Z (Telljohann et al., 2006), additional edges are established by a combination of topological field annotation and special edge labels. As an example, Fig. 1 shows a tree from TüBa-D/Z with the annotation of (1). Note here the edge label ON-MOD on the relative clause which indicates that the subject of the sentence (*alle Attribute*) is modified.

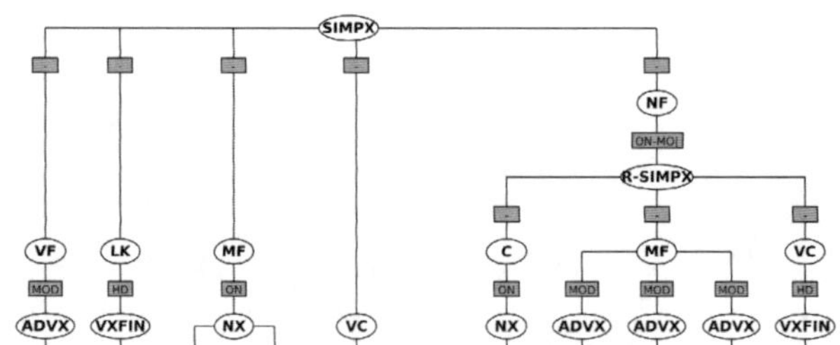


Figure 1: A tree from TüBa-D/Z

However, in a few other treebanks, such as the German NeGra and TIGER treebanks (Skut et al., 1997; Brants et al., 2002), crossing branches are allowed. This way, all dependents of a long-distance dependency can be grouped under a single node.



*Proceedings of the NAACL HLT 2010 First Workshop on Statistical Parsing of Morphologically-Rich Languages*, pages 58–66,
Los Angeles, California, June 2010. ©2010 Association for Computational Linguistics

Fig. 2 shows a tree from NeGra with the annotation of (3).

(3) Noch nie habe ich so viel gewählt
Yet never have I so much chosen
'Never have I had that much choice.'

Note the direct annotation of the discontinuous VP.

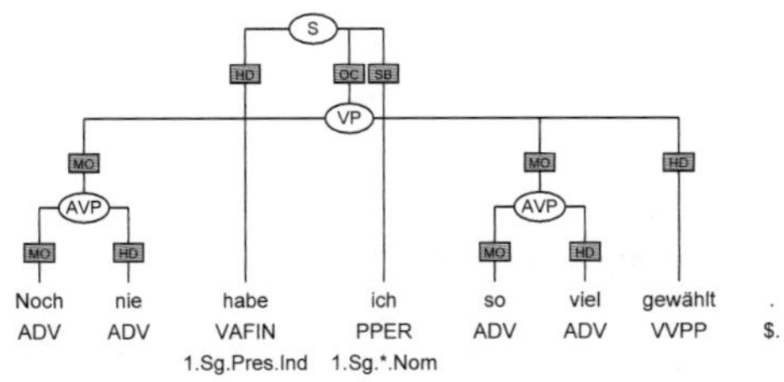


Figure 2: A tree from NeGra

Since in general, the annotation mechanisms for non-local dependencies lie beyond the expressivity of Context-Free Grammar, non-local information is inaccessible for PCFG parsing and therefore generally discarded. In NeGra/TIGER annotation, e.g., tree transformation algorithms are applied before parsing in order to resolve the crossing branches. See, e.g., Kübler et al. (2008) and Boyd (2007) for details. If one wants to avoid the loss of annotation information which is implied with such transformations, one possibility is to use a probabilistic parser for a formalism which is more expressive than CFG.

In this paper, we tackle the question if qualitatively good results can be achieved when parsing German with such a parser. Concretely, we use a parser for Probabilistic Linear Context-Free Rewriting Systems (PLCFRS) (Kallmeyer and Maier, 2010). LCFRS (Vijay-Shanker et al., 1987) are a natural extension of CFG in which a single non-terminal node can dominate more than one continuous span of terminals. We can directly interpret NeGra-style trees as its derivation structures, i.e., we can extract grammars without making further linguistic assumptions (Maier and Lichte, 2009) (see Sect. 2.3), as it is necessary for other formalisms such as Probabilistic Tree Adjoining Grammars (Chiang, 2003). Since the non-local dependencies are immediately accessible in NeGra and TIGER, we choose these treebanks as our data source. In order to judge parser output quality, we use four different evaluation types. We use an EVALB-style measure, adapted for LCFRS, in order to compare our parser to previous work on parsing German treebanks. In order to address the known shortcomings of EVALB, we perform an additional evaluation using the tree distance metric of Zhang and Shasha (1989), which works independently of the fact if there are crossing branches in the trees or not, and a dependency evaluation (Lin, 1995), which has also be applied before in the context of parsing German (Kübler et al., 2008). Last, we evaluate certain difficult phenomena by hand on TePaCoC (Kübler et al., 2008), a set of sentences hand-picked from TIGER. The evaluations show that with a PLCFRS parser, competitive results can be achieved.

The remainder of the article is structured as follows. In Sect. 2, we present the formalism, the parser, and how we obtain our grammars. In Sect. 3, we discuss the evaluation methods we employ. Sect. 4 contains our experimental results. Sect. 5 is dedicated to related work. Sect. 6 contains the conclusion and presents some possible future work.

## 2 A Parser for PLCFRS

### 2.1 Probabilistic Linear Context-Free Rewriting Systems

LCFRS are an extension of CFG where the non-terminals can span not only single strings but, instead, tuples of strings. We will notate LCFRS with the syntax of **simple Range Concatenation Grammars** (SRCG) (Boullier, 1998), a formalism that is equivalent to LCFRS.

A LCFRS (Vijay-Shanker et al., 1987) is a tuple $G = (N, T, V, P, S)$ where

a) $N$ is a finite set of non-terminals with a function $dim$: $N \to \mathbb{N}$ that determines the **fan-out** of each $A \in N$;

b) $T$ and $V$ are disjoint finite sets of terminals and variables;

c) $S \in N$ is the start symbol with $dim(S) = 1$;

d) $P$ is a finite set of rewriting rules

$$A(\alpha_1, \ldots, \alpha_{dim(A)}) \to A_1(X_1^{(1)}, \ldots, X_{dim(A_1)}^{(1)}) \cdots A_m(X_1^{(m)}, \ldots, X_{dim(A_m)}^{(m)})$$

for $m \geq 0$ where $A, A_1, \ldots, A_m \in N$, $X_j^{(i)} \in V$ for $1 \leq i \leq m, 1 \leq j \leq dim(A_i)$ and $\alpha_i \in (T \cup V)^*$ for $1 \leq i \leq dim(A)$. For all $r \in P$, it holds that every variable $X$ occurring in $r$ occurs exactly once in the left-hand side (LHS) and exactly once in the right-hand side (RHS).

The **fan-out** of an LCFRS $G$ is the maximal fan-out of all non-terminals in $G$. Furthermore, the RHS length of a rewriting rules $r \in P$ is called the **rank** of $r$ and the maximal rank of all rules in $P$ is called the **rank** of $G$. An LCFRS is called **ordered** if for every $r \in P$ and every RHS non-terminal $A$ in $r$ and each pair $X_1$, $X_2$ of arguments of $A$ in the RHS of $r$, $X_1$ precedes $X_2$ in the RHS iff $X_1$ precedes $X_2$ in the LHS.

Borrowed from SRCG, we specify the language of an LCFRS based on the notion of ranges. For some input word $w = w_1 \cdots w_n$, a range is a pair $\langle i, j \rangle$ of integers with $0 \leq i \leq n$ denoting the substring $w_{i+1} \cdots w_j$. Note that a range denotes $\varepsilon$ iff $i = j$. Only consecutive ranges can be concatenated into new ranges. We can replace the variables and terminals of the rewriting rules with ranges. E.g., $A(\langle g, h \rangle) \rightarrow B(\langle g+1, h-1 \rangle)$ is a replacement of the clause $A(aX_1b) \rightarrow B(X_1)$ if the input word $w$ is such that $w_{g+1} = a$ and $w_h = b$. A rewriting rule in which all elements of all arguments have been consistently replaced by ranges is called an **instantiated rule**. A derivation is built by successively rewriting the LHSs of instantiated rules with its RHSs. The language $L(G)$ of some LCFRS $G$ consists of all words $w = w_1 \cdots w_n$ for which it holds that there is a rule with the start symbol on the LHS which can be instantiated to $\langle 0, n \rangle$ and rewritten to $\varepsilon$.

A **probabilistic LCFRS** (PLCFRS) is a tuple $\langle N, T, V, P, S, p \rangle$ such that $\langle N, T, V, P, S \rangle$ is a LCFRS and $p : P \rightarrow [0..1]$ a function such that for all $A \in N$: $\Sigma_{A(\vec{x}) \rightarrow \vec{\Phi} \in P} p(A(\vec{x}) \rightarrow \vec{\Phi}) = 1$. There are possibly other ways to extend LCFRS with probabilities. This definition is supported by the fact that probabilistic MCFGs[1] have been defined in the same way (Kato et al., 2006).

[1]MCFGs are equivalent to LCFRSs and SRCGs (Boullier, 1998).

Scan: $\dfrac{}{0 : [A, \langle\langle i, i+1 \rangle\rangle]}$ $A$ POS tag of $w_{i+1}$

Unary: $\dfrac{in : [B, \vec{\rho}]}{in + |log(p)| : [A, \vec{\rho}]}$ $p : A(\vec{\rho}) \rightarrow B(\vec{\rho}) \in P$

Binary: $\dfrac{in_B : [B, \vec{\rho_B}], in_C : [C, \vec{\rho_C}]}{in_B + in_C + log(p) : [A, \vec{\rho_A}]}$

where $p : A(\vec{\rho_A}) \rightarrow B(\vec{\rho_B})C(\vec{\rho_C})$ is an instantiated rule.

Goal: $[S, \langle\langle 0, n \rangle\rangle]$

Figure 3: Weighted CYK deduction system

## 2.2 A CYK Parser for PLCFRS

We use the parser of Kallmeyer and Maier (2010). It is a probabilistic CYK parser (Seki et al., 1991), using the technique of weighted deductive parsing (Nederhof, 2003). While for symbolic parsing, other elaborate algorithms exist (Kallmeyer and Maier, 2009), for probabilistic parsing, CYK is a natural choice.

It is assumed for the parser that our LCFRSs are of rank 2 and do not contain rules where some of the LHS components are $\varepsilon$. Both assumptions can be made without loss of generality since every LCFRS can be binarized (Gómez-Rodríguez et al., 2009) and $\varepsilon$-components on LHS of rules can be removed (Boullier, 1998). We make the assumption that POS tagging is done before parsing. The POS tags are special non-terminals of fan-out 1. Consequently, the rules are either of the form $A(a) \rightarrow \varepsilon$ where $A$ is a POS tag and $a \in T$ or of the form $A(\vec{\alpha}) \rightarrow B(\vec{x})$ or $A(\vec{\alpha}) \rightarrow B(\vec{x})C(\vec{y})$ where $\vec{\alpha} \in (V^+)^{dim(A)}$, i.e., only the rules for POS tags contain terminals in their LHSs.

The parser items have the form $[A, \vec{\rho}]$, with $A \in N$ and $\vec{\rho}$ a vector of ranges characterizing all components of the span of $A$. We specify the set of weighted parse items via the deduction rules in Fig. 3.

Parsing time can be reduced by reordering the agenda during parsing such that those items are processed first which lead to a complete parse more quickly than others (Klein and Manning, 2003a). The parser uses for this purpose an admissible, but not monotonic estimate called **LR estimate**. It gives (relative to a sentence length) an estimate of the outside probability of some non-terminal $A$ with a span of a certain length (the sum of the lengths of all the components of the span), a certain number of terminals to the left of the first and to the right of the last component and a certain number of terminals *gaps* in between the components of the $A$ span, i.e., filling the gaps. A discussion of other estimates is presented at length in Kallmeyer and Maier (2010).

### 2.3 LCFRS for Modeling Discontinuities

We use the algorithm from Maier and Søgaard (2008) to extract LCFRS rules from our data sets. For all nonterminals $A_0$ with the children $A_1 \cdots A_m$ (i.e., for all non-terminals which are not preterminals), we create a clause $\psi_0 \rightarrow \psi_1 \cdots \psi_m$ with $\psi_i$, $0 \leq i \leq m$, labeled $A_i$. The arguments of each $\psi_i$, $1 \leq i \leq m$, are single variables, one for each of the continuous yield part dominated by the node $A_i$. The arguments of $\psi_0$ are concatenations of these variables that describe how the discontinuous parts of the yield of $A_0$ are obtained from the yields of its daughters. For all preterminals $A$ dominating some terminal $a$, we extract a production $A(a) \rightarrow \varepsilon$. Since by definition, a label is associated with a certain fan-out, we distinguish the labels by corresponding subscripts. Note that this extraction algorithm yields only ordered LCFRS. Furthermore, note that for trees without crossing branches, this algorithm yields a PLCFRS with fan-out 1, i.e., a PCFG.

As mentioned before, the advantage of using LCFRS is that grammar extraction is straightforward and that no separate assumptions must be made. Note that unlike, e.g., Range Concatenation Grammar (RCG) (Boullier, 1998), LCFRS cannot model re-entrancies, i.e., nodes with more than one incoming edge. While those do not occur in NeGra-style annotation, some of the annotation in the PTB, e.g., the annotation for right node raising, can be interpreted as re-entrancies. This topic is left for future work. See Maier and Lichte (2009) for further details, especially on how treebank properties relate to properties of extracted grammars.

Before parsing, we binarize our grammar. We first mark the head daughters of all non-terminal nodes using Collins-style head rules based on the NeGra rules of the Stanford Parser (Klein and Manning, 2003b) and the reorder the RHSs of all LCFRS rules such that sequence of elements to the right of the head daughter is reversed and moved to the beginning of the RHS. From this point, the binarization works like the transformation into Chomsky Normal Form for CFGs. For each rule with an RHS of length $\geq 3$, we introduce a new non-terminal which covers the RHS without the first element and continue successively from left to right. The rightmost new rule, which covers the head daughter, is binarized to unary.

We markovize the grammar as in the CFG case. To the new symbols introduced during the binarization, a variable number of symbols from the vertical and horizontal context of the original rule is added. Following the literature, we call the respective quantities $v$ and $h$. As an example, Fig. 4 shows the output for the production for the VP in the left tree in Fig. 2.

After extraction and head marking:
VP2($X_1$,$X_2X_3$) $\rightarrow$ AVP1($X_1$) AVP1($X_2$) VVPP1'($X_3$)

After binarization and markovization with $v = 1, h = 2$:
VP2($X_1$,$X_2$) $\rightarrow$ AVP1($X_1$) @-VP2$^v$-AVP1$^h$-VVPP1$^h$($X_2$)
@-VP2$^v$-AVP1$^h$-VVPP1$^h$($X_1X_2$)
$\rightarrow$ AVP1($X_1$) @-VP2$^v$-VVPP1$^h$($X_2$)
@-VP2$^v$-VVPP1$^h$($X_1$) $\rightarrow$ VVPP1($X_1$)
After binarization and markovization with $v = 2, h = 1$:
VP2($X_1$,$X_2$) $\rightarrow$ AVP1($X_1$) @-VP2$^v$-S2$^v$-AVP1$^h$($X_2$)
@-VP2$^v$-S2$^v$-AVP1$^h$($X_1X_2$)
$\rightarrow$ AVP1($X_1$) @-VP2$^v$-S2$^v$-VVPP1$^h$($X_2$)
@-VP2$^v$-S2$^v$-VVPP1$^h$($X_1$) $\rightarrow$ VVPP1($X_1$)

Figure 4: Grammar extraction and binarization example

The probabilities are then computed based on the number of occurrences of rules in the transformed treebank, using a Maximum Likelihood estimator.

## 3 Evaluation methods

We assess the quality of our parser output using different methods.

The first is an **EVALB-style metric** (henceforth **EVALB**), i.e., we compare phrase boundaries. In spite of its shortcomings (Rehbein and van Genabith, 2007), it allows us to compare to previous work on parsing NeGra. In the context of LCFRS, we compare sets of tuples of the form $[A, (i_l^1, i_r^1), \ldots, (i_l^k, i_r^k)]$, where $A$ is a non-terminal in some derivation tree with $dim(A) = k$ and each $(i_l^m, i_r^m)$, $1 \leq m \leq k$, is a tuple of indices denoting a continuous sequence of terminals dominated by $A$. One set is obtained from the parser output, and

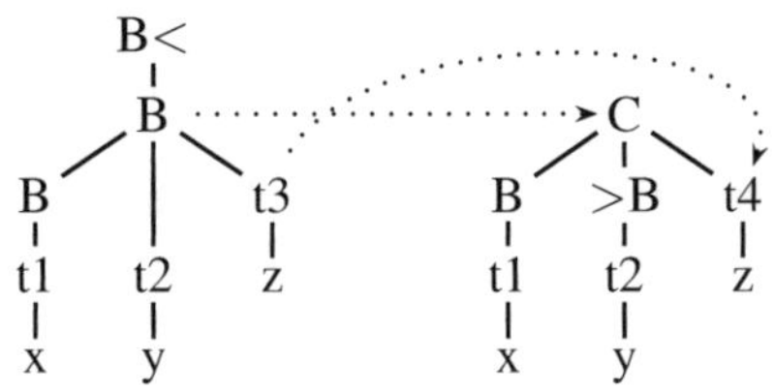


Figure 5: TDIST example

one from the corresponding treebank trees. Using these tuple sets, we compute labeled and unlabeled recall (LR/UR), precision (LP/UP), and the $F_1$ measure (L$F_1$/U$F_1$) in the usual way. Note that if $k = 1$, our metric is identical to its PCFG version.

EVALB does not necessarily reflect parser output quality (Rehbein and van Genabith, 2007; Emms, 2008; Kübler et al., 2008). One of its major problems is that attachment errors are penalized too hard. As the second evaluation method, we therefore choose the **tree-distance measure** (henceforth **TDIST**) (Zhang and Shasha, 1989), which levitates this problem. It has been proposed for parser evaluation by Emms (2008). TDIST is an ideal candidate for evaluation of the output of a PLCFRS, since it the fact if trees have crossing branches or not is not relevant to it. Two trees $\tau_k$ and $\tau_A$ are compared on the basis of **$T$-mappings** from $\tau_k$ to $\tau_A$. A $T$-mapping is a partial mapping $\sigma$ of nodes of $\tau_k$ to nodes of $\tau_A$ where all node mappings preserve left-to-right order and ancestry. Within the mappings, node insertion, node deletion, and label swap operations are identified, represented resp. by the sets $\mathcal{I}$, $\mathcal{D}$ and $\mathcal{S}$. Furthermore, we consider the set $\mathcal{M}$ representing the matched (i.e., unchanged) nodes. The cost of a $T$-mapping is the total number of operations, i.e. $|\mathcal{I}|+|\mathcal{D}|+|\mathcal{S}|$. The **tree distance** between two trees $\tau_K$ and $\tau_A$ is the cost of the cheapest $T$-mapping. Fig. 5, borrowed from Emms, shows an example for a $T$-mapping. Inserted nodes are prefixed with $>$, deleted nodes are suffixed with $<$, and nodes with swapped labels are linked with arrows. Since in total, four operations are involved, to this $T$-mapping, a cost of 4 is assigned. For more details, especially on algorithms which compute TDIST, refer to Bille (2005). In order to convert the tree distance measure into a similarity measure like EVALB, we use the macro-averaged Dice and Jaccard normalizations as defined by Emms. Let $\tau_K$ and $\tau_A$ be two trees with $|\tau_K|$ and $|\tau_A|$ nodes, respectively. For a $T$-mapping $\sigma$ from $\tau_K$ to $\tau_A$ with the sets $\mathcal{D}$, $\mathcal{I}$, $\mathcal{S}$ and $\mathcal{M}$, we compute them as follows.

$$dice(\sigma) = 1 - \frac{|\mathcal{D}| + |\mathcal{I}| + |\mathcal{S}|}{|\tau_K| + |\tau_A|}$$

$$jaccard(\sigma) = 1 - \frac{|\mathcal{D}| + |\mathcal{I}| + |\mathcal{S}|}{|\mathcal{D}| + |\mathcal{I}| + |\mathcal{S}| + |\mathcal{M}|}$$

where, in order to achieve macro-averaging, we sum the numerators and denominators over all tree pairs before dividing. See Emms (2008) for further details.

The third method is **dependency evaluation** (henceforth **DEP**), as described by Lin (1995). It consists of comparing dependency graphs extracted from the gold data and from the parser output. The dependency extraction algorithm as given by Lin does also not rely on trees to be free of crossing branches. It only relies on a method to identify the head of each phrase. We use our own implementation of the algorithm which is described in Sect. 4 of Lin (1995), combined with the head finding algorithm of the parser. Dependency evaluation abstracts away from another bias of EVALB. Concretely, it does not prefer trees with a high node/token ratio, since two dependency graphs to be compared necessarily have the same number of (terminal) nodes. In the context of parsing German, this evaluation has been employed previously by Kübler et al. (2008).

Last, we evaluate on **TePaCoC** (**Te**sting **Pa**rser **P**erformance **o**n **Co**mplex Grammatical **C**onstructions), a set of particularly difficult sentences hand-picked from TIGER (Kübler et al., 2008).

## 4 Experiments

Our data sources are the German NeGra (Skut et al., 1997) and TIGER (Brants et al., 2002) treebanks. In a preprocessing step, following common practice, we attach all punctuation to nodes within the tree, since it is not included in the NeGra annotation. In a first pass, using heuristics, we attach all nodes to the in each case highest available phrasal node such that ideally, we do not introduce new crossing branches. In a second pass, parentheses and quotation marks are preferably attached to the same node. Grammatical function labels are discarded. After this preprocessing step, we create a separate version of the data set, in which we resolve the crossing branches in the trees, using the common approach of re-attaching nodes to higher constituents. We use the first 90% of our data sets for training and the remaining 10% for testing. Due to memory limitations, we restrict ourselves to sentences of a maximal length of 30 words. Our TIGER data sets (TIGER and T-CF) have 31,568 sentences of an average length of 14.81, splitted into 31,568 sentences for training and 3,508 sentences for testing. Our NeGra data sets (NeGra and N-CF) have 18,335 sentences, splitted into 16,501 sentences for training and 1,834 sentences for testing.

We parse the data sets described above with activated LR estimate. For all our experiments, we use the markovization settings $v = 2$ and $h = 1$, which have proven to be successful in previous work on parsing NeGra (Rafferty and Manning, 2008). We provide the parser with the gold tagging. Fig. 6 shows the average parsing times for all data sets on an AMD Opteron node with 8GB of RAM (pure Java implementation), Tab. 1 shows the percentage of parsed sentences.

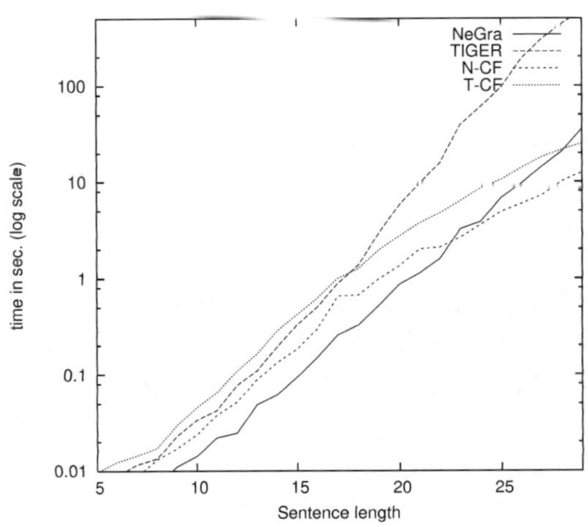


Figure 6: Parsing times

| | NeGra | TIGER | N-CF | T-CF |
|---|---|---|---|---|
| total | 1834 | 3508 | 1834 | 3508 |
| parsed | 1779 | 3462 | 1804 | 3462 |
| | (97.0%) | (98.7%) | (98.4%) | (98.7%) |

Table 1: Parsed sentences

### 4.1 Evaluation Using EVALB

Tab. 2 shows the evaluation of the parser output using EVALB, as described in the previous section. We report labeled and unlabeled precision, recall and $F_1$ measure.

| | LP | LR | $LF_1$ | UP | UR | $UF_1$ |
|---|---|---|---|---|---|---|
| NeGra | 72.39 | 70.68 | 71.52 | 76.01 | 74.22 | 75.10 |
| TIGER | 74.97 | 71.95 | 73.43 | 78.58 | 75.42 | 76.97 |
| N-CF | 74.85 | 73.26 | 74.04 | 78.11 | 76.45 | 77.28 |
| T-CF | 77.51 | 73.73 | 75.57 | 80.59 | 76.66 | 78.57 |

Table 2: EVALB results

Not surprisingly, reconstructing discontinuities is hard. Therefore, when parsing without crossing branches, the results are slightly better. In order to see the influence of discontinuous structures during parsing on the underlying phrase structure, we resolve the crossing branches in the parser output of NeGra and TIGER and compare it to the respective gold test data of N-CF and T-CF. Tab. 3 shows the results.

| | LP | LR | $LF_1$ | UP | UR | $UF_1$ |
|---|---|---|---|---|---|---|
| NeGra | 72.75 | 71.04 | 71.89 | 76.38 | 74.58 | 75.47 |
| TIGER | 75.28 | 72.25 | 73.74 | 78.81 | 75.64 | 77.20 |

Table 3: EVALB results (resolved crossing branches)

The results deteriorate slightly in comparison with N-CF and T-CF, however, they are slightly higher than for than for NeGra and TIGER. This is due to the fact that during the transformation, some errors in the LCFRS parses get "corrected": Wrongly attached phrasal nodes are re-attached to unique higher positions in the trees.

In order to give a point of comparison with previous work on parsing TIGER and NeGra, in Tab. 4, we report some of the results from the literature. All of them were obtained using PCFG parsers: Kübler (2005) (Tab. 1, plain PCFG for NeGra), Kübler et al. (2008) (Tab. 3, plain PCFG and Stanford parser with markovization $v = 2$ and $h = 1$ for TIGER), and Petrov and Klein (2007) (Tab. 1, Berkeley parser, latent variables). We include the results for N-CF and T-CF.

Our results are slightly better than for the plain PCFG models. We would expect the result for T-CF to be closer to the corresponding result for the Stanford parser, since we are using a comparable

| | plain | **this work** | markov. | latent |
|---|---|---|---|---|
| NeGra | 69.94 | **74.04** | – | 80.1 |
| TIGER | 74.00 | **75.57** | 77.30 | – |

Table 4: PCFG parsing of NeGra, Labeled $F_1$

model. This difference is mostly likely due to losses induced by the LR estimate. All items to which the estimate assigns an outside log probability estimate of $-\infty$ get blocked and are not put on the agenda. This blocking has an extremely beneficial effect on parser speed. However, it is paid by a worse recall, as experiments with smaller data sets have shown. A complete discussion of the effects of estimates, as well as a discussion of other possible optimizations, is presented in Kallmeyer and Maier (2010).

Recall finally that LCFRS parses are more informative than PCFG parses – a lower score for LCFRS EVALB than for PCFG EVALB does not necessarily mean that the PCFG parse is "better".

### 4.2 Evaluation Using Tree Distance

Tab. 5 shows the results of evaluating with TDIST, excluding unparsed sentences. We report the *dice* and *jaccard* normalizations, as well as a summary of the distribution of the tree distances between gold trees and trees from the parser output (see Sect. 3).

| | | | tree distance distrib. | | |
|---|---|---|---|---|---|
| | dice | jaccard | 0 | $\leq 3$ | $\geq 10$ |
| NeGra | 88.86 | 79.79 | 31.65 | 53.77 | 15.08 |
| TIGER | 89.47 | 80.84 | 29.87 | 56.78 | 18.18 |
| N-CF | 92.50 | 85.99 | 33.43 | 61.92 | 6.71 |
| T-CF | 92.70 | 86.46 | 31.80 | 63.81 | 4.56 |

Table 5: Tree distance evaluation

Again, we can observe that parsing LCFRS is harder than parsing PCFG. As for EVALB, the results for TIGER are slightly higher than the ones for NeGra. The distribution of the tree distances shows that about a third of all sentences receive a completely correct parse. More than a half, resp. a third of all parser output trees require $\leq 3$ operations to be mapped to the corresponding gold tree, and a only a small percentage requires $\geq 10$ operations.

To our knowledge, TDIST has not been used to evaluate parser output for NeGra and TIGER. However, Emms (2008) reports results for the PTB using different parsers. Collins' Model 1 (Collins, 1999), e.g., lies at 93.62 (Dice) and 87.87 (Jaccard). For the Berkeley Parser (Petrov and Klein, 2007), 94.72 and 89.87 is reported. We see that our results lie in them same range. However, Jaccard scores are lower since this normalization punishes a higher number of edit operations more severely than Dice. In order to meaningfully interpret which treebank properties are responsible for the fact that between the gold trees and the trees from the parser, the German data requires more tree edit operations than the English data, a TDIST evaluation of the output of an off-the-shelf PCFG parser would be necessary. This is left for future work.

### 4.3 Dependency Evaluation

For the dependency evaluation, we extract dependency graphs from both the gold data and the test data and compare the unlabeled accuracy. Tab. 6 shows the results. We report unlabeled attachment score (UAS).

| | UAS |
|---|---|
| NeGra | 76.50 |
| TIGER | 77.84 |
| N-CF | 77.52 |
| T-CF | 78.67 |

Table 6: Dependency evaluation

The dependency results are consistent with the previous results in as much as the scores for PCFG parsing are again higher. The dependency results reported in Kübler et al. (2008) however are much higher (85.6 UAS for the markovized Stanford parser). While a part of the losses can again be attributed to the LR estimate, another reason lies undoubtedly in the different dependency conversion method which we employ, and in further treebank transformations which Kübler et al. perform. In order to get a more fine grained result, in future work, we will consider graph modifications as proposed by Lin (1995) as well as including annotation-specific information from NeGra/TIGER in our conversion procedure.

### 4.4 TePaCoC

The TePaCoC data set (Kübler et al., 2008) provides 100 hand-picked sentences from TIGER which contain constructions that are especially difficult to parse. Out of these 100 sentences, we only consider 69. The remaining 31 sentences are either longer than 30 words or not included in the TIGER 2003 release (Kübler et al. use the 2005 release). The data is partitioned in groups of sentences with extraposed relative clauses (ERC), forward conjunction reduction (FCR), noun PP attachment (PPN), verb PP attachment (PPV), subject gap with finite/fronted verbs (SGF) and coordination of unlike constituents (CUC). Tab. 7 shows the EVALB results for the (discontinuous) TePaCoC. We parse these sentences using the same training set as before with all TePaCoC sentences removed.

| | LP | LR | $LF_1$ | UP | UR | $UF_1$ |
|---|---|---|---|---|---|---|
| ERC | 59.34 | 61.36 | 60.34 | 64.84 | 67.05 | 65.92 |
| FCR | 78.03 | 76.70 | 77.36 | 82.66 | 81.25 | 81.95 |
| PPN | 72.15 | 72.15 | 72.15 | 75.95 | 75.95 | 75.95 |
| PPV | 73.33 | 73.33 | 73.33 | 76.66 | 76.66 | 76.66 |
| CUC | 58.76 | 57.58 | 58.16 | 69.07 | 67.68 | 68.37 |
| SGF | 82.67 | 81.05 | 81.85 | 85.33 | 83.66 | 84.49 |
| all | 72.27 | 71.83 | 72.05 | 77.26 | 76.78 | 77.02 |

Table 7: EVALB scores for TePaCoC

While we cannot compare our results directly with the PCFG results (using grammatical function labels) of Kübler et al., their results nevertheless give an orientation.

We take a closer look at all sentence groups. Our result for ERC is more than 15 points worse than the result of Kübler et al. The relative clause itself is mostly recognized as a sentence (though not explicitly marked as a relative clause, since we do not consider grammatical functions). However, it is almost consistently attached too high (on the VP or on clause level). While this is correct for Kübler et al., with crossing branches, it treated as an error and punished especially hard by EVALB. FCR is parsed mostly well and with comparable results to Kübler et al. There are too few sentences to make a strong claim about PP attachment. However, in both PPN and PPV flat phrases seem to be preferred, which has as a consequence that in PPN, PPs are attached too high and in PPV too low. Our output confirms the claim of Kübler et al.'s that unlike coordinations is the most difficult of all TePaCoC phenomena. The conjuncts themselves are correctly identified in most cases, however then coordinated at the wrong level. SGF is parsed best. Kübler et al. report for this group only 78.6 labeled $F_1$ for the Stanford Parser. Our overall results are slightly worse than the results of Kübler et al., but show less variance.

To sum up, not surprisingly, getting the right attachment positions seems to be hard for LCFRS, too. Additionally, with crossing branches, the output is rated worse, since some attachments are not present anymore without crossing branches. Since especially for the relative clauses, attachment positions are in fact a matter of discussion from a syntactic point of view, we will consider in future studies to selectively resolve some of the crossing branches, e.g., by attaching relative clauses to higher positions.

## 5 Related Work

The use of formalisms with a high expressivity has been explored before (Plaehn, 2004; Levy, 2005). To our knowledge, Plaehn is the only one to report evaluation results. He uses the formalism of Discontinuous Phrase Structure Grammar (DPSG). Limiting the sentence length to 15, he obtains 73.16 labeled $F_1$ on NeGra. Evaluating all sentences of our NeGra data with a length of up to 15 words results, however, in 81.27 labeled $F_1$. For a comparison between DPSG and LCFRS, refer to Maier and Søgaard (2008).

## 6 Conclusion and Future Work

We have investigated the possibility of using Probabilistic Linear Context-Free Rewriting Systems for direct parsing of discontinuous constituents. Consequently, we have applied a PLCFRS parser on the German NeGra and TIGER treebanks. Our evaluation, which used different metrics, showed that a PLCFRS parser can achieve competitive results.

In future work, all of the presented evaluation methods will be investigated to greater detail. In order to do this, we will parse our data sets with current state-of-the-art systems. Especially a more elaborate dependency conversion should enable a more informative comparison between the output of PCFG parsers and the output of the PLCFRS parser. Last, since an algorithm is available which extracts LCFRSs from dependency structures (Kuhlmann and Satta, 2009), the parser is instantly ready for parsing them. We are currently performing the corresponding experiments.

## References


Philip Bille. 2005. A survey on tree edit distance and related problems. *Theoretical Computer Science*, 337.

Pierre Boullier. 1998. A Proposal for a Natural Language Processing Syntactic Backbone. Technical Report 3342, INRIA.

Adriane Boyd. 2007. Discontinuity revisited: An improved conversion to context-free representations. In *The Linguistic Annotation Workshop at ACL 2007*.

Sabine Brants, Stefanie Dipper, Silvia Hansen, Wolfgang Lezius, and George Smith. 2002. The TIGER Treebank. In *Proceedings of Treebanks and Linguistic Theories*.

David Chiang. 2003. Statistical parsing with an automatically extracted Tree Adjoining Grammar. In *Data-Oriented Parsing*. CSLI Publications.

Michael Collins. 1999. *Head-driven statistical models for natural language parsing*. Ph.D. thesis, University of Pennsylvania.

Martin Emms. 2008. Tree Distance and some other variants of Evalb. In *Proceedings of LREC 08*.

Carlos Gómez-Rodríguez, Marco Kuhlmann, Giorgio Satta, and David Weir. 2009. Optimal reduction of rule length in linear context-free rewriting systems. In *Proceedings of NAACL-HLT*.

Laura Kallmeyer and Wolfgang Maier. 2009. An incremental earley parser for simple range concatenation grammar. In *Proceedings of IWPT 09*.

Laura Kallmeyer and Wolfgang Maier. 2010. Data-driven parsing with probabilistic linear context-free rewriting systems. Unpublished Manuscript.

Yuki Kato, Hiroyuki Seki, and Tadao Kasami. 2006. RNA pseudoknotted structure prediction using stochastic multiple context-free grammar. *IPSJ Digital Courier*, 2.

Dan Klein and Christopher D. Manning. 2003a. A* Parsing: Fast Exact Viterbi Parse Selection. In *Proceedings of NAACL-HLT*.

Dan Klein and Christopher D. Manning. 2003b. Fast exact inference with a factored model for natural language parsing. In *In Advances in Neural Information Processing Systems 15 (NIPS)*. MIT Press.

Sandra Kübler, Wolfgang Maier, Ines Rehbein, and Yannick Versley. 2008. How to compare treebanks. In *Proceedings of LREC 08*.

Sandra Kübler. 2005. How do treebank annotation schemes influence parsing results? Or how not to compare apples and oranges. In *Proceedings of RANLP 2005*.

Marco Kuhlmann and Giorgio Satta. 2009. Treebank grammar techniques for non-projective dependency parsing. In *Proceedings of EACL*.

Roger Levy. 2005. *Probabilistic Models of Word Order and Syntactic Discontinuity*. Ph.D. thesis, Stanford University.

Dekang Lin. 1995. A dependency-based method for evaluating broad-coverage parsers. In *Proceedings of IJCAI 95*.

Wolfgang Maier and Timm Lichte. 2009. Characterizing discontinuity in constituent treebanks. In *Proceedings of Formal Grammar 2009*.

Wolfgang Maier and Anders Søgaard. 2008. Treebanks and mild context-sensitivity. In *Proceedings of Formal Grammar 2008*.

Mitchell Marcus, Grace Kim, Mary Ann Marcinkiewicz, Robert MacIntyre, Ann Bies, Mark Ferguson, Karen Katz, and Britta Schasberger. 1994. The Penn Treebank: Annotating predicate argument structure. In *Proceedings of HLT*.

Mark-Jan Nederhof. 2003. Weighted Deductive Parsing and Knuth's Algorithm. *Computational Linguistics*, 29(1).

Slav Petrov and Dan Klein. 2007. Improved inference for unlexicalized parsing. In *Proceedings of HLT-NAACL 2007*.

Oliver Plaehn. 2004. Computing the most probable parse for a discontinuous phrase-structure grammar. In *New developments in parsing technology*. Kluwer.

Anna Rafferty and Christopher D. Manning. 2008. Parsing three German treebanks: Lexicalized and unlexicalized baselines. In *Proceedings of the Workshop on Parsing German at ACL 2008*.

Ines Rehbein and Josef van Genabith. 2007. Evaluating evaluation measures. In *Proceedings of NODALIDA 2007*.

Hiroyuki Seki, Takahashi Matsumura, Mamoru Fujii, and Tadao Kasami. 1991. On multiple context-free grammars. *Theoretical Computer Science*, 88(2).

Wojciech Skut, Brigitte Krenn, Thorten Brants, and Hans Uszkoreit. 1997. An annotation scheme for free word order languages. In *Proceedings of ANLP*.

Heike Telljohann, Erhard Hinrichs, Sandra Kübler, and Heike Zinsmeister. 2006. Stylebook for the Tübingen Treebank of Written German (TüBa-D/Z). Technischer Bericht, Universität Tübingen.

K. Vijay-Shanker, David J. Weir, and Aravind K. Joshi. 1987. Characterizing structural descriptions produced by various grammatical formalisms. In *Proceedings of ACL*.

Kaizhong Zhang and Dennis Shasha. 1989. Simple fast algorithms for the editing distance between trees and related problems. *SIAM Journal of Computing*, 18.

# Handling Unknown Words in Statistical Latent-Variable Parsing Models for Arabic, English and French

**Mohammed Attia, Jennifer Foster, Deirdre Hogan, Joseph Le Roux, Lamia Tounsi, Josef van Genabith***
National Centre for Language Technology
School of Computing, Dublin City University
{mattia,jfoster,dhogan,jleroux,ltounsi,josef}@computing.dcu.ie

## Abstract

This paper presents a study of the impact of using simple and complex morphological clues to improve the classification of rare and unknown words for parsing. We compare this approach to a language-independent technique often used in parsers which is based solely on word frequencies. This study is applied to three languages that exhibit different levels of morphological expressiveness: Arabic, French and English. We integrate information about Arabic affixes and morphotactics into a PCFG-LA parser and obtain state-of-the-art accuracy. We also show that these morphological clues can be learnt automatically from an annotated corpus.

## 1 Introduction

For a parser to do a reasonable job of analysing free text, it must have a strategy for assigning part-of-speech tags to words which are not in its lexicon. This problem, also known as the problem of unknown words, has received relatively little attention in the vast literature on Wall-Street-Journal (WSJ) statistical parsing. This is likely due to the fact that the proportion of unknown words in the standard English test set, Section 23 of the WSJ section of Penn Treebank, is quite small. The problem manifests itself when the text to be analysed comes from a different domain to the text upon which the parser has been trained, when the treebank upon which the parser has been trained is limited in size and when the language to be parsed is heavily inflected. We concentrate on the latter case, and examine the problem of unknown words for two languages which lie on opposite ends of the spectrum of morphological expressiveness and for one language which lies somewhere in between: Arabic, English and French.

In our experiments we use a Berkeley-style latent-variable PCFG parser and we contrast two techniques for handling unknown words within the generative parsing model: one in which no language-specific information is employed and one in which morphological clues (or signatures) are exploited. We find that the improvement accrued from looking at a word's morphology is greater for Arabic and French than for English. The morphological clues we use for English are taken directly from the Berkeley parser (Petrov et al., 2006) and those for French from recent work on French statistical parsing with the Berkeley parser (Crabbé and Candito, 2008; Candito et al., 2009). For Arabic, we present our own set of heuristics to extract these signatures and demonstrate a statistically significant improvement of 3.25% over the baseline model which does not employ morphological information.

We next try to establish to what extent these clues can be learnt automatically by extracting affixes from the words in the training data and ranking these using information gain. We show that this automatic method performs quite well for all three languages.

The paper is organised as follows: In Section 2 we describe latent variable PCFG parsing models. This is followed in Section 3 by a description of our three datasets, including statistics on the extent of the unknown word problem in each. In Section 4, we

*Author names are listed in alphabetical order. For further correspondence, contact L. Tounsi, D. Hogan or J. Foster.



*Proceedings of the NAACL HLT 2010 First Workshop on Statistical Parsing of Morphologically-Rich Languages*, pages 67–75,
Los Angeles, California, June 2010. ©2010 Association for Computational Linguistics

present results on applying a version of the parser which uses a simple, language-agnostic, unknown-word handling technique to our three languages. In Section 5, we show how this technique is extended to include morphological information and present parsing results for English and French. In Section 6, we describe the Arabic morphological system and explain how we used heuristic rules to cluster words into word-classes or signatures. We present parsing results for the version of the parser which uses this information. In Section 7, we describe our attempts to automatically determine the signatures for a language and present parsing results for the three languages. Finally, in Section 8, we discuss how this work might be fruitfully extended.

## 2 Latent Variable PCFG Parsing

Johnson (1998) showed that refining treebank categories with parent information leads to more accurate grammars. This was followed by a collection of linguistically motivated propositions for manual or semi-automatic modifications of categories in treebanks (Klein and Manning, 2003). In PCFG-LAs, first introduced by Matsuzaki *et al.* (2005), the refined categories are learnt from the treebank using unsupervised techniques. Each base category – and this includes part-of-speech tags – is augmented with an annotation that refines its distributional properties.

Following Petrov *et al.* (2006) latent annotations and probabilities for the associated rules are learnt incrementally following an iterative process consisting of the repetition of three steps.

1. Split each annotation of each symbol into $n$ (usually 2) new annotations and create rules with the new annotated symbols. Estimate[1] the probabilities of the newly created rules.
2. Evaluate the impact of the newly created annotations and discard the least useful ones. Re-estimate probabilities with the new set of annotations.
3. Smooth the probabilities to prevent overfitting.

We use our own parser which trains a PCFG-LA using the above procedure and parses using the max-rule parsing algorithm (Petrov et al., 2006; Petrov and Klein, 2007). PCFG-LA parsing is relatively language-independent but has been shown to be very effective on several languages (Petrov, 2009). For our experiments, we set the number of iterations to be 5 and we test on sentences less than or equal to 40 words in length. All our experiments, apart from the final one, are carried out on the development sets of our three languages.

## 3 The Datasets

**Arabic** We use the the Penn Arabic Treebank (ATB) (Bies and Maamouri, 2003; Maamouri and Bies., 2004). The ATB describes written Modern Standard Arabic newswire and follows the style and guidelines of the English Penn-II treebank. We use the part-of-speech tagset defined by Bikel and Bies (Bikel, 2004). We employ the usual treebank split (80% training, 10% development and 10% test).

**English** We use the Wall Street Journal section of the Penn-II Treebank (Marcus et al., 1994). We train our parser on sections 2-21 and use section 22 concatenated with section 24 as our development set. Final testing is carried out on Section 23.

**French** We use the French Treebank (Abeillé et al., 2003) and divide it into 80% for training, 10% for development and 10% for final results. We follow the methodology defined by Crabbé and Candito (2008): compound words are merged and the tagset consists of base categories augmented with morphological information in some cases[2].

Table 1 gives basic unknown word statistics for our three datasets. We calculate the proportion of words in our development sets which are unknown or rare (specified by the cutoff value) in the corresponding training set. To control for training set size, we also provide statistics when the English training set is reduced to the size of the Arabic and French training sets and when the Arabic training set is reduced to the size of the French training set. In an ideal world where training set sizes are the same for all languages, the problem of unknown words will be greatest for Arabic and smallest for English. It is

[1]Estimation of the parameters is performed by running Expectation/Maximisation on the training corpus.

[2]This is called the CC tagset: base categories with verbal moods and extraction features

| language | cutoff | #train | #dev | #unk | %unk | language | #train | #dev | #unk | %unk |
|---|---|---|---|---|---|---|---|---|---|---|
| Arabic | 0 | 594,683 | 70,188 | 3794 | 5.40 | Reduced English | 597,999 | 72,970 | 2627 | 3.60 |
| - | 1 | - | - | 6023 | 8.58 | (Arabic Size) | - | - | 3849 | 5.27 |
| - | 5 | - | - | 11,347 | 16.17 | - | - | - | 6700 | 9.18 |
| - | 10 | - | - | 15,035 | 21.42 | - | - | - | 9083 | 12.45 |
| English | 0 | 950,028 | 72,970 | 2062 | 2.83 | Reduced Arabic | 266,132 | 70,188 | 7027 | 10.01 |
| - | 1 | - | - | 2983 | 4.09 | (French Size) | - | - | 10,208 | 14.54 |
| - | 5 | - | - | 5306 | 7.27 | - | - | - | 16,977 | 24.19 |
| - | 10 | - | - | 7230 | 9.91 | - | - | - | 21,434 | 30.54 |
| French | 0 | 268,842 | 35,374 | 2116 | 5.98 | Reduced English | 265,464 | 72,970 | 4188 | 5.74 |
| - | 1 | - | - | 3136 | 8.89 | (French Size) | - | - | 5894 | 8.08 |
| - | 5 | - | - | 5697 | 16.11 | - | - | - | 10,105 | 13.85 |
| - | 10 | - | - | 7584 | 21.44 | - | - | - | 13,053 | 17.89 |

Table 1: Basic Unknown Word Statistics for Arabic, French and English

reasonable to assume that the levels of inflectional richness have a role to play in these differences.

## 4 A Simple Lexical Probability Model

The simplest method for handling unknown words within a generative probabilistic parsing/tagging model is to reserve a proportion of the lexical rule probability mass for such cases. This is done by mapping rare words in the training data to a special UNKNOWN terminal symbol and estimating rule probabilities in the usual way. We illustrate the process with the toy unannotated PCFG in Figures 1 and 2. The lexical rules in Fig. 1 are the original rules and the ones in Fig. 2 are the result of applying the rare-word-to-unknown-symbol transformation. Given the input sentence *The shares recovered*, the word *recovered* is mapped to the UNKNOWN token and the three edges corresponding to the rules $NNS \rightarrow$ UNKNOWN, $VBD \rightarrow$ UNKNOWN and $JJ \rightarrow$ UNKNOWN are added to the chart at this position. The disadvantage of this simple approach is obvious: all unknown words are treated equally and the tag whose probability distribution is most dominated by rare words in the training will be deemed the most likely (JJ for this example), regardless of the characteristics of the individual word. Apart from its ease of implementation, its main advantage is its language-independence - it can be used off-the-shelf for any language for which a PCFG is available.[3]

One parameter along which the simple lexical probability model can vary is the threshold used to decide whether a word in the training data is rare or "unknown". When the threshold is set to *n*, a word in the training data is considered to be unknown if it occurs *n* or fewer times. We experiment with three thresholds: 1, 5 and 10. The result of this experiment for our three languages is shown in Table 2.

The general trend we see in Table 2 is that the number of training set words considered to be unknown should be minimized. For all three languages, the worst performing grammar is the one obtained when the threshold is increased to 10. This result is not unexpected. With this simple lexical probability model, there is a trade-off between obtaining good guesses for words which do not occur in the training data and obtaining reliable statistics for words which do. The greater the proportion of the probability mass that we reserve for the unknown word section of the grammar, the more performance suffers on the known yet rare words since these are the words which are mapped to the UNKNOWN symbol. For example, assume the word *restructuring* occurs 10 times in the training data, always tagged as a *VBG*. If the unknown threshold is less than ten and if the word occurs in the sentence to be parsed, a *VBG* edge will be added to the chart at this word's position with the probability 10/#VBG. If, however, the threshold is set to 10, the word (in the training set and the input sentence) will be mapped to UNKNOWN and more possibilities will be explored (an edge for each $TAG \rightarrow$ UNKNOWN rule in the grammar). We can see from Table 1 that at threshold 10, one fifth

[3]Our simple lexical model is equivalent to the Berkeley simpleLexicon option.

```
VBD -> fell 50/153
VBD -> reoriented 2/153
VBD -> went 100/153
VBD -> latched 1/153
NNS -> photofinishers 1/201
NNS -> shares 200/201
JJ  -> financial 20/24
JJ  -> centrist 4/24
DT  -> the 170/170
```

Figure 1: The original toy PCFG

```
VBD -> fell 50/153
VBD -> UNKNOWN 3/153
VBD -> went 100/153
NNS -> UNKNOWN 1/201
NNS -> shares 200/201
JJ  -> financial 20/24
JJ  -> UNKNOWN 4/24
DT  -> the 170/170
```

Figure 2: Rare → UNKNOWN

```
VBD -> fell 50/153
VBD -> UNK-ed 3/153
VBD -> went 100/153
NNS -> UNK-s 1/201
NNS -> shares 200/201
JJ  -> financial 20/24
JJ  -> UNK-ist 4/24
DT  -> the 170/170
```

Figure 3: Rare → UNKNOWN+SIGNATURE

| **Unknown Threshold** | **Recall** | **Precision** | **F-Score** | **Tagging Accuracy** |
|---|---|---|---|---|
| | | | **Arabic** | |
| **1** | 78.60 | 80.49 | **79.53** | 94.03 |
| **5** | 77.17 | 79.81 | 78.47 | 91.16 |
| **10** | 75.32 | 78.69 | 76.97 | 89.06 |
| | | | **English** | |
| **1** | 89.20 | 89.73 | **89.47** | 95.60 |
| **5** | 88.91 | 89.74 | 89.33 | 94.66 |
| **10** | 88.00 | 88.97 | 88.48 | 93.61 |
| | | | **French** | |
| **1** | 83.60 | 84.17 | **83.88** | 94.90 |
| **5** | 82.31 | 83.10 | 82.70 | 92.99 |
| **10** | 80.87 | 82.05 | 81.45 | 91.56 |

Table 2: Varying the Unknown Threshold with the Simple Lexical Probability Model

of the words in the Arabic and French development sets are unknown, and this is reflected in the drop in parsing performance at these thresholds.

## 5 Making use of Morphology

Unknown words are not all the same. We exploit this fact by examining the effect on parsing accuracy of clustering rare training set words using cues from the word's morphological structure. Affixes have been shown to be useful in part-of-speech tagging (Schmid, 1994; Tseng et al., 2005) and have been used in the Charniak (Charniak, 2000), Stanford (Klein and Manning, 2003) and Berkeley (Petrov et al., 2006) parsers. In this section, we contrast the effect on parsing accuracy of making use of such information for our three languages of interest.
Returning to our toy English example in Figures 1 and 2, and given the input sentence *The shares recovered*, we would like to use the fact that the unknown word *recovered* ends with the past tense suffix *-ed* to boost the probability of the lexical rule $VBD \rightarrow$ *UNKNOWN*. If we specialise the `UNKNOWN` terminal using information from English morphology, we can do just that, resulting in the grammar in Figure 3. Now the word *recovered* is mapped to the symbol `UNK-ed` and the only edge which is added to the chart at this position is the one corresponding to the rule $VBD \rightarrow$ `UNK-ed`.

For our English experiments we use the unknown word classes (or *signatures*) which are used in the Berkeley parser. A signature indicates whether a words contains a digit or a hyphen, if a word starts with a capital letter or ends with one of the following English suffixes (both derivational and inflectional): *-s*, *-ed*, *-ing*, *-ion*, *-er*, *-est*, *-ly*, *-ity*, *-y* and *-al*.

For our French experiments we employ the same signature list as Crabbé and Candito (2008), which itself was adapted from Arun and Keller (2005). This list consists of (a) conjugation suffixes of regular verbs for common tenses (eg. *-ons*, *-ez*, *-ent*...) and (b) derivational suffixes for nouns, adverbs and adjectives (eg. *-tion*, *-ment*, *-able*...).

The result of employing signature information for French and English is shown in Table 3. Beside each f-score the absolute improvement over the `UNKNOWN` baseline (Table 2) is given. For both languages there is an improvement at all unknown thresholds. The improvement for English is statistically significant at unknown thresholds 1 and 10.[4] The improvement is more marked for French and is statistically significant at all levels.

In the next section, we experiment with signature lists for Arabic.[5]

## 6 Arabic Signatures

In order to use morphological clues for Arabic we go further than just looking at suffixes. We exploit all the richness of the morphology of this language which can be expressed through morphotactics.

### 6.1 Handling Arabic Morphotactics

Morphotactics refers to the way morphemes combine together to form words (Beesley, 1998; Beesley and Karttunen, 2003). Generally speaking, morphotactics can be concatenative, with morphemes either prefixed or suffixed to stems, or non-concatenative, with stems undergoing internal alternations to convey morphosyntactic information. Arabic is considered a typical example of a language that employs non-concatenative morphotactics.

Arabic words are traditionally classified into three types: verbs, nouns and particles. Adjectives take almost all the morphological forms of, and share the same templatic structures with, nouns. Adjectives, for example, can be definite, and are inflected for case, number and gender.

There are a number of indicators that tell us whether the word is a verb or a noun. Among these indicators are prefixes, suffixes and word templates. A template (Beesley and Karttunen, 2003) is a kind of vocalization mould in which a word fits. In derivational morphology Arabic words are formed through the amalgamation of two tiers, namely, root and template. A root is a sequence of three (rarely two or four) consonants which are called radicals, and the template is a pattern of vowels, or a combination of consonants and vowels, with slots into which the radicals of the root are inserted.

For the purpose of detection we use the reverse of this information. Given that we have a word, we try to extract the stem, by removing prefixes and suffixes, and match the word against a number of verbal and nominal templates. We found that most Arabic templatic structures are in complementary distribution, i.e. they are either restricted to nominal or verbal usage, and with simple regular expression matching we can decide whether a word form is a noun or a verb.

### 6.2 Noun Indicators

In order to detect that a word form is a noun (or adjective), we employ heuristic rules related to Arabic prefixes/suffixes and if none of these rules apply we attempt to match the word against templatic structures. Using this methodology, we are able to detect 95% of ATB nouns.[6]

We define a list of 42 noun templates which are used to indicate active/passive participle nouns, verbal nouns, nouns of instrument and broken plural nouns (see Table 4 for some examples). Note that templates ending with taa marboutah "ap" or starting with meem madmoumah "mu" are not considered since they are covered by our suffix/prefix rules, which are as follows:

1- The definite article prefix ال or in Buckwalter transliteration "Al".
2- The tanween suffix اً, اٍ, اٌ or "N", "F", "K", "AF".
3- The feminine plural suffix ات, or "+At".
4- The taa marboutah ending ة or "ap" whether as a

[4]Statistical significance was determined using the stratified shuffling method. The software used to perform the test was downloaded from `http://www.cis.upenn.edu/~dbikel/software.html`.

[5]An inspection of the Berkeley Arabic grammar (available at `http://code.google.com/p/berkeleyparser/downloads/list`) shows that no Arabic-specific signatures were employed. The Stanford parser uses 9 signatures for Arabic, designed for use with unvocalised text. An immediate future goal is to test this signature list with our parser.

[6]The heuristics we developed are designed to work on diacritized texts. Although diacritics are generally ignored in modern writing, the issue of restoring diacritics has been satisfactorily addressed by different researchers. For example, Nelken and Shieber (2005) presented an algorithm for restoring diacritics to undiacritized MSA texts with an accuracy of over 90% and Habasah *et al.* (2009) reported on a freely-available toolkit (MADA-TOKAN) an accuracy of over 96%.

| Unknown Threshold | Recall | Precision | F-Score | Tagging Accuracy |
|---|---|---|---|---|
| | | | **Arabic** | |
| **1** | 80.67 | 82.19 | *81.42 (+ 1.89) | 96.32 |
| **5** | 80.66 | 82.81 | *81.72 (+ 3.25) | 95.15 |
| **10** | 79.86 | 82.49 | *81.15 (+ 4.18) | 94.38 |
| | | | **English** | |
| **1** | ***89.64 | 89.95 | **89.79** (+ 0.32) | 96.44 |
| **5** | 89.16 | 89.80 | 89.48 (+ 0.15) | 96.32 |
| **10** | 89.14 | 89.78 | **89.46 (+ 0.98) | 96.21 |
| | | | **French** | |
| **1** | 85.15 | 85.77 | ***85.46 (+ 1.58)** | 96.13 |
| **5** | 84.08 | 84.80 | *84.44 (+ 1.74) | 95.54 |
| **10** | 84.21 | 84.78 | *84.49 (+ 3.04) | 94.68 |

Table 3: Baseline Signatures for Arabic, French and English
statistically significant with *:$p < 10^{-4}$, **: $p < 10^{-3}$, ***: $p < 0.004$,

| Template Name | | Regular | Specification |
|---|---|---|---|
| Arabic | Buckwalter | Expression | |
| إنفِعَال | `{inofiEAl` | `{ino.i.A.` | verbal noun (masdar) |
| مِفعَال | `mifoEAl` | `mi.o.A.` | noun instrument |
| مُستَفعِل | `musotafoEil` | `musota.o.i.` | noun participle |
| مَفَاعِيل | `mafAEiyl` | `ma.A.iy.` | noun plural |
| إستَفعَل | `{isotafoEal` | `{isota.o.a.` | verb |
| فُوعِل | `fuwEil` | `.uw.i.` | verb passive |

Table 4: Sample Arabic Templatic Structures for Nouns and Verbs

feminine marker suffix or part of the word.
5- The genitive case marking kasrah ِ, or "+i".
6- Words of length of at least five characters ending with doubled yaa يّ or "y~".
7- Words of length of at least six characters ending with alif mamdoudah and hamzah اء or "A'".
8- Words of length of at least seven characters starting with meem madmoumah مُ or "mu".

### 6.3 Verb Indicators

In the same way, we define a list of 16 templates and we combine them with heuristic rules related to Arabic prefixes/suffixes to detect whether a word form is exclusively a verb. The prefix/suffix heuristics are as follows:
9-The plural marker suffix وَا or "uwA" indicates a verb.
10- The prefixes سَ ، أَ ، نَ ، يَ ، تَ or "sa", ">a", ">u", "na", "nu", "ya", "yu", "ta", "tu" indicate imprefective verb.
The verbal templates are less in number than the noun templates yet they are no less effective in detecting the word class (see Table 4 for examples). Using these heuristics we are able to detect 85% of ATB verbs.

### 6.4 Arabic Signatures

We map the 72 noun/verb classes that are identified using our hand-crafted heuristics into sets of signatures of varying sizes: 4, 6, 14, 21, 25, 28 and 72. The very coarse-grained set considers just 4 signatures `UNK-noun`, `UNK-verb`, `UNK-num`, and `UNK` and the most fine-grained set of 72 signatures associates one signature per heuristic. In addition, we have evaluated the effect of reordering rules and templates and also the effect of collating all signatures satisfying an unknown word. The results of using these various signatures sets in parsing

| **UNK** | | | | | |
|---|---|---|---|---|---|
| **NUM**<br>digits | **NOUN**<br>(see section 6.2) | | | | **VERB**<br>(see section 6.3) |
| | **Al_definiteness**<br>rule 1 | **tashkil**<br>rules 2 and 5 | **At_suffix**<br>rule 3 | **ap_suffix**<br>rule 4 | **imperfect**<br>rule 10 |
| | **y~_suffix**<br>rule 6 | **A'_suffix**<br>rule 7 | **mu_prefix**<br>rule 8 | **verbal_noun_templates**<br>3 groupings | **suffixes**<br>dual/plural suffixes |
| | **plural_templates**<br>4 groupings | **participle_active_templates** | **participle_passive_templates** | **instrument_templates** | **passive_templates** |
| | **other_templates** | | | | **verbal templates**<br>5 groupings |

Table 6: Arabic signatures

| **Cutoff** | **1** | **5** | **10** |
|---|---|---|---|
| 4 | 80.78 | 80.71 | 80.09 |
| 6 | 81.14 | 81.16 | 81.06 |
| 14 | 80.88 | 81.45 | 81.19 |
| 14 reorder | 81.39 | 81.01 | 80.81 |
| 21 | 81.38 | 81.55 | 81.35 |
| 21 reorder | 81.20 | 81.13 | 80.58 |
| 21 collect | 80.94 | 80.56 | 79.63 |
| 25 | 81.18 | 81.25 | 81.26 |
| **28** | 81.42 | **81.72 (+ 3.25)** | 81.15 |
| 72 | 79.64 | 78.87 | 77.58 |

Table 5: Baseline Signatures for Arabic

our Arabic development set are presented in Table 5. We achieve our best labeled bracketing f-score using 28 signatures with an unknown threshold of five. In fact we get an improvement of 3.25% over using no signatures at all (see Table 2). Table 3 describes in more detail the scores obtained using the 28 signatures present in Table 6. Apart from the set containing 72 signatures, all of the baseline signature sets in Table 5 yield a statistically significant improvement over the generic `UNKNOWN` results ($p < 10^{-4}$).

## 7 Using Information Gain to Determine Signatures

It is clear that dividing the `UNKNOWN` terminal into more fine-grained categories based on morphological information helps parsing for our three languages. In this section we explore whether useful morphological clues can be learnt automatically. If they can, it means that a latent-variable PCFG parser can be adapted to any language without knowledge of the language in question since the only language-specific component in such a parser is the unknown-signature specification.

In a nutshell, we extract affix features from training set words[7] and then use information gain to rank these features in terms of their predictive power in a POS-tagging task. The features deemed most discriminative are then used as signatures, replacing our baseline signatures described in Sections 5 and 6. We are not going as far as actual POS-tagging, but rather seeing whether the affixes that make good features for a part-of-speech tagger also make good unknown word signatures.

We experiment with English and French suffixes of length 1-3 and Arabic prefixes and suffixes of various lengths as well as stem prefixes and suffixes of length 2, 4 and 6. For each of our languages we experiment with several information gain thresholds on our development sets and we fix on an English signature list containing 24 suffixes, a French list containing 48 suffixes and an Arabic list containing 38 prefixes and suffixes.

Our development set results are presented in Table 7. For all three languages, the information gain signatures perform at a comparable level to the baseline hand-crafted signatures (Table 3). For each of the three unknown-word handling techniques, no signature (`UNKNOWN`), hand-crafted signatures and information gain signatures, we select the best unknown threshold for each language's development set and apply these grammars to our test sets. The f-scores are presented in Table 8, along with the upper bounds obtained by parsing with these grammars in gold-tag mode. For French, the effect of tagging accuracy on overall parse accuracy is striking. The improvements that we get from using morphological signatures are greatest for Arabic[8] and smallest for

[7] We omit all function words and high frequency words because we are interested in the behaviour of words which are likely to be similar to rare words.

[8] Bikel's parser trained on the same Arabic data and tested on the same input achieves an f-score of 76.50%. We trained a 5-split-merge-iteration Berkeley grammar and parsed with the

| Unknown Threshold | Recall | Precision | F-Score | Tagging Accuracy |
|---|---|---|---|---|
| | | | **Arabic IG** | |
| **1** | 80.10 | 82.15 | *81.11 (+ 1.58) | 96.53 |
| **5** | 80.03 | 82.49 | ***81.32 (+ 2.85)** | 95.30 |
| **10** | 80.17 | 82.40 | *81.27 (+ 4.3) | 94.66 |
| | | | **English IG** | |
| **1** | 89.38 | 89.87 | 89.63 (+ 0.16) | 96.45 |
| **5** | 89.54 | 90.22 | *****89.88 (+ 0.55)** | 96.41 |
| **10** | 89.22 | 90.05 | *89.63 (+ 1.15) | 96.19 |
| | | | **French IG** | |
| **1** | 84.78 | 85.36 | ***85.07 (+ 1.19)** | 96.17 |
| **5** | 84.63 | 85.24 | **84.93 (+ 2.23) | 95.30 |
| **10** | 84.18 | 84.80 | *84.49 (+ 3.09) | 94.68 |

Table 7: Information Gain Signature Results
statistically significant with *:$p < 10^{-4}$, **: $p < 2 \cdot 10^{-4}$, ***: $p < 0.005$

| Language | No Sig | Baseline Sig | IG Sig |
|---|---|---|---|
| Arabic | 78.34 | *81.59 | *81.33 |
| Arabic Gold Tag | 81.46 | 82.43 | 81.90 |
| English | 89.48 | 89.65 | 89.77 |
| English Gold Tag | 89.94 | 90.10 | 90.23 |
| French | 83.74 | *85.77 | **85.55 |
| French Gold Tag | 88.82 | 88.41 | 88.86 |

statistically significant with *: $p < 10^{-4}$, **: $p < 10^{-3}$

Table 8: F-Scores on Test Sets

English. The results for the information gain signatures are promising and warrant further exploration.

## 8 Conclusion

We experiment with two unknown-word-handling techniques in a statistical generative parsing model, applying them to Arabic, French and English. One technique is language-agnostic and the other makes use of some morphological information (signatures) in assigning part-of-speech tags to unknown words. The performance differences from the two techniques are smallest for English, the language with the sparsest morphology of the three and the smallest proportion of unknown words in its development set. As a result of carrying out these experiments, we have developed a list of Arabic signatures which can be used with any statistical parser which does its own tagging. We also present results which show that signatures can be learnt automatically.

Our experiments have been carried out using gold tokens. Tokenisation is an issue particularly for Arabic, but also for French (since the treebank contains merged compounds) and to a much lesser extent for English (unedited text with missing apostrophes). It is important that the experiments in this paper are repeated on untokenised text using automatic tokenisation methods (e.g. MADA-TOKAN).

The performance improvements that we demonstrate for Arabic unknown-word handling are obviously just the tip of the iceberg in terms of what can be done to improve performance on a morphologically rich language. The simple generative lexical probability model we use can be improved by adopting a more sophisticated approach in which known and unknown word counts are combined when estimating lexical rule probabilities for rare words (see Huang and Harper (2009) and the Berkeley sophisticatedLexicon training option). Further work will also include making use of a lexical resource external to the treebank (Goldberg et al., 2009; Habash, 2008) and investigating clustering techniques to reduce data sparseness (Candito and Crabbé, 2009).

## Acknowledgements

This research is funded by Enterprise Ireland (CFTD/07/229 and PC/09/037) and the Irish Research Council for Science Engineering and Technology (IRCSET). We thank Marie Candito and our three reviewers for their very helpful suggestions.

Berkeley parser, achieving an f-score of 75.28%. We trained the Berkeley parser with the *-treebank SINGLEFILE* option so that English signatures were not employed.

## References


Anne Abeillé, Lionel Clément, and François Toussenel, 2003. *Treebanks: Building and Using Parsed Corpora*, chapter Building a Treebank for French. Kluwer, Dordrecht.

Abhishek Arun and Frank Keller. 2005. Lexicalization in crosslinguistic probabilistic parsing: The case of French. In *ACL*. The Association for Computer Linguistics.

Kenneth R. Beesley and Lauri Karttunen. 2003. *Finite State Morphology*. CSLI studies in computational linguistics.

Kenneth R. Beesley. 1998. Arabic morphology using only finite-state operations. In *The Workshop on Computational Approaches to Semitic Languages*.

Ann Bies and Mohammed Maamouri. 2003. Penn Arabic Treebank guidelines. Technical Report TB-1-28-03.

Dan Bikel. 2004. *On the Parameter Space of Generative Lexicalized Parsing Models*. Ph.D. thesis, University of Pennslyvania.

Marie Candito and Benoit Crabbé. 2009. Improving generative statistical parsing with semi-supervised word clustering. In *Proceedings of IWPT'09*.

Marie Candito, Benoît Crabbé, and Djamé Seddah. 2009. On statistical parsing of French with supervised and semi-supervised strategies. In *Proceedings of the EACL 2009 Workshop on Computational Linguistic Aspects of Grammatical Inference*, pages 49–57, Athens, Greece, March.

Eugene Charniak. 2000. A maximum-entropy-inspired parser. In *Proceedings of the Annual Meeting of the North American Association for Computational Linguistics (NAACL-00)*, pages 132–139, Seattle, Washington.

Benoît Crabbé and Marie Candito. 2008. Expériences d'analyse syntaxique statistique du français. In *Actes de TALN*.

Yoav Goldberg, Reut Tsarfaty, Meni Adler, and Michael Elhadad. 2009. Enhancing unlexicalized parsing performance using a wide coverage lexicon, fuzzy tag-set mapping, and EM-HMM-based lexical probabilities. In *EACL*, pages 327–335. The Association for Computer Linguistics.

Nizar Habash, Owen Rambow, and Ryan Roth. 2009. Mada+tokan: A toolkit for Arabic tokenization, diacritization, morphological disambiguation, pos tagging, stemming and lemmatization. In *Proceedings of the 2nd International Conference on Arabic Language Resources and Tools (MEDAR)*.

Nizar Habash. 2008. Four techniques for online handling of out-of-vocabulary words in arabic-english statistical machine translation. In *Proceedings of Association for Computational Linguistics*, pages 57–60.

Zhongqiang Huang and Mary Harper. 2009. Self-training pcfg grammars with latent annotations across languages. In *Proceedings of the 2009 Conference on Empirical Methods in Natural Language Processing*, Singapore, August.

Mark Johnson. 1998. PCFG models of linguistic tree representations. *Computational Linguistics*, 24(4):613–632.

Dan Klein and Chris Manning. 2003. Accurate unlexicalised parsing. In *Proceedings of the 41st Annual Meeting of the ACL*.

Mohammed Maamouri and Ann Bies. 2004. Developing an Arabic Treebank: Methods, guidelines, procedures, and tools. In *Workshop on Computational Approaches to Arabic Script-based Languages, COLING*.

Mitchell Marcus, Grace Kim, Mary Ann Marcinkiewicz, Robert MacIntyre, Ann Bies, Mark Ferguson, Karen Katz, and Britta Schasberger. 1994. The Penn Treebank: Annotating predicate argument structure. In *Proceedings of the 1994 ARPA Speech and Natural Language Workshop*, pages 114–119, Princeton, New Jersey.

Takuya Matsuzaki, Yusuke Miyao, and Jun'ichi Tsujii. 2005. Probabilistic CFG with latent annotations. In *Proceedings of the 43rd Annual Meeting of the ACL*, pages 75–82, Ann Arbor, June.

Rani Nelken and Stuart M. Shieber. 2005. Arabic diacritization using weighted finite-state transducers. In *ACL-05 Workshop on Computational Approaches to Semitic Languages*.

Slav Petrov and Dan Klein. 2007. Improved inference for unlexicalized parsing. In *Proceedings of HLT-NAACL*, Rochester, NY, April.

Slav Petrov, Leon Barrett, Romain Thibaux, and Dan Klein. 2006. Learning accurate, compact and interpretable tree annotation. In *Proceedings of the 21st International Conference on Computational Linguistics and the 44th Annual Meeting of the ACL*, Sydney, Australia, July.

Slav Petrov. 2009. *Coarse-to-Fine Natural Language Processing*. Ph.D. thesis, University of California at Berkeley, Berkeley, CA, USA.

Helmut Schmid. 1994. Probabilistic part-of-speech tagging using decision trees. In *Proceedings of the International Conference on New Methods in Language Processing (NeMLaP-1)*, pages 44–49.

Huihsin Tseng, Daniel Jurafsky, and Christopher Manning. 2005. Morphological features help POS tagging of unknown words across language varieties. In *Proceedings of the Fourth SIGHAN Workshop on Chinese Language Processing*.

# Parsing word clusters

**Marie Candito**[⋆] **and Djamé Seddah**[⋆⋄]
⋆ Alpage (Université Paris 7/INRIA), 30 rue du château des rentiers 75013 Paris, France
⋄ Université Paris-Sorbonne, 28, rue Serpente, 75006 Paris, France

## Abstract

We present and discuss experiments in statistical parsing of French, where terminal forms used during training and parsing are replaced by more general symbols, particularly clusters of words obtained through unsupervised linear clustering. We build on the work of Candito and Crabbé (2009) who proposed to use clusters built over slightly coarsened French inflected forms. We investigate the alternative method of building clusters over lemma/part-of-speech pairs, using a raw corpus automatically tagged and lemmatized. We find that both methods lead to comparable improvement over the baseline (we obtain $F_1$=86.20% and $F_1$=86.21% respectively, compared to a baseline of $F_1$=84.10%). Yet, when we replace gold lemma/POS pairs with their corresponding cluster, we obtain an upper bound ($F_1$=87.80) that suggests room for improvement for this technique, should tagging/lemmatisation performance increase for French.
We also analyze the improvement in performance for both techniques with respect to word frequency. We find that replacing word forms with clusters improves attachment performance for words that are originally either unknown or low-frequency, since these words are replaced by cluster symbols that tend to have higher frequencies. Furthermore, clustering also helps significantly for medium to high frequency words, suggesting that training on word clusters leads to better probability estimates for these words.

## 1 Introduction

Statistical parsing techniques have dramatically improved over the last 15 years, yet lexical data sparseness remains a critical problem. And the richer the morphology of a language, the sparser the treebank-driven lexicons will be for that language.

Koo et al. (2008) have proposed to use word clusters as features to improve graph-based statistical dependency parsing for English and Czech. Their clusters are obtained using unsupervised clustering, which makes it possible to use a raw corpus containing several million words. Candito and Crabbé (2009) applied clustering to generative constituency parsing for French. They use a *desinflection* step that removes some inflection marks from word forms and then replaces them with word clusters, resulting in a significant improvement in parsing performance. Clustering words seems useful as a way of addressing the lexical data sparseness problem, since counts on clusters are more reliable and lead to better probability estimates. Clustering also appears to address the mismatch of vocabularies between the original treebank and any external, potentially out-of-domain corpus: clusters operate as an intermediary between words from the treebank and words from the external corpus used to compute clusters. Furthermore, parsing word clusters instead of word forms augments the known vocabulary.

However, depending on the clustering method, clusters are either not very reliable or are available only for very frequent words. In order to parse word clusters one needs to determine which word clusters are reliable enough to be beneficial, so the tuning of parameters such as cluster granularity and cluster reliability becomes very important.

The aim of this paper is to give an in-depth study of the "parsing word clusters" technique. In particular, starting from the Candito and Crabbé (2009) experiments, we investigate the use of clustering lem-



*Proceedings of the NAACL HLT 2010 First Workshop on Statistical Parsing of Morphologically-Rich Languages*, pages 76–84,
Los Angeles, California, June 2010. ©2010 Association for Computational Linguistics

mas instead of *desinflected* forms. We also provide an analysis of the performance gains obtained with respect to word frequency (frequent words, rare words, unknown words).

In the next section, we describe the French treebank used as the basis for all of our experiments. We describe in section 3 the statistical parser used for training and testing. We then describe the desinflection process used prior to unsupervised clustering (section 4), and the Brown algorithm we use for unsupervised clustering (section ). We describe our experiments and results in section 6, and provide a discussion in section 7. We then point out some related work and conclude in section 9.

## 2 French Treebank

For our experiments, we used the French Treebank (Abeillé et al., 2003), which contains 12531 sentences, 350931 tokens, from the newspaper *Le Monde*. We used the treebank instantiation (hereafter FTB-UC) as first described in (Candito and Crabbé, 2009), where :
(i) the rich original annotation containing morphological and functional information is mapped to a simpler phrase-structure treebank with a tagset of 28 part-of-speech tags, and no functional annotation
(ii) some compounds with regular syntax are broken down into phrases containing several simple words
(iii) the remaining sequences annotated as compound words in the FTB are merged into a single token, whose components are separated with an underscore

For all experiments in this paper (tagging and parsing) we used the same partition of the treebank as these authors : first 10% for test, next 10% for dev and the rest for training[1].

## 3 Berkeley Parser

We report here experiments using the Berkeley PCFG parser with latent annotations (Petrov et al., 2006), hereafter BKY, which is a constituent parser that has been proven to perform well for French (Crabbé and Candito, 2008; Seddah et al., 2009), though a little lower than a combination of a tagger plus the dependency-based MST parser (Candito et al., 2010). Though PCFG-style parsers operate on too narrow a domain of locality, splitting symbols according to structural and/or lexical properties is known to help parsing (Klein and Manning., 2003). Following (Matsuzaki et al., 2005), the BKY algorithm uses EM to estimate probabilities on symbols that are automatically augmented with latent annotations, a process which can be viewed as symbol splitting. It iteratively evaluates each such split and merges back the less beneficial ones. Crabbé and Candito (2008) show that some of the information carried by the latent annotations is lexical, since replacing words by their gold part-of-speech tag leads to worse results than the corresponding perfect tagging test, with words unchanged. This is a clear indication that lexical distinctions are used, and percolate up the parse tree via the latent annotations.

We now describe how the BKY software handles rare and unknown words, as this is pertinent to our discussion in section 6. $P(w|tag)$ is calculated using Bayes' rule, as $P(tag|w)P(w)/P(tag)$. Relative frequency estimates are used for words that are sufficiently frequent. For rare words (appearing less than 10 times in our settings), $P(tag|w)$ is smoothed using the proportion of tokens in the second half of the training set that were not seen in the first half, and that have this tag. For unknown words, words signatures are used: these are word classes determined by information such as the word suffix, whether the word is capitalized, whether it contains digits, etc. $P(w|tag)$ is estimated with $P(signature(w)|tag)$, and is also smoothed in the same way rare words are.

## 4 Morphological clustering

A first approach to word clustering is to cluster forms on a morphological basis. In the case of a relatively morphologically rich language such as French, this is an obvious way to reduce lexical sparseness caused by inflection.

(Candito and Crabbé, 2009) proposed the use of a *desinflection* method, without resorting to part-of-speech tagging. We propose an alternate method here, which uses lemmas and part-of-speech tags that are output by a tagger/lemmatizer. Because

[1] More precisely the partition is : first 1235 sentences for test, next 1235 sentences for development, and remaining 9881 sentences for training.

counts on lemmas are more reliable, clustering over lemmas presumably produces clusters that are more reliable than those produced by clustering over desinflected forms. However, this approach does create a constraint in which automatically tagged and lemmatized text is required as input to the parser, leading to the introduction of tagging errors.

Both morphological clustering methods make use of the L*efff* lexicon (Sagot, 2010). Before we describe these two methods, we briefly give basic information on French inflectional morphology and on the L*efff*.

### 4.1 French inflection and the L*efff* lexicon

French nouns appear in singular and plural forms, and have an intrinsic gender. The number and gender of a noun determines the number and gender of determiners, adjectives, past participles that depend on it. Hence in the general case, past participles and adjectives have four different forms. The major inflectional variation appears for finite verbs that vary for tense, mood, person and number. A regular verb may correspond to more than 60 inflected forms if all tenses and mood are included. In practice, some forms occur very rarely, because some tense/mood pairs are rare, and further, in the case of newspaper text for instance, the first and second persons are also rare. So for instance in the FTB-UC, there are 33 different forms for the highly frequent verb and auxiliary *avoir* (*to have*), that appears 4557 times. The medium frequency verb *donner* (*to give*) occurs 155 times, under 15 different forms. In the whole treebank, there are 27130 unique word forms, corresponding to 17570 lemmas.

The L*efff* is a freely available rich morphological and syntactic French lexicon (Sagot, 2010). It contains $110,477$ lemmas (simple and compounds) and $536,375$ inflected forms. The coverage on the FTB-UC is high : around $96\%$ of the tokens, and $80,1\%$ of the types are present in the L*efff* (leaving out punctuation and numeric tokens, and ignoring case differences).

### 4.2 Desinflection

The aim of the desinflection step is to reduce lexical data sparseness caused by inflection, without hurting parsability and without committing oneself as far as lexical ambiguity is concerned. The idea is to leave unchanged the parser's task in disambiguating part-of-speech tags. In that case, morphological clustering using lemmas is not an option, since lemma assignment presupposes POS disambiguation. Furthermore, useful information such as verb mood (which is needed to capture, for instance, that infinitive verbs have no overt subject or that participial clauses are sentence modifiers) is discarded during lemmatization, though it is encoded in the FTB with different projections for finite verbs (projecting sentences) versus non finite verbs (projecting VPpart or VPinf).

The intuition of Candito and Crabbé (2009) is that other inflectional markers in French (gender and number for determiners, adjectives, pronouns and nouns, or tense and person for verbs) are not crucial for inferring the correct phrase-structure projection for a given word. Consequently, they proposed to achieve morphological clustering by *desinflection*, namely by removing unneeded inflectional markers, identified using the L*efff*. This lexicon-based technique can be viewed as an intermediate method between stemming and lemmatization.

The desinflection process is as follows: for a token $t$ to *desinflect*, if it is known in the lexicon, then for each inflected lexical entry $le$ of $t$, try to get a corresponding singular entry. If corresponding singular entries exist for all such $le$ and all have the same form, then replace $t$ by the corresponding form. For instance for $wt$=*entrées* (ambiguous between *entrances* and *entered*, fem, plural), the two lexical entries are *[entrées/N/fem/plu]* and *[entrées/V/fem/plu/part/past]*[2], each have a corresponding singular lexical entry, with form *entrée*.

The same process is used to map feminine forms to corresponding masculine forms. This allows one to change *mangée* (*eaten*, fem, sing) into *mangé* (*eaten*, masc, sing). But for the form *entrée*, ambiguous between N and Vpastpart entries, only the participle has a corresponding masculine entry (with form *entré*). In that case, in order to preserve the original part-of-speech ambiguity, *entrée* is not replaced by *entré*. Finite verb forms, when unambiguous with other parts-of-speech, are mapped to second person plural present indicative corresponding forms. This choice was made in order to avoid cre-

[2] This is just an example and not the real Lefff format.

| Dev set | Overall | Overall (-punct) | Unseen (4.8) |
|---|---|---|---|
| POS acc | 97.38 | 96.99 | 91.95 |
| Lemma acc | 98.20 | 97.93 | 92.52 |
| Joint acc | 96.35 | 95.81 | 87.16 |
| **Test set** | **Overall** | **Overall (-punct)** | **Unseen (4.62)** |
| POS acc | 97.68 | 97.34 | 90.52 |
| Lemma acc | 98.36 | 98.12 | 91.54 |
| Joint acc | 96.74 | 96.26 | 85.28 |

Table 1: MORFETTE performance on the FTB-UC dev and test sets (with and without punctuation)

ating ambiguity: the second person plural forms end with a very typical *-ez* suffix, and the resulting form is very unlikely ambiguous. For the first token of a sentence, if it is unknown in the lexicon, the algorithm tries to desinflect the corresponding lowercase form.

This desinflection process reduces the number of distinct tokens in the FTB-UC training set from 24110 to 18052.

### 4.3 Part-of-speech tagging and lemmatization

In order to assign morphological tags and lemmas to words we use a variation of the MORFETTE model described in (Chrupała et al., 2008). It is a sequence labeling model which combines the predictions of two classification models (one for morphological tagging and one for lemmatization) at decoding time, using a beam search.
While (Chrupała et al., 2008) use Maximum Entropy training to learn $P_M$ and $P_L$, we use the MORFETTE models described in (Seddah et al., 2010), that are trained using the Averaged Sequence Perceptron algorithm (Freund and Schapire, 1999). The two classification models incorporate additional features calculated using the *Lefff* lexicon.

Table 1 shows detailed results on dev set and test set of the FTB-UC, when MORFETTE is trained on the FTB-UC training set. To the best of our knowledge the parts-of-speech tagging performance is state-of-the-art for French[3] and the lemmatization performance has no comparable results.

## 5 Unsupervised clustering

We use the Brown et al. (1992) hard clustering algorithm, which has proven useful for various NLP tasks such as dependency parsing (Koo et al., 2008) and named entity recognition (Liang, 2005). The algorithm to obtain C clusters is as follows: each of the C most frequent tokens of the corpus is assigned its own distinct cluster. For the $(C+1)^{th}$ most frequent token, create a $(C+1)^{th}$ cluster. Then for each pair among the $C+1$ resulting clusters, merge the pair that minimizes the loss in the likelihood of the corpus, according to a bigram language model defined on the clusters. Repeat this operation for the $(C+2)^{th}$ most frequent token, etc. The result is a hard clustering of words in the corpus into $C$ distinct clusters, though the process can be continued to further merge pairs of clusters among the $C$ clusters, ending with a single cluster for the entire vocabulary. A binary tree hierarchy of merges for the $C$ clusters can be obtained by tracing the merging process, with each cluster identified by its path within this binary tree. Clusters can thus be used at various levels of granularity.

## 6 Experiments and results

### 6.1 Clustering

For the Brown clustering algorithm, we used Percy Liang's code[4], run on the *L'Est Républicain* corpus, a 125 million word journalistic corpus, freely available at CNRTL[5]. The corpus was first tokenized and segmented into sentences. For compound words, the 240 most frequent compounds of the FTB-UC were systematically recognized as one token. We tried out the two alternate morphological clustering processes described in section 4 as a preprocessing step before the unsupervised clustering algorithm was run on the *L'Est Républicain* corpus :
(i) word forms were replaced by corresponding desinflected form
(ii) word forms were replaced by a concatenation of the part-of-speech tag and lemma obtained with MORFETTE[6].

[3] A pure MAXENT based tagger is described in (Denis and Sagot, 2009), that also uses the *Lefff*, under the form of features for the known categories of a word in the lexicon. The authors report 97.70% of accuracy and 90.01% for unseen data.

[4] *http://www.eecs.berkeley.edu/ pliang/software*

[5] *http://www.cnrtl.fr/corpus/estrepublicain*

[6] Because these experiments were first run with a version of Morfette that was not yet optimized for lemmatization, we chose to overide the MORFETTE lemma when the *Lefff* lemma is available for a given form and part-of-speech tag pair supplied by Morfette. Morfette's current results (version 0.3.1) in

| Name | Terminal symbols in training set | Vocabulary size in training set | Terminal symbols in dev/test sets |
|---|---|---|---|
| BASELINE | wf | 24110 | wf |
| DFL | Desinflected wf | 18052 | Desinflected wf |
| DFL+CLUST>X | $Cluster_1$(desinflected wf) | 1773 ($X = 200$) | $Cluster_1$(desinflected wf) |
| GOLDCATLEMMA | Gold POS+lemma | 18654 | Gold POS+lemma |
| AUTOCATLEMMA | Gold POS+lemma | 18654 | Automatic POS+lemma |
| GOLDCATLEMMA+CLUST>X | $Cluster_2$(gold POS+lemma) | 1298 ($X = 200$) | $Cluster_2$(gold POS+lemma) |
| AUTOCATLEMMA+CLUST>X | $Cluster_2$(gold POS+lemma) | 1298 ($X = 200$) | $Cluster_2$(automatic POS+lemma) |

Table 2: Types of terminal symbols used for training and parsing

In the first case we obtain clusters of desinflected forms, whereas in the second case we obtain clusters of tag+lemma pairs. Note that lemmas alone could be used, but as noted earlier, important syntactic information would be lost, particularly for verb mood. We did try using clusters of lemmas, coupled with a few suffixes to record the verb mood, but this resulted in more or less the same performance as clusters of tag+lemma pairs.

### 6.2 Berkeley parser settings

For BKY we used Slav Petrov's code, adapted for French by Crabbé and Candito (2008) by modifying the suffixes used to classify unknown words. We use the partition between training, development and test sets introduced in section 2. Note though that the BKY algorithm itself uses two sets of sentences at training: a learning set and a smaller validation set for tuning model hyperparameters. In all experiments in this paper, we used 2% of the training set as as a validation set, and 98% as a learning set. This differs from (Candito and Crabbé, 2009), where the dev set was used as a validation set.

### 6.3 Experiments

We then tested several settings differing only in the terminal symbols used in the training set, and in the dev and test sets. We list these settings in table 2. For the settings involving unsupervised linear clustering:

**DFL+CLUST>X**: Each desinflected form *df* is replaced by $Cluster_1(df)$ : if *df* occurred more than X times in the *L'Est Républicain* corpus, it is replaced by its cluster id, otherwise, a special cluster UNKC is used. Further, a _c suffix is added if the desinflected form starts with a capital letter, and additional features are appended, capturing whether the form is all digits, ends with *ant*, or *r*, or *ez* (cf. this is the ending of the desinflected forms of unambiguous finite verbs). (Candito and Crabbé, 2009) showed that these additional features are needed because clusters are noisy: linear context clustering sometimes groups together items that belong to different parts-of-speech.

**GOLDCATLEMMA+CLUST>X**: The terminal form used is the gold part-of-speech concatenated to the cluster id of the gold POS+lemma, or UNKC if that pair did not occur more than X times in the *L'Est Républicain* corpus.

**AUTOCATLEMMA+CLUST>X**: For the training set, the same setting as GOLDCATLEMMA+CLUST>X is used. But for the dev and test sets, predicted parts-of-speech and lemmas are used, as output by the MORFETTE tagger/lemmatizer: the terminal form is the predicted part-of-speech concatenated with the cluster id of the predicted POS+lemma, or UNKC if that pair was not frequent enough.

For the CLUST>X experiments, we report results with $X = 200$. We have found empirically that varying $X$ between 20 and 700 has very little effect on performance gains, both for clustering of desinflected forms and clustering of tag+lemma pairs. Also, all results are with a maximum number of clusters set to 1000, and we found that limiting the number of clusters (by taking only a prefix of the cluster bit string) degrades results.

### 6.4 Evaluation metrics

We evaluate parsing performance using labeled F-Measure (combining labeled precision and labeled

lemmatization renders this step obsolete.

| **DEV SET** | | | | |
|---|---|---|---|---|
| **TERMINAL SYMBOLS** | $F_1$<40 | $F_1$ | UAS | Tagging Acc. |
| BASELINE | 86.06 | **83.81** | **89.23** | 96.44 |
| DFL | 86.65 | 84.67 (+0.86) | 89.86 | 96.52 |
| DFL+CLUST>200 | 87.57 | **85.53** (+1.72) | **90.68** | 96.47 |
| AUTOCATLEMMA | 86.77 | 84.52 (+0.71) | 89.97 | 96.25 |
| AUTOCATLEMMA+CLUST>200 | 87.53 | **85.19** (+1.38) | **90.39** | 96.78 |
| GOLDCATLEMMA | 87.74 | 85.53 (+1.72) | 91.42 | 98.49 |
| GOLDCATLEMMA+CLUST>200 | 88.83 | 86.52 (+2.71) | 92.11 | 99.46 |

| **TEST SET** | | | | |
|---|---|---|---|---|
| **TERMINAL SYMBOLS** | $F_1$<40 | $F_1$ | UAS | Tagging Acc. |
| BASELINE | 86.16 | **84.10** | **89.57** | 96.97 |
| DFL | 87.13 | 85.07 (+0.93) | 90.45 | 97.08 |
| DFL+CLUST>200 | 88.22 | **86.21** (+2.11) | **90.96** | 96.98 |
| AUTOCATLEMMA | 86.85 | 84.83 (+0.73) | 90.30 | 96.58 |
| AUTOCATLEMMA+CLUST>200 | 87.99 | **86.20** (+2.10) | **91.22** | 97.11 |
| GOLDCATLEMMA | 88.16 | 85.90 (+1.80) | 91.52 | 98.54 |
| GOLDCATLEMMA+CLUST>200 | 89.93 | 87.80 (+3.70) | 92.83 | 99.41 |

Table 3: Parsing performance on the dev set/test set when training and parsing make use of clustered terminal symbols. $F_1$<40 is the F-Measure combining labeled precision and labeled recall for sentences of less than 40 words. All other metrics are for all sentences of the dev set/test set. UAS = Unlabeled attachement score of converted constituency trees into surface dependency trees. All metrics ignore punctuation tokens.

recall) both for sentences of less than 40 words, and for all sentences[7]. We also use the unlabeled attachment score (UAS), obtained when converting the constituency trees output by the BKY parsers into surface dependency trees, using the conversion procedure and software of (Candito et al., 2010)[8]. Punctuation tokens are ignored in all metrics.

## 7 Discussion

Results are shown in table 3. Our hope was that using lemmatization would improve overall accuracy of unsupervised clustering, hence leading to better parsing performance. However, results using both methods are comparable.

Table 3 shows that both morphological clustering techniques (DFL and AUTOCATLEMMA) slightly improve performance (+0.97 and +0.73 $F_1$ over the baseline for the test set)[9]. In the case of AUTOCATLEMMA, morphological ambiguity is totally absent in training set: each terminal symbol is the gold POS+lemma pair, and hence appears with a unique part-of-speech in the whole training set. But at parsing time, the terminal symbols are the POS+lemma pairs predicted by MORFETTE, which are wrong for approximately 3% of the tokens. So when comparing the impact on parsing of the two morphological clustering techniques, it seems that the advantage of lemmatization (a sounder morphological clustering compared to the desinflection process) is counterbalanced by tagging errors that lead to wrong POS+lemma pairs. Indeed, it can be verified that

[7] Note that often for statistical constituent parsing results are given for sentences of less than 40 words, whereas for dependency parsing, there is no such limitation. The experiment DFL and DFL+CLUST>200 are reproduced from the previous work (Candito and Crabbé, 2009). More precisely, this previous work reports $F_1 = 88.29$ on the test set, but for sentences $\leq 40$ words, for a DFL+CLUST>20 experiment, and as previously mentioned, the dev set was used as validation set for the BKY algorithm. We report now $F_1 = 88.22$ for the same less-than-40-words sentences, leaving dev set unused at training time.

[8] The conversion uses head propagation rules to find the head on the right-hand side of the CFG rules, first proposed for English in (Magerman, 1995). Hence the process is highly sensitive to part-of-speech tags.

[9] We have computed p-values for pairs of results, using Dan Bikel's statistical significance tester for evalb output (http://www.cis.upenn.edu/ dbikel/software.html). All experiments have a p-value $< 0.05$ both for recall and precision when compared to the baseline. The differences between DFL and AUTOCATLEMMA, and between DFL+CLUST>200 and AUTOCATLEMMA+CLUST>200 are not statistically significant ($p - value > 0.2$). The gain obtained by adding the unsupervised clustering is clearly significant ($p - value > 0.005$), both when comparing AUTOCATLEMMA and AUTOCATLEMMA+CLUST>200, and DFL and DFL+CLUST>200.

| | | BASELINE | | DFL+CLUST>200 | | AUTOCATLEMMA+CLUST>200 | |
|---|---|---|---|---|---|---|---|
| **FREQUENCY RANGE** in original training set | #tokens in dev set | UAS | Tagging | UAS | Tagging | UAS | Tagging |
| any | 31733 (100%) | 89.23 | 96.43 | 90.68 | 96.45 | 90.39 | 96.78 |
| 0 (original unseen) | 1892 (5.96%) | 84.78 | 82.56 | 88.79 | 89.22 | 88.64 | 91.17 |
| $0 < x \leq 5$ | 3376 (10.64%) | 86.49 | 94.52 | 88.68 | 93.13 | 88.33 | 95.41 |
| $5 < x \leq 10$ | 1906 (6.01%) | 90.35 | 96.59 | 91.50 | 95.02 | 91.55 | 96.12 |
| $10 < x \leq 20$ | 2248 (7.08%) | 89.55 | 96.71 | 91.37 | 95.42 | 90.57 | 95.91 |
| $20 < x \leq 50$ | 3395 (10.70%) | 91.87 | 96.35 | 92.40 | 95.96 | 91.72 | 95.94 |
| $x \geq 50$ | 18916 (59.61%) | 89.53 | 98.12 | 90.75 (+1.22) | 98.12 | 90.56 (+1.03) | 97.91 |

Table 4: Tagging accuracy and UAS scores for words in the dev set, grouped by ranges of frequencies in the **original** training set.

when parsing the gold POS+lemma pairs (the non realistic GOLDCATLEMMA setting[10]), performance is greatly improved ($+1.80$ $F_1$ over the baseline).

Replacing morphological clusters by their corresponding unsupervised clusters leads to a further improvement, both for $F_1$ score and for UAS. But here again, using desinflection or tagging+lemmatisation leads to more or less the same improvement. But while the former method is unlikely improvable, the latter method might reveal more effective if the performance of the tagging/lemmatisation phase improves. The GOLDCATLEMMA+CLUST>200 experiment gives the upper bound performance : it leads to a $+3.70 F_1$ increase over the baseline, for the test set. In that case, the terminal symbols are made of the perfect POS plus the cluster of the perfect POS+lemma pair. Very few such terminal symbols are unseen in training set, and all are unambiguous with respect to part-of-speech (hence the 99.46% tagging accuracy).

In order to better understand the causes of improvement, we have broken down the tagging accuracy scores and the UAS scores according to various ranges of word frequencies. For word forms in the dev set that occur x times *in the original training set*, for x in a certain range, we look at how many are correctly tagged by the parsers, and how many receive the correct head when constituents are converted into surface dependencies.

The results are shown in table 4. Unseen words and rare words are much better handled (about $+4$ points for UAS for unseen words, and $+2$ points for forms appearing less than 5 times). This is simply obtained because the majority of original rare or unknowns are replaced by terminal symbols (either a cluster id or the UNKC token, plus suffixes) that are shared by many forms in the treebank, leading to higher counts. This can be verified by analyzing tagging accuracies and UAS scores for various frequency ranges for the *modified* terminal symbols : the symbols that replace the word forms in the training set for DFL+CLUST>X and AUTOCATLEMMA+CLUST>X experiments. This is shown in table 5. It can be seen that the majority of the tokens have now high-frequency. For instance for the DFL+CLUST>200 experiment, there are only 0.09% terminal symbols in the dev set that are unseen in training set, and 92.62% appear more than 50 times. The parsers do not perform very well on low-frequency modified terminal symbols, but they are so few that it has little impact on the overall performance.

Hence, in our parsing word clusters experiments, there are almost no real unseen anymore, there are only terminal symbols made of a cluster id or UNKC (plus suffixes). More precisely, for instance about 30% of the original unseen in the dev set, are replaced by a UNKC* symbol, which means that 70% are replaced by a cluster-based symbol and are thus "connected" to the known vocabulary.

Interestingly, the improvement in performance is also evident for words with high frequency in the original treebank: for the forms appearing more than 50 times in the original training set, the UAS increases by $+1.22$ with DFL+CLUST>200 and $+1.03$ with AUTOCATLEMMA+CLUST>200 (table 4). This means that despite any imperfections in the

[10]The GOLDCATLEMMA experiment leads to high tagging accuracy, though not perfect, because of POS+lemma pairs present in dev/test sets but missing in the training set.

| | DFL+CLUST>200 | | | AUTOCATLEMMA+CLUST>200 | | |
|---|---|---|---|---|---|---|
| **FREQUENCY RANGE** in modified training set | percentage of dev set | UAS | Tagging | percentage of dev set | UAS | Tagging |
| any | 100 | 90.68 | 96.45 | 100 | 90.39 | 96.78 |
| 0 (effective unseen) | 0.09 | 86.21 | 58.62 | 0.08 | 84.00 | 40.00 |
| $0 < x \leq 5$ | 0.45 | 88.19 | 86.81 | 0.32 | 70.30 | 70.30 |
| $5 < x \leq 10$ | 0.64 | 90.69 | 91.18 | 0.37 | 92.24 | 79.31 |
| $10 < x \leq 20$ | 1.31 | 90.12 | 94.22 | 0.87 | 89.53 | 88.09 |
| $20 < x \leq 50$ | 4.88 | 88.64 | 92.19 | 3.30 | 86.44 | 92.65 |
| $x \geq 50$ | 92.62 | 90.81 | 96.83 | 95.07 | 90.60 | 97.21 |
| replaced by UNKC* | 8.58 | 90.64 | 88.10 | 8.73 | 89.67 | 90.07 |

Table 5: Tagging accuracy and UAS scores for modified terminal symbols in the dev set, grouped by ranges of frequencies in the modified training sets. The "replaced by UNKC*" line corresponds to the case where the desinflected form or the POS+lemma pair does not appear more than 200 times in the *L'est Républicain* corpus.

unsupervised Brown clustering, which uses very local information, the higher counts lead to better estimates even for high-frequency words.

## 8 Related work

We have already cited the previous work of Koo et al. (2008) which has directly inspired ours. Sagae and Gordon (2009) explores the use of syntactic clustering to improve transition-based dependency parsing for English : using an available 30 million word corpus parsed with a constituency parser, words are represented as vectors of paths within the obtained constituency parses. Words are then clustered using a similarity metric between vectors of syntactic paths. The clusters are used as features to help a transition-based dependency parser. Note that the word representation for clustering is more complex (paths in parse trees), thus these authors have to cluster a smaller vocabulary : the top 5000 most frequent words are clustered.

Agirre et al. (2008) use the same approach of replacing words by more general symbols, but these symbols are semantic classes. They test various methods to assign semantic classes (gold semantic class, most-frequent sense in sense-tagged data, or a fully unsupervised sense tagger). Though the method is very appealing, the reported improvement in parsing is rather small, especially for the fully unsupervised method.

Versley and Rehbein (2009) cluster words according to linear context features, and use the clusters as features to boost discriminative German parsing for unknown words. Another approach to augment the known vocabulary for a generative probabilistic parser is the one pursued in (Goldberg et al., 2009). Within a plain PCFG, the lexical probabilities for words that are rare or absent in the treebank are taken from an external lexical probability distribution, estimated using a lexicon and the Baulm-Welch training of an HMM tagger. This is proven useful to better parse Hebrew.

## 9 Conclusion and future work

We have provided a thorough study of the results of parsing word clusters for French. We showed that the clustering improves performance both for unseen and rare words and for medium- to high-frequency words. For French, preprocessing words with desinflection or with tagging+lemmatisation lead to comparable results. However, the method using POS tagging is expected to yield higher performance should a better tagger become available in the future.

One avenue for further improvement is to use a clustering technique that makes explicit use of syntactic or semantic similarity, instead of simple linear context sharing. While the Brown clustering algorithm can be run on large raw corpus, it uses extremely local information (bigrams). The resulting clusters are thus necessarily noisy, and semantic or syntactic clustering would certainly be more appropriate. Since resource-based semantic clustering is difficult for French due to a lack of resources, clustering based on distributional syntactic similarity is a worthwhile technique to investigate in the future.

## Acknowledgments

This work was supported by the ANR Sequoia (ANR-08-EMER-013). We are grateful to our anonymous reviewers for their comments and to Grzegorz Chrupala for helping us with Morfette.

## References

Anne Abeillé, Lionel Clément, and François Toussenel, 2003. *Building a Treebank for French*. Kluwer, Dordrecht.

Eneko Agirre, Timothy Baldwin, and David Martinez. 2008. Improving parsing and PP attachment performance with sense information. In *Proceedings of ACL-08: HLT*, pages 317–325, Columbus, Ohio, June. Association for Computational Linguistics.

Peter F. Brown, Vincent J. Della, Peter V. Desouza, Jennifer C. Lai, and Robert L. Mercer. 1992. Class-based n-gram models of natural language. *Computational linguistics*, 18(4):467–479.

Marie Candito and Benoît Crabbé. 2009. Improving generative statistical parsing with semi-supervised word clustering. In *Proceedings of the 11th International Conference on Parsing Technologies (IWPT'09)*, pages 138–141, Paris, France, October. Association for Computational Linguistics.

Marie Candito, Benoit Crabbé, and Pascal Denis. 2010. Statistical french dependency parsing : Treebank conversion and first results. In *Proceedings of LREC'2010*, Valletta, Malta.

Grzegorz Chrupała, Georgiana Dinu, and Josef van Genabith. 2008. Learning morphology with morfette. In *In Proceedings of LREC 2008*, Marrakech, Morocco. ELDA/ELRA.

Benoit Crabbé and Marie Candito. 2008. Expériences d'analyse syntaxique statistique du français. In *Actes de la 15ème Conférence sur le Traitement Automatique des Langues Naturelles (TALN'08)*, pages 45–54, Avignon, France.

Pascal Denis and Benoît Sagot. 2009. Coupling an annotated corpus and a morphosyntactic lexicon for state-of-the-art pos tagging with less human effort. In *Proc. of PACLIC*, Hong Kong, China.

Yoav Freund and Robert E. Schapire. 1999. Large margin classification using the perceptron algorithm. *Machine learning*, 37(3):277–296.

Yoav Goldberg, Reut Tsarfaty, Meni Adler, and Michael Elhadad. 2009. Enhancing unlexicalized parsing performance using a wide coverage lexicon, fuzzy tag-set mapping, and EM-HMM-based lexical probabilities. In *Proc. of EACL-09*, pages 327–335, Athens, Greece.

Dan Klein and Christopher D. Manning. 2003. Accurate unlexicalized parsing. In *Proceedings of the 41st Meeting of the Association for Computational Linguistics*.

Terry Koo, Xavier Carreras, and Michael Collins. 2008. Simple semi-supervised dependency parsing. In *Proceedings of ACL-08*, pages 595–603, Columbus, USA.

Percy Liang. 2005. Semi-supervised learning for natural language. In *MIT Master's thesis*, Cambridge, USA.

D.M. Magerman. 1995. Statistical decision-tree models for parsing. In *Proc. of ACL'95*, pages 276–283, Morristown, NJ, USA.

Takuya Matsuzaki, Yusuke Miyao, and Jun'ichi Tsujii. 2005. Probabilistic cfg with latent annotations. In *Proceedings of the 43rd Annual Meeting of the Association for Computational Linguistics (ACL)*, pages 75–82.

Slav Petrov, Leon Barrett, Romain Thibaux, and Dan Klein. 2006. Learning accurate, compact, and interpretable tree annotation. In *Proc. of ACL-06*, Sydney, Australia.

Kenji Sagae and Andrew S. Gordon. 2009. Clustering words by syntactic similarity improves dependency parsing of predicate-argument structures. In *Proceedings of the 11th International Conference on Parsing Technologies (IWPT'09)*, pages 192–201, Paris, France, October. Association for Computational Linguistics.

Benoît Sagot. 2010. The Le*fff*, a freely available and large-coverage morphological and syntactic lexicon for french. In *Proceedings of LREC'10*, Valetta, Malta.

Djamé Seddah, Marie Candito, and Benoit Crabbé. 2009. Cross parser evaluation and tagset variation: A French Treebank study. In *Proceedings of the 11th Internation Conference on Parsing Technologies (IWPT'09)*, pages 150–161, Paris, France, October. Association for Computational Linguistics.

Djamé Seddah, Grzegorz Chrupała, Ozlem Cetinoglu, Josef van Genabith, and Marie Candito. 2010. Lemmatization and statistical lexicalized parsing of morphologically-rich languages. In *Proceedings of the NAACL/HLT Workshop on Statistical Parsing of Morphologically Rich Languages (SPMRL 2010)*, Los Angeles, CA.

Yannick Versley and Ines Rehbein. 2009. Scalable discriminative parsing for german. In *Proceedings of the 11th International Conference on Parsing Technologies (IWPT'09)*, pages 134–137, Paris, France, October. Association for Computational Linguistics.

# Lemmatization and Lexicalized Statistical Parsing of Morphologically Rich Languages: the Case of French

**Djamé Seddah**
Alpage Inria & Univ. Paris-Sorbonne
Paris, France

**Grzegorz Chrupała**
Spoken Language System, Saarland Univ.
Saarbrücken, Germany

**Özlem Çetinoğlu** and **Josef van Genabith**
NCLT & CNGL, Dublin City Univ.
Dublin, Ireland

**Marie Candito**
Alpage Inria & Univ. Paris 7
Paris, France

## Abstract

This paper shows that training a lexicalized parser on a lemmatized morphologically-rich treebank such as the French Treebank slightly improves parsing results. We also show that lemmatizing a similar in size subset of the English Penn Treebank has almost no effect on parsing performance with gold lemmas and leads to a small drop of performance when automatically assigned lemmas and POS tags are used. This highlights two facts: (i) lemmatization helps to reduce lexicon data-sparseness issues for French, (ii) it also makes the parsing process sensitive to correct assignment of POS tags to unknown words.

## 1 Introduction

Large parse-annotated corpora have led to an explosion of interest in statistical parsing methods, including the development of highly successful models for parsing English using the Wall Street Journal Penn Treebank (PTB, (Marcus et al., 1994)). Over the last 10 years, parsing performance on the PTB has hit a performance plateau of 90-92% f-score using the PARSEVAL evaluation metric. When adapted to other language/treebank pairs (such as German, Hebrew, Arabic, Italian or French), to date these models have performed much worse.

A number of arguments have been advanced to explain this performance gap, including limited amounts of training data, differences in treebank annotation schemes, inadequacies of evaluation metrics, linguistic factors such as the degree of word order variation, the amount of morphological information available to the parser as well as the effects of syncretism prevalent in many morphologically rich languages.

Even though none of these arguments in isolation can account for the systematic performance gap, a pattern is beginning to emerge: morphologically rich languages tend to be susceptible to parsing performance degradation.

Except for a residual clitic case system, French does not have explicit case marking, yet its morphology is considerably richer than that of English, and French is therefore a candidate to serve as an instance of a morphologically rich language (MRL) that requires specific treatment to achieve reasonable parsing performance.

Interestingly, French also exhibits a limited amount of word order variation occurring at different syntactic levels including (i) the word level (e.g. pre or post nominal adjective, pre or post verbal adverbs); (ii) phrase level (e.g. possible alternations between post verbal NPs and PPs). In order to avoid discontinuous constituents as well as traces and coindexations, treebanks for this language, such as the French Treebank (FTB, (Abeillé et al., 2003)) or the Modified French Treebank (MFT, (Schluter and van Genabith, 2007)), propose a flat annotation scheme with a non-configurational distinction between adjunct and arguments.

Finally, the extraction of treebank grammars from the French treebanks, which contain less than a third of the annotated data as compared to PTB, is subject to many data sparseness issues that contribute to a performance ceiling, preventing the statistical parsing of French to reach the same level of performance as for PTB-trained parsers (Candito et al., 2009).

This data sparseness bottleneck can be summarized as a problem of optimizing a parsing model along two axes: the grammar and the lexicon. In both cases, the goal is either to get a more compact grammar at the rule level or to obtain a consider-



*Proceedings of the NAACL HLT 2010 First Workshop on Statistical Parsing of Morphologically-Rich Languages*, pages 85–93,
Los Angeles, California, June 2010. ©2010 Association for Computational Linguistics

ably less sparse lexicon. So far, both approaches have been tested for French using different means and with different degrees of success.

To obtain better grammars, Schluter and van Genabith (2007) extracted a subset of an early release of the FTB and carried out extensive restructuring, extensions and corrections (referred to as the Modified French Treebank MFT) to support grammar acquisition for PCFG-based LFG Parsing (Cahill et al., 2004) while Crabbé and Candito (2008) slightly modified the original FTB POS tagset to optimize the grammar with latent annotations extracted by the Berkeley parser (BKY, (Petrov et al., 2006)).

Moreover, research oriented towards adapting more complex parsing models to French showed that lexicalized models such as Collins' model 2 (Collins, 1999) can be tuned to cope effectively with the flatness of the annotation scheme in the FTB, with the Charniak model (Charniak, 2000) performing particularly well, but outperformed by the BKY parser on French data (Seddah et al., 2009).

Focusing on the lexicon, experiments have been carried out to study the impact of different forms of word clustering on the BKY parser trained on the FTB. Candito et al. (2009) showed that using gold lemmatization provides a significant increase in performance. Obviously, less sparse lexical data which retains critical pieces of information can only help a model to perform better. This was shown in (Candito and Crabbé, 2009) where distributional word clusters were acquired from a 125 million words corpus and combined with inflectional suffixes extracted from the training data. Training the BKY parser with 1000 clusters boosts its performance to the current state-of-the-art with a PARSEVAL $F_1$ score of 88.28% (baseline was 86.29 %).

We performed the same experiment using the CHARNIAK parser and recorded only a small improvement (from 84.96% to 85.51%). Given the fact that lexical information is crucial for lexicalized parsers in the form of bilexical dependencies, this result raises the question whether this kind of clustering is in fact too drastic for lexicalized parsers as it may give rise to head-to-head dependencies which are too coarse. To answer this question, in this paper we explore the impact of lemmatization, as a (rather limited) constrained form of clustering, on a state-of-the-art lexicalized parser (CHARNIAK). In order to evaluate the influence of lemmatization on this parser (which is known to be highly tuned for English) we carry out experiments on both the FTB and on a lemmatized version of the PTB. We used gold lemmatization when available and an automatic statistical morphological analyzer (Chrupała, 2010) to provide more realistic parsing results.
The idea is to verify whether lemmatization will help to reduce data sparseness issues due to the French rich morphology and to see if this process, when applied to English will harm the performance of a parser optimized for the limited morphology of English.
Our results show that the key issue is the way unseen tokens (lemmas or words) are handled by the CHARNIAK parser. Indeed, using pure lemma is equally suboptimal for both languages. On the other hand, feeding the parser with both lemma and part-of-speech slightly enhances parsing performance for French.

We first describe our data sets in Section 2, introduce our data driven morphology process in Section 3, then present experiments in Section 4. We discuss our results in Section 5 and compare them with related research in Section 6 before concluding and outlining further research.

## 2 Corpus

THE FRENCH TREEBANK is the first annotated and manually corrected treebank for French. The data is annotated with labeled constituent trees augmented with morphological annotations and functional annotations of verbal dependents. Its key properties, compared with the PTB, are the following :

*Size:* The FTB consists of 350,931 tokens and 12,351 sentences, that is less than a third of the size of PTB. The average length of a sentence is 28.41 tokens. By contrast, the average sentence length in the Wall Street Journal section of the PTB is 25.4 tokens.

*A Flat Annotation Scheme:* Both the FTB and the PTB are annotated with constituent trees. However, the annotation scheme is flatter in the FTB. For instance, there are no VPs for finite verbs and only one sentential level for clauses or sentences whether or not they are introduced by a complementizer. Only the *verbal nucleus* (VN) is annotated and comprises the verb, its clitics, auxiliaries, adverbs and negation.

*Inflection:* French morphology is richer than English and leads to increased data sparseness for statistical parsing. There are 24,098 lexical types in the FTB, with an average of 16 tokens occurring for each type.

*Compounds:* Compounds are explicitly annotated and very frequent in the treebank: 14.52% of tokens are part of a compound. Following Candito and Crabbé (2009), we use a variation of the treebank where compounds with regular syntactic patterns have been expanded. We refer to this instance as FTB-UC.

*Lemmatization:* Lemmas are included in the treebank's morphological annotations and denote an abstraction over a group of inflected forms. As there is no distinction between semantically ambiguous lexemes at the word form level, polysemic homographs with common inflections are associated with the same lemma (Abeillé et al., 2003). Thus, except for some very rare cases, a pair consisting of a word form and its part-of-speech unambiguously maps to the same lemma.

### 2.1 Lemmatizing the Penn Treebank

Unlike the FTB, the PTB does not have gold lemmas provided within the treebank. We use the finite state morphological analyzer which comes within the English ParGram Grammar (Butt et al., 1999) for lemmatization. For open class words (nouns, verbs, adjectives, adverbs) the word form is sent to the morphological analyzer. The English ParGram morphological analyzer outputs all possible analyses of the word form. The associated gold POS from the PTB is used to disambiguate the result. The same process is applied to closed class words where the word form is different from the lemma (e.g. 'll for will). For the remaining parts of speech the word form is assigned to the lemma.

Since gold lemmas are not available for the PTB, a large-scale automatic evaluation of the lemmatizer is not possible. Instead, we conducted two manual evaluations. First, we randomly extracted 5 samples of 200 <POS,word> pairs from Section 23 of the PTB. Each data set is fed into the lemmatization script, and the output is manually checked. For the 5x200 <POS,word> sets the number of incorrect lemmas is 1, 3, 2, 0, and 2. The variance is small indicating that the results are fairly stable. For the second evaluation, we extracted each unseen word from Section 23 and manually checked the accuracy of the lemmatization. Of the total of 1802 unseen words, 394 words are associated with an incorrect lemma (331 unique) and only 8 with an incorrect <POS,lemma> pair (5 unique). For an overall unseen word percentage of 3.22%, the lemma accuracy is 77.70%. If we assume that all seen words are correctly lemmatized, overall accuracy would be 99.28%.

### 2.2 Treebank properties

In order to evaluate the influence of lemmatization on comparable corpora, we extracted a random subset of the PTB with properties comparable to the FTB-UC (mainly with respect to CFG size and number of tokens). We call this PTB subset S.PTB. Table 1 presents a summary of some relevant features of those treebanks.

| | FTBUC | S.PTB | PTB |
|---|---|---|---|
| # of tokens | 350,931 | 350,992 | 1,152,305 |
| # of sentences | 12,351 | 13,811 | 45,293 |
| average length | 28,41 | 25.41 | 25.44 |
| CFG size | 607,162 | 638,955 | 2,097,757 |
| # unique CFG rules | 43,413 | 46,783 | 91,027 |
| # unique word forms | 27,130 | 26,536 | 47,678 |
| # unique lemmas | 17,570 | 20,226 | 36,316 |
| ratio words/lemma | 1.544 | 1.311 | 1.312 |

Table 1. French and Penn Treebanks properties

Table 1 shows that the average number of word forms associated with a lemma (i.e. the lemma ratio) is higher in the FTB-UC (1.54 words/lemma) than in the PTB (1.31). Even though the PTB ratio is lower, it is still large enough to suggest that even the limited English morphology should be taken into account when aiming at reducing lexicon sparseness.

Trying to learn French and English morphology in a data driven fashion in order to predict lemma from word forms is the subject of the next section.

## 3 Morphology learning

In order to assign morphological tags and lemmas to words we use the MORFETTE model (Chrupała, 2010), which is a variation of the approach described in (Chrupała et al., 2008).

MORFETTE is a sequence labeling model which combines the predictions of two classification models (one for morphological tagging and one for lemmatization) at decoding time, using beam search.

### 3.1 Overview of the Morfette model

The morphological classes correspond simply to the (fine-grained) POS tags. Lemma classes are edit scripts computed from training data: they specify which string manipulations (such as character deletions and insertions) need to be performed in order to transform the input string (word form) into the corresponding output string (lemma).

The best sequence of lemmas and morphological tags for input sentence $\mathbf{x}$ is defined as:

$$(\hat{\mathbf{l}}, \hat{\mathbf{m}}) = \arg\max_{(\mathbf{l},\mathbf{m})} P(\mathbf{l}, \mathbf{m}|\mathbf{x})$$

The joint probability is decomposed as follows:

$$P(l_0...l_i, m_0...m_i|\mathbf{x}) = P_L(l_i|m_i, \mathbf{x}) P_M(m_i|\mathbf{x}) \times P(m_0...m_{i-1}, l_0...l_{i-1}|\mathbf{x})$$

where $P_L(l_i|m_i, \mathbf{x})$ is the probability of lemma class $l$ at position $i$ according to the lemma classifier, $P_M(m_i|\mathbf{x})$ is the probability of the tag $m$ at position $i$ according to the morphological tag classifier, and $\mathbf{x}$ is the sequence of words to label.

While Chrupała et al. (2008) use Maximum Entropy training to learn $P_M$ and $P_L$, here we learn them using Averaged Perceptron algorithm due to Freund and Schapire (1999). It is a much simpler algorithm which in many scenarios (including ours) performs as well as or better than MaxEnt.

We also use the general Edit Tree instantiation of the edit script as developed in (Chrupała, 2008). We find the longest common substring (LCS) between the form $w$ and the lemma $w'$. The portions of the string in the word form before (prefix) and after (suffix) the LCS need to be modified in some way, while the LCS (stem) stays the same. If there is no LCS, then we simply record that we need to replace $w$ with $w'$ . As for the modifications to the prefix and the suffix, we apply the same procedure recursively: we try to find the LCS between the prefix of $w$ and the prefix of $w'$. If we find one, we recurse; if we do not, we record the replacement; we do the same for the suffix.

### 3.2 Data Set

We trained MORFETTE on the standard splits of the FTB with the first 10% as test set, the next 10% for the development set and the remaining for training (i.e. 1235/1235/9881 sentences). Lemmas and part-of-speech tags are given by the treebank annotation scheme.

As pointed out in section 2.1, PTB's lemmas have been automatically generated by a deterministic process, and only a random subset of them have been manually checked. For the remainder of this paper, we treat them as gold, regardless of the errors induced by our PTB lemmatizer.

The S.PTB follows the same split as the FTB-UC, first 10% for test, next 10% for dev and the last 80% for training (i.e. 1380/1381/11050 sentences).

MORFETTE can optionally use a morphological lexicon to extract features. For French, we used the extended version of *Lefff* (Sagot et al., 2006) and for English, the lexicon used in the Penn XTAG project (Doran et al., 1994). We reduced the granularity of the XTAG tag set, keeping only the bare categories. Both lexicons contain around 225 thousands word form entries.

### 3.3 Performance on French and English

Table 2 presents results of MORFETTE applied to the development and test sets of our treebanks. Part-of-speech tagging performance for French is state-of-the-art on the FTB-UC, with an accuracy of 97.68%, on the FTB-UC test set, only 0.02 points (absolute) below the MaxEnt POS tagger of Denis and Sagot (2009). Comparing MORFETTE's tagging performance for English is a bit more challenging as we only trained on one third of the full PTB and evaluated on approximately one section, whereas results reported in the literature are usually based on training on sections 02-18 and evaluating on either sections 19-21 or 22-24. For this setting, state-of-the-art POS accuracy for PTB tagging is around 97.33%. On our PTB sample, MORFETTE achieves 96.36% for all words and 89.64 for unseen words.
Comparing the lemmatization performance for both languages on the same kind of data is even more difficult as we are not aware of any data driven lemmatizer on the same data. However, with an overall accuracy above 98% for the FTB-UC (91.5% for un-

seen words) and above 99% for the S.PTB (95% for unseen words), lemmatization performs well enough to properly evaluate parsing on lemmatized data.

| | FTBUC | | S.PTB | |
|---|---|---|---|---|
| DEV | All | Unk. (4.8) | All | Unk. (4.67) |
| POS acc | 97.38 | 91.95 | 96.36 | 88.90 |
| Lemma acc | 98.20 | 92.52 | 99.11 | 95.51 |
| Joint acc | 96.35 | 87.16 | 96.26 | 87.05 |
| TEST | All | Unk. (4.62) | All | Unk. (5.04) |
| POS acc | 97.68 | 90.52 | 96.53 | 89.64 |
| Lemma acc | 98.36 | 91.54 | 99.13 | 95.72 |
| Joint acc | 96.74 | 85.28 | 96.45 | 88.49 |

Table 2: POS tagging and lemmatization performance on the FTB and on the S.PTB

## 4 Parsing Experiments

In this section, we present the results of two sets of experiments to evaluate the impact of lemmatization on the lexicalized statistical parsing of two languages, one morphologically rich (French), but with none of its morphological features exploited by the CHARNIAK parser, the other (English) being quite the opposite, with the parser developed mainly for this language and PTB annotated data. We show that lemmatization results in increased performance for French, while doing the same for English penalizes parser performance.

### 4.1 Experimental Protocol

**Data** The data sets described in section 3.2 are used throughout. The version of the CHARNIAK parser (Charniak, 2000) was released in August 2005 and recently adapted to French (Seddah et al., 2009).

**Metrics** We report results on sentences of length less than 40 words, with three evaluation metrics: the classical PARSEVAL Labeled brackets $F_1$ score, POS tagging accuracy (excluding punctuation tags) and the Leaf Ancestor metric (Sampson and Babarczy, 2003) which is believed to be somewhat more neutral with respect to the treebank annotation scheme than PARSEVAL (Rehbein and van Genabith, 2007).

**Treebank tag sets** Our experiments involve the inclusion of POS tags directly in tokens. We briefly describe our treebank tag sets below.

- FTB-UC TAG SET: "CC" This is the tag set developed by (Crabbé and Candito, 2008) (Table 4), known to provide the best parsing performance for French (Seddah et al., 2009). Like in the FTB, preterminals are the main categories, but they are also augmented with a WH flag for A, ADV, PRO and with the mood for verbs (there are 6 moods). No information is propagated to non-terminal symbols.

ADJ ADJWH ADV ADVWH CC CLO CLR CLS CS DET DETWH ET I NC NPP P P+D P+PRO PONCT PREF PRO PROREL PROWH V VIMP VINF VPP VPR VS

Table 4: CC tag set

- THE PTB TAG SET This tag set is described at length in (Marcus et al., 1994) and contains supplementary morphological information (e.g. number) over and above what is represented in the CC tag set for French. Note that some information is marked at the morphological level in English (superlative, "the greatest (JJS)") and not in French (" le plus (ADV) grand (ADJ)").

CC CD DT EX FW IN JJ JJR JJS LS MD NN NNP NNPS NNS PDT POS PRP PRP$ RB RBR RBS RP SYM TO UH VB VBD VBG VBN VBP VBZ WDT WP WP$ WRB

Table 5: PTB tag set

### 4.2 Cross token variation and parsing impact

From the source treebanks, we produce 5 versions of tokens: tokens are generated as either simple POS tag, gold lemma, gold lemma+gold POS, word form, and word form+gold POS. The token versions successively add more morphological information. Parsing results are presented in Table 3.

**Varying the token form** The results show that having no lexical information at all (POS-only) results in a small drop of PARSEVAL performance for French compared to parsing lemmas, while the corresponding Leaf Ancestor score is actually higher. For English having no lexical information at all leads to a drop of 2 points in PARSEVAL. The *so-called* impoverished morphology of English appears to bring enough morphological information to raise tagging performance to 95.92% (from POS-only to word-only).

For French the corresponding gain is only 2 points of POS tagging accuracy. Moreover, between these

| | French Treebank UC | | | Sampled Penn Treebank | | |
|---|---|---|---|---|---|---|
| Tokens | $F_1$ score | Pos acc. | leaf-Anc. | $F_1$ score | Pos acc. | leaf-Anc. |
| POS-only | 84.48 | 100 | 93.97 | 85.62 | 100 | 94.02 |
| lemma-only | 84.77 | 94.23 | 93.76 | 87.69 | 89.22 | 94.92 |
| word-only | 84.96 | 96.26 | 94.08 | 88.64 | 95.92 | 95.10 |
| **lemma-POS** | **86.83**$^{(1)}$ | **98.79** | **94.65** | **89.59**$^{(3)}$ | **99.97** | **95.41** |
| word-POS | 86.13$^{(2)}$ | 98.4 | 94.46 | 89.53$^{(4)}$ | 99.96 | 95.38 |

Table 3: Parsing performance on the FTB-UC and the S.PTB with tokens variations using gold lemmas and gold POS. *( p-value* (1) *&* (2) $= 0.007$*; p-value* (3) *&* (4) $= 0.146$*. All other configurations are statistically significant.)*

two tokens variations, POS-only and word-only, parsing results gain only half a point in PARSEVAL and almost nothing in leaf Ancestor.

Thus, it seems that encoding more morphology (i.e. including word forms) in the tokens does not lead to much improvement for parsing French as opposed to English. The reduction in data sparseness due to the use of lemmas alone is thus not sufficient to counterbalance the lack of morphological information.

However, the large gap between POS tagging accuracy seen between lemma-only and word-only for English indicates that the parser makes use of this information to provide at least reasonable POS guesses.

For French, only 0.2 points are gained for PARSEVAL results between lemma-only to word-only, while POS accuracy benefits a bit more from including richer morphological information.

This raises the question whether the FTB-UC provides enough data to make its richer morphology informative enough for a parsing model.

**Suffixing tokens with POS tags** It is only when gold POS are added to the lemmas that one can see the advantage of a reduced lexicon for French. Indeed, performance peaks for this setting (lemma-POS). The situation is not as clear for English, where performance is almost identical when gold POS are added to lemmas or words. POS Tagging is nearly perfect, thus a performance ceiling is reached. The very small differences between those two configurations (most noticeable with the Leaf Ancestor score of 95.41 vs. 95.38) indicates that the reduced lemma lexicon is actually of some limited use but its impact is negligible compared to perfect tagging.

While the lemma+POS setting clearly boosts performance for parsing the FTB, the situation is less clear for English. Indeed, the lemma+POS and the word+POS gold variations give almost the same results. The fact that the POS tagging accuracy is close to 100% in this mode shows that the key parameter for optimum parsing performance in this experiment is the ability to guess POS for unknown words well.

In fact, the CHARNIAK parser uses a two letter suffix context for its tagging model, and when gold POS are suffixed to any type of token (being lemma or word form), the PTB POS tagset is used as a substitute for lack of morphology.

It should also be noted that the FTB-UC tag set does include some discriminative features (such as PART, INF and so on) but those are expressed by more than two letters, and therefore a two letter suffix tag cannot really be useful to discriminate a richer morphology. For example, in the PTB, the suffix BZ, as in VBZ, always refers to a verb, whereas the FTB pos tag suffix PP, as in NPP (Proper Noun) is also found in POS labels such as VPP (past participle verb).

### 4.3 Realistic Setup: Using Morfette to help parsing

Having shown that parsing French benefits from a reduced lexicon is not enough as results imply that a key factor is POS tag guessing. We therefore test our hypothesis in a more realistic set up. We use MORFETTE to lemmatize and tag raw words (instead of the "gold" lemma-based approach described above), and the resulting corpus is then parsed using the corresponding training set.

In order to be consistent with PARSEVAL POS evaluation, which does not take punctuation POS into account, we provide a summary of MORFETTE's performance for such a configuration in (Table 6).

Results shown in Table 7 confirm our initial hy-

| | POS acc | Lemma acc | Joint acc |
|---|---|---|---|
| FTB-UC | 97.34 | 98.12 | 96.26 |
| S.PTB | 96.15 | 99.04 | 96.07 |

Table 6: PARSEVAL Pos tagging accuracy of treebanks test set

pothesis for French. Indeed, parsing performance peaks with a setup involving automatically generated lemma and POS pairs, even though the difference with raw words+auto POS is not statistically significant for the PARSEVAL $F_1$ metric[1]. Note that parser POS accuracy does not follow this pattern. It is unclear exactly why this is the case. We speculate that the parser is helped by the reduced lexicon but that performance suffers when a <lemma,POS> pair has been incorrectly assigned by MORFETTE, leading to an increase in unseen tokens. This is confirmed by parsing the same lemma but with gold POS. In that case, parsing performance does not suffer too much from CHARNIAK's POS guessing on unseen data.

For the S.PTB, results clearly show that both the automatic <lemma,POS> and <word,POS> configurations lead to very similar results (yet statistically significant with a $F_1$ $p$-value = 0.027); having the same POS accuracy indicates that most of the work is done at the level of POS guessing for unseen tokens, and in this respect the CHARNIAK parser clearly takes advantage of the information included in the PTB tag set.

| | $F_1$ score | Pos acc. | leaf-Anc. |
|---|---|---|---|
| S.PTB | | | |
| auto lemma only | 87.11 | 89.82 | 94.71 |
| auto lemma+auto pos (a) | 88.15 | 96.21 | 94.85 |
| **word +auto pos** (b) | **88.28** | **96.21** | **94.88** |
| *$F_1$ p-value: (a) and (b)* | *0.027* | | |
| *auto lemma+gold pos* | *89.51* | *99.96* | *95,36* |
| FTB-UC | | | |
| auto lemma only | 83.92 | 92.98 | 93.53 |
| **auto lemma+auto pos** (c) | **85.06** | 96.04 | **94.14** |
| word +auto pos (d) | 84.99 | **96.47** | 94.09 |
| *$F_1$ p-value: (c) and (d)* | *0.247* | | |
| *auto lemma+gold pos* | *86.39* | *97.35* | *94.68* |

Table 7: Realistic evaluation of parsing performance

[1]Statistical significance is computed using Dan Bikel's stratified shuffling implementation: www.cis.upenn.edu/~dbikel/software.html.

## 5 Discussion

When we started this work, we wanted to explore the benefit of lemmatization as a means to reduce data sparseness issues underlying statistical lexicalized parsing of small treebanks for morphologically rich languages, such as the FTB. We showed that the expected benefit of lemmatization, a less sparse lexicon, was in fact hidden by the absence of inflectional information, as required by e.g. the CHARNIAK parser to provide good POS guesses for unseen words. Even the inclusion of POS tags generated by a state-of-the-art tagger (MORFETTE) did not lead to much improvement compared to a parser run in a regular bare word set up.

An unexpected effect is that the POS accuracy of the parser trained on the French data does not reach the same level of performance as our tagger (96.47% for <word, auto POS> vs. 97.34% for MORFETTE). Of course, extending the CHARNIAK tagging model to cope with lemmatized input should be enough, because its POS guessing model builds on features such as capitalization, hyphenation and a two-letter suffix (Charniak, 2000). Those features are not present in our current lemmatized input and thus cannot be properly estimated.

CHARNIAK also uses the probability that a given POS is realized by a previously unobserved word. If any part of a <lemma,POS> pair is incorrect, the number of unseen words in the test set would be higher than the one estimated from the training set, which only contained correct lemmas and POS tags in our setting. This would lead to unsatisfying POS accuracy. This inadequate behavior of the unknown word tagging model may be responsible for the POS accuracy result for <auto lemma> (cf. Table 7, lines <auto lemma only> for both treebanks).

We believe that this performance degradation (or in this case the somewhat less than expected improvement in parsing results) calls for the inclusion of all available lexical information in the parsing model. For example, nothing prevents a parsing model to condition the generation of a head upon a lemma, while the probability to generate a POS would depend on both morphological features and (potentially) the supplied POS.

## 6 Related Work

A fair amount of recent research in parsing morphologically rich languages has focused on coping with unknowns words and more generally with the small and limited lexicons acquired from treebanks. For instance, Goldberg et al. (2009) augment the lexicon for a generative parsing model by including lexical probabilities coming from an external lexicon. These are estimated using an HMM tagger with Baum-Welch training. This method leads to a significant increase of parsing performance over previously reported results for Modern Hebrew. Our method is more stratified: external lexical resources are included as features for MORFETTE and therefore are not directly seen by the parser besides generated lemma and POS.

For parsing German, Versley and Rehbein (2009) cluster words according to linear context features. The clusters are then integrated as features to boost a discriminative parsing model to cope with unknown words. Interestingly, they also include all possible information: valence information, extracted from a lexicon, is added to verbs and preterminal nodes are annotated with case/number. This leads their discriminative model to state-of-the-art results for parsing German.

Concerning French, Candito and Crabbé (2009) present the results of different clustering methods applied to the parsing of FTB with the BKY parser. They applied an unsupervised clustering algorithm on the 125 millions words "Est Republicain" corpus to get a reduced lexicon of 1000 clusters which they then augmented with various features such as capitalization and suffixes. Their method is the best current approach for the probabilistic parsing of French with a $F_1$ score (<=40) of 88.29% on the standard test set. We run the CHARNIAK parser on their clusterized corpus. Table 8 summarizes the current state-of-the-art for lexicalized parsing on the FTB-UC.[2] Clearly, the approach consisting in extending clusters with features and suffixes seems to improve CHARNIAK's performance more than our method. In that case, the lexicon is drastically reduced, as well as the amount of out of vocabulary words (OOVs). Nevertheless, the relatively low POS accuracy, with only 36 OOVs, for this configuration confirms that POS guessing is the current bottleneck if a process of reducing the lexicon increases POS assignment ambiguities.

| tokens | $F_1$ | Pos acc | % of OOVs |
|---|---|---|---|
| raw word (a) | 84.96 | 96.26 | 4.89 |
| auto <lemma,pos> (b) | 85.06 | 96.04 | 6.47 |
| disinflected (c) | 85.45 | 96.51 | 3.59 |
| cluster+caps+suffixes (d) | 85.51 | 96.89 | 0.10 |

Table 8: CHARNIAK parser performance summary on the FTB-UC test set *(36340 tokens). Compared to (a), all $F_1$ results, but (b), are statistically significant (p-values < 0.05), differences between (c) & (d), (b) & (c) and (b) & (d) are not (p-values are resp. 0.12, 0.41 and 0.11). Note that the (b) & (d) p-value for all sentences is of 0.034, correlating thus the observed gap in parsing performance between these two configuration.*

## 7 Conclusion

We showed that while lemmatization can be of some benefit to reduce lexicon size and remedy data sparseness for a MRL such as French, the key factor that drives parsing performance for the CHARNIAK parser is the amount of unseen words resulting from the generation of <lemma,POS> pairs for the FTB-UC. For a sample of the English PTB, morphological analysis did not produce any significant improvement.

Finally, even if this architecture has the potential to help out-of-domain parsing, adding morphological analysis on top of an existing highly tuned statistical parsing system can result in suboptimal performance. Thus, in future we will investigate tighter integration of the morphological features with the parsing model.

## Acknowledgments

D. Seddah and M. Candito were supported by the ANR Sequoia (ANR-08-EMER-013); Ö. Çetinoğlu and J. van Genabith by the Science Foundation Ireland (Grant 07/CE/I1142) as part of the Centre for Next Generation Localisation at Dublin City University; G. Chrupała by BMBF project NL-Search (contract 01IS08020B).

[2] For this comparison, we also trained the CHARNIAK parser on a *disinflected* variation of the FTB-UC. *Disinflection* is a deterministic, lexicon based process, standing between stemming and lemmatization, which preserves POS assignment ambiguities (Candito and Crabbé, 2009).

## References


Anne Abeillé, Lionel Clément, and François Toussenel, 2003. *Building a Treebank for French*. Kluwer, Dordrecht.

Miriam Butt, María-Eugenia Niño, and Frédérique Segond. 1999. *A Grammar Writer's Cookbook*. CSLI Publications, Stanford, CA.

Aoife Cahill, Michael Burke, Ruth O'Donovan, Josef van Genabith, and Andy Way. 2004. Long-Distance Dependency Resolution in Automatically Acquired Wide-Coverage PCFG-Based LFG Approximations. In *Proceedings of the 42nd Annual Meeting of the Association for Computational Linguistics*, pages 320–327, Barcelona, Spain.

Marie Candito and Benoît Crabbé. 2009. Improving generative statistical parsing with semi-supervised word clustering. In *Proceedings of the 11th International Conference on Parsing Technologies (IWPT'09)*, pages 138–141, Paris, France, October. Association for Computational Linguistics.

Marie Candito, Benoit Crabbé, and Djamé Seddah. 2009. On statistical parsing of french with supervised and semi-supervised strategies. In *EACL 2009 Workshop Grammatical inference for Computational Linguistics*, Athens, Greece.

Eugene Charniak. 2000. A maximum entropy inspired parser. In *Proceedings of the First Annual Meeting of the North American Chapter of the Association for Computational Linguistics (NAACL 2000)*, pages 132–139, Seattle, WA.

Grzegorz Chrupała, Georgiana Dinu, and Josef van Genabith. 2008. Learning morphology with morfette. In *In Proceedings of LREC 2008*, Marrakech, Morocco. ELDA/ELRA.

Grzegorz Chrupała. 2008. *Towards a machine-learning architecture for lexical functional grammar parsing*. Ph.D. thesis, Dublin City University.

Grzegorz Chrupała. 2010. Morfette: A tool for supervised learning of morphology. `http://sites.google.com/site/morfetteweb/`. Version 0.3.1.

Michael Collins. 1999. *Head Driven Statistical Models for Natural Language Parsing*. Ph.D. thesis, University of Pennsylvania, Philadelphia.

Benoit Crabbé and Marie Candito. 2008. Expériences d'analyse syntaxique statistique du français. In *Actes de la 15ème Conférence sur le Traitement Automatique des Langues Naturelles (TALN'08)*, pages 45–54, Avignon, France.

Pascal Denis and Benoît Sagot. 2009. Coupling an annotated corpus and a morphosyntactic lexicon for state-of-the-art pos tagging with less human effort. In *Proc. of PACLIC*, Hong Kong, China.

Christy Doran, Dania Egedi, Beth Ann Hockey, B. Srinivas, and Martin Zaidel. 1994. Xtag system: A wide coverage grammar for english. In *Proceedings of the 15th conference on Computational linguistics*, pages 922–928, Morristown, NJ, USA. Association for Computational Linguistics.

Yoav Freund and Robert E. Schapire. 1999. Large margin classification using the perceptron algorithm. *Machine learning*, 37(3):277–296.

Yoav Goldberg, Reut Tsarfaty, Meni Adler, and Michael Elhadad. 2009. Enhancing unlexicalized parsing performance using a wide coverage lexicon, fuzzy tag-set mapping, and EM-HMM-based lexical probabilities. In *Proc. of EACL-09*, pages 327–335, Athens, Greece.

Mitchell P. Marcus, Beatrice Santorini, and Mary Ann Marcinkiewicz. 1994. Building a large annotated corpus of English: The Penn TreeBank. *Computational Linguistics*, 19(2):313–330.

Slav Petrov, Leon Barrett, Romain Thibaux, and Dan Klein. 2006. Learning accurate, compact, and interpretable tree annotation. In *Proceedings of the 21st International Conference on Computational Linguistics and 44th Annual Meeting of the Association for Computational Linguistics*, Sydney, Australia, July. Association for Computational Linguistics.

Ines Rehbein and Josef van Genabith. 2007. Treebank annotation schemes and parser evaluation for german. In *Proceedings of the 2007 Joint Conference on Empirical Methods in Natural Language Processing and Computational Natural Language Learning (EMNLP-CoNLL)*, Prague.

Benoit Sagot, Lionel Clément, Eric V. de La Clergerie, and Pierre Boullier. 2006. The lefff 2 syntactic lexicon for french: Architecture, acquisition, use. *Proc. of LREC 06, Genoa, Italy*.

Geoffrey Sampson and Anna Babarczy. 2003. A test of the leaf-ancestor metric for parse accuracy. *Natural Language Engineering*, 9(04):365–380.

Natalie Schluter and Josef van Genabith. 2007. Preparing, restructuring, and augmenting a French Treebank: Lexicalised parsers or coherent treebanks? In *Proc. of PACLING 07*, Melbourne, Australia.

Djamé Seddah, Marie Candito, and Benoit Crabbé. 2009. Cross parser evaluation and tagset variation: A French Treebank study. In *Proceedings of the 11th International Conference on Parsing Technologies (IWPT'09)*, pages 150–161, Paris, France, October. Association for Computational Linguistics.

Yannick Versley and Ines Rehbein. 2009. Scalable discriminative parsing for german. In *Proceedings of the 11th International Conference on Parsing Technologies (IWPT'09)*, pages 134–137, Paris, France, October. Association for Computational Linguistics.

# On the Role of Morphosyntactic Features in Hindi Dependency Parsing

**Bharat Ram Ambati*, Samar Husain*, Joakim Nivre† and Rajeev Sangal***
*Language Technologies Research Centre, IIIT-Hyderabad, India.
†Department of Linguistics and Philology, Uppsala University, Sweden.
{bharat,samar}@research.iiit.ac.in, joakim.nivre@lingfil.uu.se, sangal@mail.iiit.ac.in

## Abstract

This paper analyzes the relative importance of different linguistic features for data-driven dependency parsing of Hindi, using a feature pool derived from two state-of-the-art parsers. The analysis shows that the greatest gain in accuracy comes from the addition of morphosyntactic features related to case, tense, aspect and modality. Combining features from the two parsers, we achieve a labeled attachment score of 76.5%, which is 2 percentage points better than the previous state of the art. We finally provide a detailed error analysis and suggest possible improvements to the parsing scheme.

## 1 Introduction

The dependency parsing community has since a few years shown considerable interest in parsing morphologically rich languages with flexible word order. This is partly due to the increasing availability of dependency treebanks for such languages, but it is also motivated by the observation that the performance obtained for these languages has not been very high (Nivre et al., 2007a). Attempts at handling various non-configurational aspects in these languages have pointed towards shortcomings in traditional parsing methodologies (Tsarfaty and Sima'an, 2008; Eryigit et al., 2008; Seddah et al., 2009; Husain et al., 2009; Gadde et al., 2010). Among other things, it has been pointed out that the use of language specific features may play a crucial role in improving the overall parsing performance. Different languages tend to encode syntactically relevant information in different ways, and it has been hypothesized that the integration of morphological and syntactic information could be a key to better accuracy. However, it has also been noted that incorporating these language specific features in parsing is not always straightforward and many intuitive features do not always work in expected ways.

In this paper, we are concerned with Hindi, an Indian language with moderately rich morphology and relatively free word order. There have been several previous attempts at parsing Hindi as well as other Indian languages (Bharati et al., 1995, Bharati et al., 2009b). Many techniques were tried out recently at the ICON09 dependency parsing tools contest (Husain, 2009). Both the best performing system (Ambati et al., 2009a) and the system in second place (Nivre, 2009b) used a transition-based approach to dependency parsing, as implemented in MaltParser (Nivre et al., 2007b). Other data driven parsing efforts for Indian languages in the past have been Bharati et al. (2008), Husain et al. (2009), Mannem et al. (2009b) and Gadde et al. (2010).

In this paper, we continue to explore the transition-based approach to Hindi dependency parsing, building on the state-of-the-art results of Ambati et al. (2009a) and Nivre (2009b) and exploring the common pool of features used by those systems. Through a series of experiments we select features incrementally to arrive at the best parser features. The primary purpose of this investigation is to study the role of different morphosyntactic features in Hindi dependency parsing, but we also want to improve the overall parsing accuracy. Our final results are 76.5% labeled and 91.1% unlabeled attachment score, improving previous results by 2 and 1 percent absolute, respectively. In addition to this, we also provide an error analysis, isolating specific linguistic phenomena and/or other factors that impede the overall parsing performance, and suggest possible remedies for these problems.



*Proceedings of the NAACL HLT 2010 First Workshop on Statistical Parsing of Morphologically-Rich Languages*, pages 94–102,
Los Angeles, California, June 2010. ©2010 Association for Computational Linguistics

## 2 The Hindi Dependency Treebank

Hindi is a free word order language with SOV as the default order. This can be seen in (1), where (1a) shows the constituents in the default order, and the remaining examples show some of the word order variants of (1a).

(1) a. malaya ne sameer ko kitaba dii.
Malay ERG Sameer DAT book gave
"Malay gave the book to Sameer" (S-IO-DO-V)[1]
b. malaya ne kitaba sameer ko dii. (S-DO-IO-V)
c. sameer ko malaya ne kitaba dii. (IO-S-DO-V)
d. sameer ko kitaba malaya ne dii. (IO-DO-S-V)
e. kitaba malaya ne sameer ko dii. (DO-S-IO-V)
f. kitaba sameer ko malaya ne dii. (DO-IO-S-V)

Hindi also has a rich case marking system, although case marking is not obligatory. For example, in (1), while the subject and indirect object are explicitly marked for the ergative (ERG) and dative (DAT) cases, the direct object is unmarked for the accusative.

The Hindi dependency treebank (Begum et al., 2008) used for the experiment was released as part of the ICON09 dependency parsing tools contest (Husain, 2009). The dependency framework (Bharati et al., 1995) used in the treebank is inspired by Panini's grammar of Sanskrit. The core labels, called *karakas*, are syntactico-semantic relations that identify the participant in the action denoted by the verb. For example, in (1), 'Malay' is the agent, 'book' is the theme, and 'Sameer' is the beneficiary in the activity of 'give'. In the treebank, these three labels are marked as k1, k2, and k4 respectively. Note, however, that the notion of *karaka* does not capture the 'global' semantics of thematic roles; rather it captures the elements of the 'local semantics' of a verb, while also taking cues from the surface level morpho-syntactic information (Vaidya et al., 2009). The syntactic relational cues (such as case markers) help identify many of the karakas. In general, the highest available karaka,[2] if not case-marked, agrees with the verb in an active sentence. In addition, the tense, aspect and modality (TAM) marker can many a times control the case markers that appear on k1. For example, in (1) 'Malay' takes an ergative case because of the past perfective TAM marker (that appears as a suffix in this case) of the main verb 'gave'. Many dependency relations other than karakas are purely syntactic. These include relations such as noun modifier (nmod), verb modifier (vmod), conjunct relation (ccof), etc.

Each sentence is manually chunked and then annotated for dependency relations. A chunk is a minimal, non-recursive structure consisting of correlated groups of words (Bharati et al., 2006). A node in a dependency tree represents a chunk head. Each lexical item in a sentence is also annotated with its part-of-speech (POS). For all the experiments described in this paper we use gold POS and chunk tags. Together, a group of lexical items with some POS tags within a chunk can be utilized to automatically compute coarse grained morphosyntactic information. For example, such information can represent the postposition/case-marking in the case of noun chunks, or it may represent the TAM information in the case of verb chunks. In the experiments conducted for this paper this local information is automatically computed and incorporated as a feature of the head of a chunk. As we will see later, such information proves to be extremely crucial during dependency parsing.

For all the experiments discussed in section 4, the training and development data size was 1500 and 150 sentences respectively. The training and development data consisted of ~22k and ~1.7k words respectively. The test data consisted of 150 sentences (~1.6k words). The average sentence length is 19.85.

## 3 Transition-Based Dependency Parsing

A transition-based dependency parser is built of two essential components (Nivre, 2008):

- A transition system for mapping sentences to dependency trees
- A classifier for predicting the next transition for every possible system configuration

[1] S=Subject; IO=Indirect Object; DO=Direct Object; V=Verb; ERG=Ergative; DAT=Dative

[2] These are the *karta karaka* (k1) and *karma karaka* (k2). k1 and k2 can be roughly translated as 'agent' and 'theme' respectively. For a complete description of the tagset and the dependency scheme, see Begum et al. (2008) and Bharati et al. (2009a).

| | PTAG | CTAG | FORM | LEMMA | DEPREL | CTAM | OTHERS |
|---|---|---|---|---|---|---|---|
| Stack: *top* | 1 | 5 | 1 | 7 | | 9 | |
| Input: *next* | 1 | 5 | 1 | 7 | | 9 | |
| Input: *next*+1 | 2 | 5 | 6 | 7 | | | |
| Input: *next*+2 | 2 | | | | | | |
| Input: *next*+3 | 2 | | | | | | |
| Stack: *top*-1 | 3 | | | | | | |
| String: predecessor of *top* | 3 | | | | | | |
| Tree: head of *top* | 4 | | | | | | |
| Tree: leftmost dep of *next* | 4 | 5 | 6 | | | | |
| Tree: rightmost dep of *top* | | | | | 8 | | |
| Tree: left sibling of rightmost dep of *top* | | | | | 8 | | |
| Merge: PTAG of *top* and *next* | | | | | | | 10 |
| Merge: CTAM and DEPREL of *top* | | | | | | | 10 |

Table 1. Feature pool based on selection from Ambati et al. (2009a) and Nivre (2009b).

Given these two components, dependency parsing can be realized as deterministic search through the transition system, guided by the classifier. With this technique, parsing can be performed in linear time for projective dependency trees. Like Ambati et al. (2009a) and Nivre (2009b), we use MaltParser, an open-source implementation of transition-based dependency parsing with a variety of transition systems and customizable classifiers.[3]

### 3.1 Transition System

Previous work has shown that the arc-eager projective transition system first described in Nivre (2003) works well for Hindi (Ambati et al., 2009a; Nivre, 2009b). A parser configuration in this system contains a stack holding partially processed tokens, an input buffer containing the remaining tokens, and a set of arcs representing the partially built dependency tree. There are four possible transitions (where *top* is the token on top of the stack and *next* is the next token in the input buffer):

- **Left-Arc(*r*)**: Add an arc labeled *r* from *next* to *top*; pop the stack.
- **Right-Arc(*r*)**: Add an arc labeled *r* from *top* to *next*; push *next* onto the stack.
- **Reduce**: Pop the stack.
- **Shift**: Push *next* onto the stack.

Although this system can only derive projective dependency trees, the fact that the trees are labeled allows non-projective dependencies to be captured using the pseudo-projective parsing technique proposed in Nivre and Nilsson (2005).

### 3.2 Classifiers

Classifiers can be induced from treebank data using a wide variety of different machine learning methods, but all experiments reported below use support vector machines with a polynomial kernel, as implemented in the LIBSVM package (Chang and Lin, 2001) included in MaltParser. The task of the classifier is to map a high-dimensional feature vector representation of a parser configuration to the optimal transition out of that configuration. The features used in our experiments represent the following attributes of input tokens:

- PTAG: POS tag of chunk head.
- CTAG: Chunk tag.
- FORM: Word form of chunk head.
- LEMMA: Lemma of chunk head.
- DEPREL: Dependency relation of chunk.
- CTAM: Case and TAM markers of chunk.

The PTAG corresponds to the POS tag associated with the head of the chunk, whereas the CTAG represent the chunk tag. The FORM is the word form of the chunk head, and the LEMMA is automatically computed with the help of a morphological analyzer. CTAM gives the local morphosyntactic features such as case markers (postpositions/suffixes) for nominals and TAM markers for verbs (cf. Section 2).

[3] MaltParser is available at http://maltparser.org.

The pool of features used in the experiments are shown in Table 1, where rows denote tokens in a parser configuration – defined relative to the stack, the input buffer, the partially built dependency tree and the input string – and columns correspond to attributes. Each non-empty cell represents a feature, and features are numbered for easy reference.

## 4 Feature Selection Experiments

Starting from the union of the feature sets used by Ambati et al. (2009a and by Nivre (2009b), we first used 5-fold cross-validation on the combined training and development sets from the ICON09 tools contest to select the pool of features depicted in Table 1, keeping all features that had a positive effect on both labeled and unlabeled accuracy. We then grouped the features into 10 groups (indicated by numbers 1–10 in Table 1) and reran the cross-validation, incrementally adding different feature groups in order to analyze their impact on parsing accuracy. The result is shown in Figure 1.

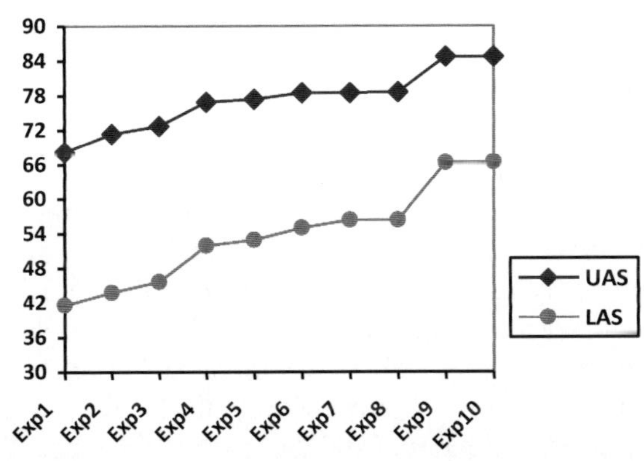


Figure 1. UAS and LAS of experiments 1-10; 5-fold cross-validation on training and development data of the ICON09 tools contest.

**Experiment 1**: Experiment 1 uses a baseline model with only four basic features: PTAG and FORM of *top* and *next*. This results in a labeled attachment score (LAS) of 41.7% and an unlabeled attachment score (UAS) of 68.2%.

**Experiments 2–3:** In experiments 2 and 3, the PTAG of contextual words of *next* and *top* are added. Of all the contextual words, *next+1*, *next+2, next+3, top-1* and predecessor of *top* were found to be useful.[4] Adding these contextual features gave a modest improvement to 45.7% LAS and 72.7% UAS.

**Experiment 4:** In experiment 4, we used the PTAG information of nodes in the partially built tree, more specifically the syntactic head of *top* and the leftmost dependent of *next*. Using these features gave a large jump in accuracy to 52% LAS and 76.8% UAS. This is because partial information is helpful in making future decisions. For example, a coordinating conjunction can have a node of any PTAG category as its child. But all the children should be of same category. Knowing the PTAG of one child therefore helps in identifying other children as well.

**Experiments 5–7:** In experiments 5, 6 and 7, we explored the usefulness of CTAG, FORM, and LEMMA attributes. These features gave small incremental improvements in accuracy; increasing LAS to 56.4% and UAS to 78.5%. It is worth noting in particular that the addition of LEMMA attributes only had a marginal effect on accuracy, given that it is generally believed that this type of information should be beneficial for richly inflected languages.

**Experiment 8:** In experiment 8, the DEPREL of nodes in the partially formed tree is used. The rightmost child and the left sibling of the rightmost child of *top* were found to be useful. This is because, if we know the dependency label of one of the children, then the search space for other children gets reduced. For example, a verb cannot have more than one k1 or k2. If we know that the parser has assigned k1 to one of its children, then it should use different labels for the other children. The overall effect on parsing accuracy is nevertheless very marginal, bringing LAS to 56.5% and UAS to 78.6%.

**Experiment 9:** In experiment 9, the CTAM attribute of *top* and *next* is used. This gave by far the greatest improvement in accuracy with a huge jump of around 10% in LAS (to 66.3%) and slightly less in UAS (to 84.7%). Recall that CTAM consists of two important morphosyntactic features, namely, case markers (as suffixes or postpositions) and TAM markers. These feature help because (a) case markers are important surface

[4] The predecessor of *top* is the word occurring immediately before *top* in the input string, as opposed to *top-1*, which is the word immediately below *top* in the current stack.

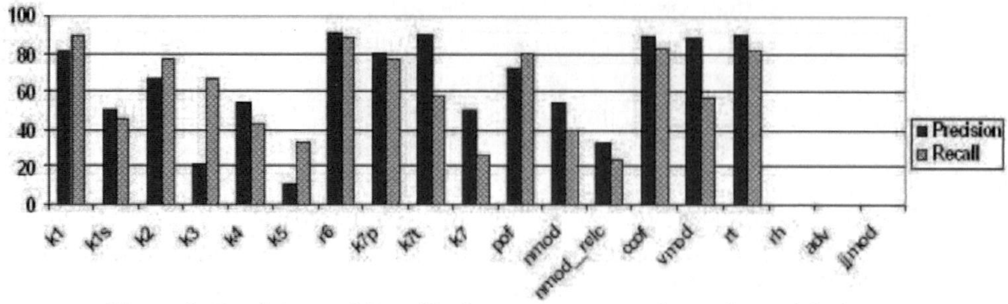


Figure 2. Precision and Recall of some important dependency labels.

cues that help identify various dependency relations, and (b) there exists a direct mapping between many TAM labels and the nominal case markers because TAMs control the case markers of some nominals. As expected, our experiments show that the parsing decisions are certainly more accurate after using these features. In particular, (a) and (b) are incorporated easily in the parsing process.

In a separate experiment we also added some other morphological features such as gender, number and person for each node. Through these features we expected to capture the agreement in Hindi. The verb agrees in gender, number and person with the highest available karaka. However, incorporating these features did not improve parsing accuracy and hence these features were not used in the final setting. We will have more to say about agreement in section 5.

**Experiment 10:** In experiment 10, finally, we added conjoined features, where the conjunction of POS of *next* and *top* and of CTAM and DEPREL of *top* gave slight improvements. This is because a child-parent pair type can only take certain labels. For example, if the child is a noun and the parent is a verb, then all the dependency labels reflecting noun, adverb and adjective modifications are not relevant. Similarly, as noted earlier, certain case-TAM combinations demand a particular set of labels only. This can be captured by the combination tried in this experiment.

Experiment 10 gave the best results in the cross-validation experiments. The settings from this experiment were used to get the final performance on the test data. Table 2 shows the final results along with the results of the first and second best performing systems in the ICON09 tools contest. We see that our system achieved an improvement of 2 percentage points in LAS and 1 percentage point in UAS over the previous state of the art reported in Ambati et al. (2009a).

| System | LAS | UAS |
|---|---|---|
| Ambati et al. (2009a) | 74.5 | 90.1 |
| Nivre (2009b) | 73.4 | 89.8 |
| Our system | 76.5 | 91.1 |

Table 2. Final results on the test data from the ICON09 tools contest.

## 5 Error Analysis

In this section we provide a detailed error analysis on the test data and suggest possible remedies for problems noted. We note here that other than the reasons mentioned in this section, small treebank size could be another reason for low accuracy of the parser. The training data used for the experiments only had ~28.5k words. With recent work on Hindi Treebanking (Bhatt et al., 2009) we expect to get more annotated data in the near future.

Figure 2 shows the precision and recall of some important dependency labels in the test data. The labels in the treebank are syntacto-semantic in nature. Morph-syntactic features such as case markers and/or TAM labels help in identifying these labels correctly. But lack of nominal postpositions can pose problems. Recall that many case markings in Hindi are optional. Also recall that the verb agrees with the highest available karaka. Since agreement features do not seem to help, if both k1 and k2 lack case markers, k1-k2 disambiguation becomes difficult (considering that word order information cannot help in this disambiguation). In the case of k1 and k2, error rates for instances that lack post-position markers are 60.9% (14/23) and 65.8% (25/38), respectively.

| | Correct | Incorrect | | | | | | | |
|---|---|---|---|---|---|---|---|---|---|
| | | k1 | k1s | k2 | pof | k7p | k7t | k7 | others |
| **k1** | 184 | 5 | 3 | 8 | 3 | | 1 | | 3 |
| **k1s** | 12 | 6 | | 1 | 6 | | | | 1 |
| **k2** | 126 | 14 | | 1 | 7 | 5 | | | 11 |
| **pof** | 54 | 1 | 8 | 4 | | | | | |
| **k7p** | 54 | 3 | | 7 | | | 1 | 2 | 3 |
| **k7t** | 27 | 3 | | 3 | 3 | | 1 | | 10 |
| **k7** | 3 | 2 | | | 2 | 4 | | | |

Table 3. Confusion matrix for important labels. The diagonal under 'Incorrect' represents attachment errors.

Table 3 shows the confusion matrix for some important labels in the test data. As the present information available for disambiguation is not sufficient, we can make use of some semantics to resolve these ambiguities. Bharati et al. (2008) and Ambati et al. (2009b) have shown that this ambiguity can be reduced using minimal semantics. They used six semantic features: human, non-human, in-animate, time, place and abstract. Using these features they showed that k1-k2 and k7p-k7t ambiguities can be resolved to a great extent. Of course, automatically extracting these semantic features is in itself a challenging task, although Øvrelid (2008) has shown that animacy features can be induced automatically from data.

In section 4 we mentioned that a separate experiment explored the effectiveness of morphological features like gender, number and person. Counter to our intuitions, these features did not improve the overall accuracy. Accuracies on cross-validated data while using these features were less than the best results with 66.2% LAS and 84.6% UAS. Agreement patterns in Hindi are not straightforward. For example, the verb agrees with k2 if the k1 has a post-position; it may also sometimes take the default features. In a passive sentence, the verb agrees only with k2. The agreement problem worsens when there is coordination or when there is a complex verb. It is understandable then that the parser is unable to learn the selective agreement pattern which needs to be followed. Similar problems with agreement features have also been noted by Goldberg and Elhadad (2009).

In the following sections, we analyze the errors due to different constructions and suggest possible remedies.

### 5.1 Simple Sentences

A simple sentence is one that has only one main verb. In these sentences, the root of the dependency tree is the main verb, which is easily identified by the parser. The main problem is the correct identification of the argument structure. Although the attachments are mostly correct, the dependency labels are error prone. Unlike in English and other more configurational languages, one of the main cues that help us identify the arguments is to be found in the nominal postpositions. Also, as noted earlier these postpositions are many times controlled by the TAM labels that appear on the verb. There are four major reasons for label errors in simple sentences: (a) absence of postpositions, (b) ambiguous postpositions, (c) ambiguous TAMs, and (d) inability of the parser to exploit agreement features. For example in (2), *raama* and *phala* are arguments of the verb *khaata*. Neither of them has any explicit case marker. This makes it difficult for the parser to identify the correct label for these nodes. In (3a) and (3b) the case marker *se* is ambiguous. It signifies 'instrument' in (3b) and 'agent' in (3a).

(2) raama phala khaata hai
'Ram' 'fruit' 'eat' 'is'
'Ram eats a fruit'

(3) a. raama se phala khaayaa nahi gaya
'Ram' INST 'fruit' 'eat' 'not' 'PAST'
'Ram could not eat the fruit'
b. raama chamach se phala khaata hai
'Ram' 'spoon' INST 'fruit' 'eat' 'is'
'Ram eats fruit with spoon'

### 5.2 Embedded Clauses

Two major types of embedded constructions involve participles and relative clause constructions. Participles in Hindi are identified through a set of TAM markers. In the case of participle embeddings, a sentence will have more than one verb, i.e., at least one participle and the matrix verb. Both the matrix (finite) verb and the participle can take their own arguments that can be identified via the case-TAM mapping discussed earlier. However, there are certain syntactic constraints that limit the type of arguments a participle can take. There are two sources of errors here: (a) argument sharing, and (b) ambiguous attachment sites.

Some arguments such as place/time nominals can be shared. Shared arguments are assigned to only one verb in the dependency tree. So the task of identifying the shared arguments, if any, and attaching them to the correct parent is a complex task. Note that the dependency labels can be identified based on the morphosyntactic features. The task becomes more complex if there is more than one participle in a sentence. 12 out of 130 instances (9.23%) of shared arguments has an incorrect attachment.

Many participles are ambiguous and making the correct attachment choice is difficult. Similar participles, depending on the context, can behave as adverbials and attach to a verb, or can behave as adjectives and attach to a noun. Take (4) as a case in point.

(4) maine daurte hue kutte ko dekhaa
'I'-ERG (while) running dog ACC 'saw'

In (4) based on how one interprets 'daurte hue', one gets either the reading that 'I saw a running dog' or that 'I saw a dog while running'. In case of the adjectival participle construction (VJJ), 2 out of 3 errors are due to wrong attachment.

### 5.3 Coordination

Coordination poses problems as it often gives rise to long-distance dependencies. Moreover, the treebank annotation treats the coordinating conjunction as the head of the coordinated structure. Therefore, a coordinating conjunction can potentially become the root of the entire dependency tree. This is similar to Prague style dependency annotation (Hajicova, 1998). Coordinating conjunctions pose additional problems in such a scenario as they can appear as the child of different heads. A coordinating conjunction takes children of similar POS category, but the parent of the conjunction depends on the type of the children.

(5) a. raama aur shyaama ne khaana khaayaa
'Ram' 'and' 'Shyam' 'ERG' 'food' 'ate'
'Ram and Shyam ate the food.'

b. raama ne khaanaa khaayaa aur paanii
'Ram' 'ERG' 'food' 'ate' 'and' 'water'
piyaa
'drank'
'Ram ate food and drank water.'

In (5a), *raama* and *shyaama* are children of the coordinating conjunction *aur*, which gets attached to the main verb *khaayaa* with the label k1. In effect, syntactically *aur* becomes the argument of the main verb. In (5b), however, the verbs *khaayaa* and *piyaa* are the children of *aur*. In this case, *aur* becomes the root of the sentence. Identifying the nature of the conjunction and its children becomes a challenging task for the parser. Note that the number of children that a coordinating conjunction can take is not fixed either. The parser could identify the correct head of the conjunctions with an accuracy of 75.7% and the correct children with an accuracy of 85.7%.

The nature of the conjunction will also affect the dependency relation it has with its head. For example, if the children are nouns, then the conjunction behaves as a noun and can potentially be an argument of a verb. By contrast, if the children are finite verbs, then it behaves as a finite verb and can become the root of the dependency tree. Unlike nouns and verbs, however, conjunctions do not have morphological features. So a child-to-head feature percolation should help make a coordinating node more transparent. For example, in (5a) the Ergative case *ne* is a strong cue for the dependency label k1. If we copy this information from one of its children (here *shyaama*) to the conjunct, then the parser can possibly make use of this information.

### 5.4 Complex Predicates

Complex predicates are formed by combining a noun or an adjective with a verbalizer *kar* or *ho*. For instance, in *taariif karanaa* 'to praise', *taariif* 'praise' is a noun and *karanaa* 'to do' is a verb. Together they form the main verb. Complex predicates are highly productive in Hindi. Combination of the light verb and the noun/adjective is dependent on not only syntax but also semantics and therefore its automatic identification is not always straightforward (Butt, 1995). A noun-verb complex predicate in the treebank is linked via the dependency label *pof*. The parser makes mistakes in identifying pof or misclassifies other labels as pof. In particular, the confusion is with k2 and k1s which are object/theme and noun complements of k1, respectively. These labels share similar contextual features like the nominal element in the verb complex. Table 3 includes the confusion matrix for pof errors.

### 5.5 Non-Projectivity

As noted earlier, MaltParser's arc-eager parsing algorithm can be combined with the pseudo-projective parsing techniques proposed in Nivre and Nilsson (2005), which potentially helps in identifying non-projective arcs. The Hindi treebank has ~14% non-projective arcs (Mannem et al., 2009a). In the test set, there were a total of 11 non-projective arcs, but the parser did not find any of them. This is consistent with earlier results showing that pseudo-projective parsing has high precision but low recall, especially when the percentage of non-projective relations is small (Nilsson et al, 2007).

Non-projectivity has proven to be one of the major problems in dependency parsing, especially for free word-order languages. In Hindi, the majority of non-projective arcs are inter-clausal (Mannem et al., 2009a), involving conjunctions and relative clauses. There have been some attempts at handling inter-clausal non-projectivity in Hindi. Husain et al. (2009) proposed a two-stage approach that can handle some of the inter-clausal non-projective structures.

### 5.6 Long-Distance Dependencies

Previous results on parsing other languages have shown that MaltParser has lower accuracy on long-distance dependencies. Our results confirm this. Errors in the case of relative clauses and coordination can mainly be explained in this way. For example, there are 8 instances of relative clauses in the test data. The system could identify only 2 of them correctly. These two are at a distance of 1 from its parent. For the remaining 6 instances the distance to the parent of the relative clause ranges from 4 to 12.

Figure 3 shows how parser performance decreases with increasing distance between the head and the dependent. Recently, Husain et al. (2009) have proposed a two-stage setup to parse inter-clausal and intra-clausal dependencies separately. They have shown that most long distance relations are inter-clausal, and therefore, using such a clause motivated parsing setup helps in maximizing both short distance and long distance dependency accuracy. In a similar spirit, Gadde et al. (2010) showed that using clausal features helps in identifying long distance dependencies. They have shown that providing clause information in the form of clause boundaries and clausal heads can help a parser make better predictions about long distance dependencies.

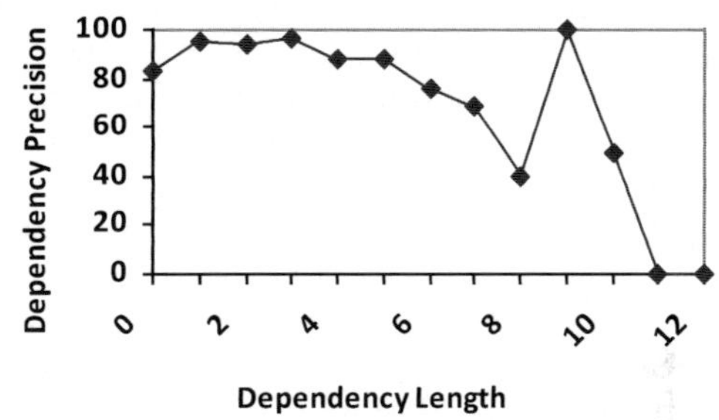


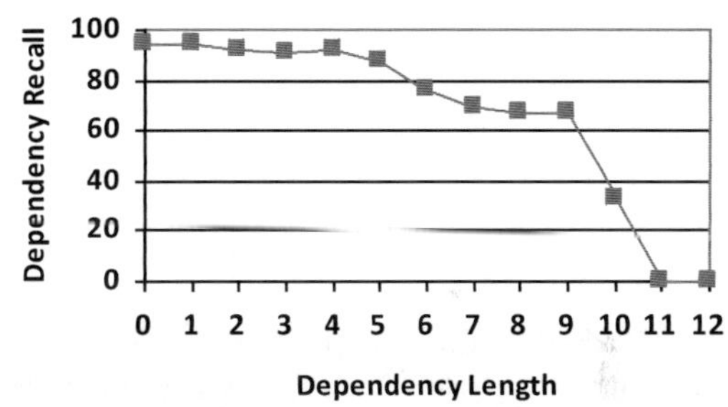


Figure 3. Dependency arc precision/recall relative to dependency length, where the length of a dependency from $w_i$ to $w_j$ is $|i-j|$ and roots are assumed to have distance 0 to their head.

## 6 Conclusion

In this paper we have analyzed the importance of different linguistic features in data-driven parsing of Hindi and at the same time improved the state of the art. Our main finding is that the combination of case markers on nominals with TAM markers on verbs is crucially important for syntactic disambiguation, while the inclusion of features such as person, number gender that help in agreement has not yet resulted in any improvement. We have also presented a detailed error analysis and discussed possible techniques targeting different error classes. We plan to use these techniques to improve our results in the near future.

## References


B. R. Ambati, P. Gadde, and K. Jindal. 2009a. Experiments in Indian Language Dependency Parsing. *Proc. of ICON09 NLP Tools Contest: Indian Language Dependency Parsing*, 32-37.

B. R. Ambati, P. Gade, C. GSK and S. Husain. 2009b. Effect of Minimal Semantics on Dependency Parsing. *Proc. of RANLP Student Research Workshop.*

R. Begum, S. Husain, A. Dhwaj, D. Sharma, L. Bai, and R. Sangal. 2008. Dependency annotation scheme for Indian languages. *Proc. of IJCNLP.*

A. Bharati, V. Chaitanya and R. Sangal. 1995. *Natural Language Processing: A Paninian Perspective,* Prentice-Hall of India, New Delhi.

A. Bharati, S. Husain, B. Ambati, S. Jain, D. Sharma, and R. Sangal. 2008. Two semantic features make all the difference in parsing accuracy. *Proc. of ICON.*

A. Bharati, R. Sangal, D. M. Sharma and L. Bai. 2006. AnnCorra: Annotating Corpora Guidelines for POS and Chunk Annotation for Indian Languages. *Technical Report (TR-LTRC-31), LTRC, IIIT-Hyderabad.*

A. Bharati, D. M. Sharma, S. Husain, L. Bai, R. Begam and R. Sangal. 2009a. AnnCorra: TreeBanks for Indian Languages, Guidelines for Annotating Hindi TreeBank. http://ltrc.iiit.ac.in/MachineTrans/research/tb/DS-guidelines/DS-guidelines-ver2-28-05-09.pdf

A. Bharati, S. Husain, D. M. Sharma and R. Sangal. 2009b. Two stage constraint based hybrid approach to free word order language dependency parsing. *In Proc. of IWPT.*

R. Bhatt, B. Narasimhan, M. Palmer, O. Rambow, D. M. Sharma and F. Xia. 2009. Multi-Representational and Multi-Layered Treebank for Hindi/Urdu. *Proc. of the Third LAW at ACL-IJCNLP,* 186-189.

M. Butt. 1995. *The Structure of Complex Predicates in Urdu.* CSLI Publications.

G. Eryigit, J. Nivre, and K. Oflazer. 2008. Dependency Parsing of Turkish. *Computational Linguistics* 34(3), 357-389.

P. Gadde, K. Jindal, S. Husain, D. M. Sharma, and R. Sangal. 2010. Improving Data Driven Dependency Parsing using Clausal Information. *Proc. of NAACL-HLT.*

Y. Goldberg and M. Elhadad. 2009. Hebrew Dependency Parsing: Initial Results. *Proc. of IWPT,* 129-133.

E. Hajicova. 1998. Prague Dependency Treebank: From Analytic to Tectogrammatical Annotation. *Proc. of TSD.*

J. Hall, J. Nilsson, J. Nivre, G. Eryigit, B. Megyesi, M. Nilsson and M. Saers. 2007. Single Malt or Blended? A Study in Multilingual Parser Optimization. *Proc. of EMNLP-CoNLL,* 933-939.

S. Husain. 2009. Dependency Parsers for Indian Languages. *Proc. of ICON09 NLP Tools Contest: Indian Language Dependency Parsing.*

S. Husain, P. Gadde, B. Ambati, D. M. Sharma and R. Sangal. 2009. A modular cascaded approach to complete parsing. *Proc. of the COLIPS International Conference on Asian Language Processing.*

P. Mannem, H. Chaudhry, and A. Bharati. 2009a. Insights into non-projectivity in Hindi. *Proc. of ACL-IJCNLP Student Research Workshop.*

P. Mannem, A. Abhilash and A. Bharati. 2009b. LTAG-spinal Treebank and Parser for Hindi. *Proceedings of International Conference on NLP, Hyderabad. 2009.*

R. McDonald, K. Lerman, and F. Pereira. 2006. Multilingual dependency analysis with a two-stage discriminative parser. *Proc. of CoNLL*, 216-220.

R. McDonald and J. Nivre. 2007. Characterizing the errors of data-driven dependency parsing models. *Proc. of EMNLP-CoNLL,* 122-131.

I. A. Mel'Cuk. 1988. *Dependency Syntax: Theory and Practice*, State University Press of New York.

J. Nilsson, J. Nivre and J. Hall. 2007. Generalizing Tree Transformations for Inductive Dependency Parsing. *Proc. of ACL*, 968-975.

J. Nivre. 2008. Algorithms for Deterministic Incremental Dependency Parsing. *Computational Linguistics* 34(4), 513-553.

J. Nivre and R. McDonald. 2008. Integrating graph-based and transition-based dependency parsers. In *Proceedings of ACL-HLT*, pp. 950-958.

J. Nivre. 2009a. Non-Projective Dependency Parsing in Expected Linear Time. *Proc. of ACL-IJCNLP*, 351-359.

J. Nivre. 2009b. Parsing Indian Languages with MaltParser. *Proc. of ICON09 NLP Tools Contest: Indian Language Dependency Parsing*, 12-18.

J. Nivre, J. Hall, S. Kubler, R. McDonald, J. Nilsson, S. Riedel and D. Yuret. 2007a. The CoNLL 2007 Shared Task on Dependency Parsing. *Proc. of EMNLP/CoNLL,* 915-932.

J. Nivre, J. Hall, J. Nilsson, A. Chanev, G. Eryigit, S. Kübler, S. Marinov and E Marsi. 2007b. MaltParser: A language-independent system for data-driven dependency parsing. *NLE*, 13(2), 95-135.

L. Øvrelid. 2008. *Argument Differentiation. Soft constraints and data-driven models.* PhD Thesis, University of Gothenburg.

D. Seddah, M. Candito and B. Crabbé. 2009. Cross parser evaluation: a French Treebanks study. *Proc. of IWPT,* 150-161.

R. Tsarfaty and K. Sima'an. 2008. Relational-Realizational Parsing. *Proc. of CoLing,* 889-896.

A. Vaidya, S. Husain, P. Mannem, and D. M. Sharma. 2009. A karaka-based dependency annotation scheme for English. *Proc. of CICLing,* 41-52.

# Easy First Dependency Parsing of Modern Hebrew

**Yoav Goldberg**[*] and **Michael Elhadad**
Ben Gurion University of the Negev
Department of Computer Science
POB 653 Be'er Sheva, 84105, Israel
{yoavg|elhadad}@cs.bgu.ac.il

## Abstract

We investigate the performance of an easy-first, non-directional dependency parser on the Hebrew Dependency treebank. We show that with a basic feature set the greedy parser's accuracy is on a par with that of a first-order globally optimized MST parser. The addition of morphological-agreement feature improves the parsing accuracy, making it on-par with a second-order globally optimized MST parser. The improvement due to the morphological agreement information is persistent both when gold-standard and automatically-induced morphological information is used.

## 1 Introduction

Data-driven Dependency Parsing algorithms are broadly categorized into two approaches (Kübler et al., 2009). *Transition based* parsers traverse the sentence from left to right[1] using greedy, local inference. *Graph based* parsers use global inference and seek a tree structure maximizing some scoring function defined over trees. This scoring function is usually decomposed over tree edges, or pairs of such edges. In recent work (Goldberg and Elhadad, 2010), we proposed another dependency parsing approach: Easy First, Non-Directional dependency parsing. Like transition based methods, the easy-first method adopts a local, greedy policy. However, it abandons the strict left-to-right processing order, replacing it with an alternative order, which attempts to make easier attachments decisions prior to harder ones. The model was applied to English dependency parsing. It was shown to be more accurate than MALTPARSER, a state-of-the-art transition based parser (Nivre et al., 2006), and near the performance of the first-order MSTPARSER, a graph based parser which decomposes its score over tree edges (McDonald et al., 2005), while being more efficient.

The easy-first parser works by making easier decisions before harder ones. Each decision can be conditioned by structures created by previous decisions, allowing harder decisions to be based on relatively rich syntactic structure. This is in contrast to the globally optimized parsers, which cannot utilize such rich syntactic structures. It was hypothesized in (Goldberg and Elhadad, 2010) that this rich conditioning can be especially beneficial in situations where informative structural information is available, such as in morphologically rich languages.

In this paper, we investigate the non-directional easy-first parser performance on Modern Hebrew, a semitic language with rich morphology, relatively free constituent order, and a small treebank compared to English. We are interested in two main questions: (a) *how well does the non-directional parser perform on Hebrew data?* and (b) *can the parser make effective use of morphological features, such as agreement?*

In (Goldberg and Elhadad, 2009), we describe a newly created Hebrew dependency treebank, and

*Supported by the Lynn and William Frankel Center for Computer Sciences, Ben Gurion University

[1]Strictly speaking, the traversal order is from start to end. This distinction is important when discussing Hebrew parsing, as the Hebrew language is written from right-to-left. We keep the left-to-right terminology throughout this paper, as this is the common terminology. However, "left" and "right" should be interpreted as "start" and "end" respectively. Similarly, "a token to the left" should be interpreted as "the previous token".



*Proceedings of the NAACL HLT 2010 First Workshop on Statistical Parsing of Morphologically-Rich Languages*, pages 103–107,
Los Angeles, California, June 2010. ©2010 Association for Computational Linguistics

report results on parsing this corpus with both MALTPARSER and first- and second- order variants of MSTPARSER. We find that the second-order MSTPARSER outperforms the first order MSTPARSER, which in turn outperforms the transition based MALTPARSER. In addition, adding morphological information to the default configurations of these parsers does not improve parsing accuracy. Interestingly, when using automatically induced (rather than gold-standard) morphological information, the transition based MALTPARSER's accuracy improves with the addition of the morphological information, while the scores of both globally optimized parsers drop with the addition of the morphological information.

Our experiments in this paper show that the accuracy of the non-directional parser on the same dataset outperforms the first-order MSTPARSER. With the addition of morphological agreement features, the parser accuracy improves even further, and is on-par with the performance of the second-order MSTPARSER. The improvement due to the morphological information persists also when automatically induced morphological information is used.

## 2 Modern Hebrew

Some aspects that make Hebrew challenging from a language-processing perspective are:

**Affixation** Common prepositions, conjunctions and articles are prefixed to the following word, and pronominal elements often appear as suffixes. The segmentation of prefixes and suffixes is often ambiguous and must be determined in a specific context only. In term of dependency parsing, this means that the dependency relations occur not between space-delimited tokens, but instead between sub-token elements which we'll refer to as segments. Furthermore, mistakes in the underlying token segmentations are sure to be reflected in the parsing accuracy.

**Relatively free constituent order** The ordering of constituents inside a phrase is relatively free. This is most notably apparent in the verbal phrases and sentential levels. In particular, while most sentences follow an SVO order, OVS and VSO configurations are also possible. Verbal arguments can appear before or after the verb, and in many ordering. For example, the message "went from Israel to Thailand" can be expressed as "went to Thailand from Israel", "to Thailand went from Israel", "from Israel went to Thailand", "from Israel to Thailand went" and "to Thailand from Israel went". This results in long and flat VP and S structures and a fair amount of sparsity, which suggests that a dependency representations might be more suitable to Hebrew than a constituency one.

**NP Structure and Construct State** While constituents order may vary, NP internal structure is rigid. A special morphological marker (*Construct State*) is used to mark noun compounds as well as similar phenomena. This marker, while ambiguous, is essential for analyzing NP internal structure.

**Case Marking** definite direct objects are marked. The case marker in this case is the function word את appearing before the direct object.[2]

**Rich templatic morphology** Hebrew has a very productive morphological structure, which is based on a root+template system. The productive morphology results in many distinct word forms and a high out-of-vocabulary rate which makes it hard to reliably estimate lexical parameters from annotated corpora. The root+template system (combined with the unvocalized writing system) makes it hard to guess the morphological analyses of an unknown word based on its prefix and suffix, as usually done in other languages.

**Unvocalized writing system** Most vowels are not marked in everyday Hebrew text, which results in a very high level of lexical and morphological ambiguity. Some tokens can admit as many as 15 distinct readings, and the average number of possible morphological analyses per token in Hebrew text is 2.7, compared to 1.4 in English (Adler, 2007).

**Agreement** Hebrew grammar forces morphological agreement between Adjectives and Nouns (which should agree in Gender and Number and definiteness), and between Subjects and Verbs (which should agree in Gender and Number).

[2]The orthographic form את is ambiguous. It can also stand for the noun "shovel" and the pronoun "you"(2nd,fem,sing).

## 3 Easy First Non Directional Parsing

Easy-First Non Directional parsing is a greedy search procedure. It works with a list of partial structures, $p_i, \ldots, p_k$, which is initialized with the $n$ words of the sentence. Each structure is a head token which is not yet assigned a parent, but may have dependants attached to it. At each stage of the parsing algorithm, two neighbouring partial structures, $(p_i, p_{i+1})$ are chosen, and one of them becomes the parent of the other. The new dependant is then removed from the list of partial structures. Parsing proceeds until only one partial structure, corresponding to the root of the sentence, is left. The choice of which neighbouring structures to attach is based on a scoring function. This scoring function is learned from data, and attempts to attach more confident attachments before less confident ones. The scoring function makes use of features. These features can be extracted from any pre-built structures. In practice, the features are defined on pre-built structures which are around the proposed attachment point. For complete details about training, features and implementation, refer to (Goldberg and Elhadad, 2010).

## 4 Experiments

We follow the setup of (Goldberg and Elhadad, 2009).

**Data** We use the Hebrew dependency treebank described in (Goldberg and Elhadad, 2009). We use Sections 2-12 (sentences 484-5724) as our training set, and report results on parsing the development set, Section 1 (sentences 0-483). As in (Goldberg and Elhadad, 2009), we do not evaluate on the test set in this work.

The data in the treebank is segmented and POS-tagged. Both the parsing models were trained on the gold-standard segmented and tagged data. When evaluating the parsing models, we perform two sets of evaluations. The first one is an oracle experiment, assuming gold segmentation and tagging is available. The second one is a real-world experiment, in which we segment and POS-tag the test-set sentences using the morphological disambiguator described in (Adler, 2007; Goldberg et al., 2008) prior to parsing.

**Parsers and parsing models** We use our freely available implementation[3] of the non-directional parser.

**Evaluation Measure** We evaluate the resulting parses in terms of unlabeled accuracy – the percent of correctly identified (child,parent) pairs[4]. To be precise, we calculate:

$$\frac{number\_of\_correctly\_identified\_pairs}{number\_of\_pairs\_in\_gold\_parse}$$

For the oracle case in which the gold-standard token segmentation is available for the parser, this is the same as the traditional unlabeled-accuracy evaluation metric. However, in the real-word setting in which the token segmentation is done automatically, the yields of the gold-standard and the automatic parse may differ, and one needs to decide how to handle the cases in which one or more elements in the identified (child,parent) pair are not present in the gold-standard parse. Our evaluation metric penalizes these cases by regarding them as mistakes.

## 5 Results

**Base Feature Set** On the first set of experiments, we used the English feature set which was used in (Goldberg and Elhadad, 2010). Our only modification to the feature set for Hebrew was not to lexicalize prepositions (we found it to work somewhat better due to the smaller treebank size, and Hebrew's rather productive preposition system).

Results of parsing the development set are summarized in Table 1. For comparison, we list the performance of the MALT and MST parsers on the same data, as reported in (Goldberg and Elhadad, 2009).

The case marker את, as well as the morphologically marked *construct nouns*, are covered by all feature models. את is a distinct lexical element in a predictable position, and all four parsers utilize such function word information. Construct nouns are differentiated from non-construct nouns already at the POS tagset level.

All models suffer from the absence of gold POS/morphological information. The easy-first non-directional parser with the basic feature set

[3] http://www.cs.bgu.ac.il/~yoavg/software/nondirparser/

[4] All the results are macro averaged.

(NonDir) outperforms the transition based Malt-Parser in all cases. It also outperforms the first order Mst1 model when gold POS/morphology information is available, and has nearly identical performance to Mst1 when automatically induced POS/-morphology information is used.

**Additional Morphology Features** Error inspection reveals that most errors are semantic in nature, and involve coordination, PP-attachment or main-verb hierarchy. However, some small class of errors reflected morphological disagreement between nouns and adjectives. These errors were either inside a simple NP, or, in some cases, could affect relative clause attachments. We were thus motivated to add specific features encoding morphological agreement to try and avoid this class of errors.

Our features are targeted specifically at capturing noun-adjective morphological agreement.[5] When attempting to score the attachment of two neighbouring structures in the list, $p_i$ and $p_{i+1}$, we inspect the pairs $(p_i, p_{i+1})$, $(p_i, p_{i+2})$, $(p_{i-1}, p_{i+1})$, $(p_{i-2}, p_i)$, $(p_{i+1}, p_{i+2})$. For each such pair, in case it is made of a noun and an adjective, we add two features: a binary feature indicating presence or absence of gender agreement, and another binary feature for number agreement.

The last row in Table 1 (NonDir+Morph) presents the parser accuracy with the addition of these agreement features. Agreement contributes to the accuracy of the parser, making it as accurate as the second-order Mst2. Interestingly, the non-directional model benefits from the agreement features also when automatically induced POS/morphology information is used (going from 75.5% to 76.2%). This is in contrast to the Mst parsers, where the morphological features hurt the parser when non-gold morphology is used (75.6 to 73.9 for Mst1 and 76.4 to 74.6 for Mst2). This can be attributed to either the agreement specific nature of the morphological features added to the non-directional parser, or to the easy-first order of the non-directional parser, and to the fact the morphological features are defined only over structurally close heads at each stage of the parsing process.

[5]This is in contrast to the morphological features used in out-of-the-box Mst and Malt parsers, which are much more general.

| | Gold Morph/POS | Auto Morph/POS |
|---|---|---|
| Malt | 80.3 | 72.9 |
| Malt+Morph | 80.7 | 73.4 |
| Mst1 | 83.6 | 75.6 |
| Mst1+Morph | 83.6 | 73.9 |
| Mst2 | 84.3 | 76.4 |
| Mst2+Morph | 84.4 | 74.6 |
| **NonDir** | 83.8 | 75.5 |
| **NonDir+Morph** | 84.2 | 76.2 |

Table 1: Unlabeled dependency accuracy of the various parsing models.

## 6 Discussion

We have verified that easy-first, non-directional dependency parsing methodology of (Goldberg and Elhadad, 2010) is successful for parsing Hebrew, a semitic language with rich morphology and a small treebank. We further verified that the model can make effective use of morphological agreement features, both when gold-standard and automatically induced morphological information is provided. With the addition of the morphological agreement features, the non-directional model is as effective as a second-order globally optimized Mst model, while being much more efficient, and easier to extend with additional structural features.

While we get adequate parsing results for Hebrew when gold-standard POS/morphology/segmentation information is used, the parsing performance in the realistic setting, in which gold POS/morphology/segmentation information is not available, is still low. We strongly believe that parsing and morphological disambiguation should be done jointly, or at least interact with each other. This is the main future direction for dependency parsing of Modern Hebrew.

## References

Meni Adler. 2007. *Hebrew Morphological Disambiguation: An Unsupervised Stochastic Word-based Approach.* Ph.D. thesis, Ben-Gurion University of the Negev, Beer-Sheva, Israel.

Yoav Goldberg and Michael Elhadad. 2009. Hebrew Dependency Parsing: Initial Results. In *Proc. of IWPT.*

Yoav Goldberg and Michael Elhadad. 2010. An efficient algorithm for easy-first non-directional dependency parsing. In *Proc. of NAACL.*

Yoav Goldberg, Meni Adler, and Michael Elhadad. 2008.

EM Can find pretty good HMM POS-Taggers (when given a good start). In *Proc. of ACL*.

Sandra Kübler, Ryan T. McDonald, and Joakim Nivre. 2009. *Dependency Parsing*. Synthesis Lectures on Human Language Technologies. Morgan & Claypool Publishers.

Ryan McDonald, Koby Crammer, and Fernando Pereira. 2005. Online large-margin training of dependency parsers. In *Proc of ACL*.

Joakim Nivre, Johan Hall, and Jens Nillson. 2006. Malt-Parser: A data-driven parser-generator for dependency parsing. In *Proc. of LREC*.

# Author Index

**Association for Computational Linguistics**
209 N. Eighth Street
Stroudsburg, Pennsylvania 18360

CURRAN ASSOCIATES INC
proceedings.com